Regina Versus Don. Report of The Trial, with Opinions of The Press, &c.

Don, John Davidson

The Making of Modern Law collection of legal archives constitutes a genuine revolution in historical legal research because it opens up a wealth of rare and previously inaccessible sources in legal, constitutional, administrative, political, cultural, intellectual, and social history. This unique collection consists of three extensive archives that provide insight into more than 300 years of American and British history. These collections include:

Legal Treatises, 1800-1926: over 20,000 legal treatises provide a comprehensive collection in legal history, business and economics, politics and government.

Trials, 1600-1926: nearly 10,000 titles reveal the drama of famous, infamous, and obscure courtroom cases in America and the British Empire across three centuries.

Primary Sources, 1620-1926: includes reports, statutes and regulations in American history, including early state codes, municipal ordinances, constitutional conventions and compilations, and law dictionaries.

These archives provide a unique research tool for tracking the development of our modern legal system and how it has affected our culture, government, business – nearly every aspect of our everyday life. For the first time, these high-quality digital scans of original works are available via print-on-demand, making them readily accessible to libraries, students, independent scholars, and readers of all ages.

The BiblioLife Network

This project was made possible in part by the BiblioLife Network (BLN), a project aimed at addressing some of the huge challenges facing book preservationists around the world. The BLN includes libraries, library networks, archives, subject matter experts, online communities and library service providers. We believe every book ever published should be available as a high-quality print reproduction; printed on-demand anywhere in the world. This insures the ongoing accessibility of the content and helps generate sustainable revenue for the libraries and organizations that work to preserve these important materials.

The following book is in the "public domain" and represents an authentic reproduction of the text as printed by the original publisher. While we have attempted to accurately maintain the integrity of the original work, there are sometimes problems with the original work or the micro-film from which the books were digitized. This can result in minor errors in reproduction. Possible imperfections include missing and blurred pages, poor pictures, markings and other reproduction issues beyond our control. Because this work is culturally important, we have made it available as part of our commitment to protecting, preserving, and promoting the world's literature.

GUIDE TO FOLD-OUTS MAPS and OVERSIZED IMAGES

The book you are reading was digitized from microfilm captured over the past thirty to forty years. Years after the creation of the original microfilm, the book was converted to digital files and made available in an online database.

In an online database, page images do not need to conform to the size restrictions found in a printed book. When converting these images back into a printed bound book, the page sizes are standardized in ways that maintain the detail of the original. For large images, such as fold-out maps, the original page image is split into two or more pages

Guidelines used to determine how to split the page image follows:

• Some images are split vertically; large images require vertical and horizontal splits.
• For horizontal splits, the content is split left to right.
• For vertical splits, the content is split from top to bottom.
• For both vertical and horizontal splits, the image is processed from top left to bottom right.

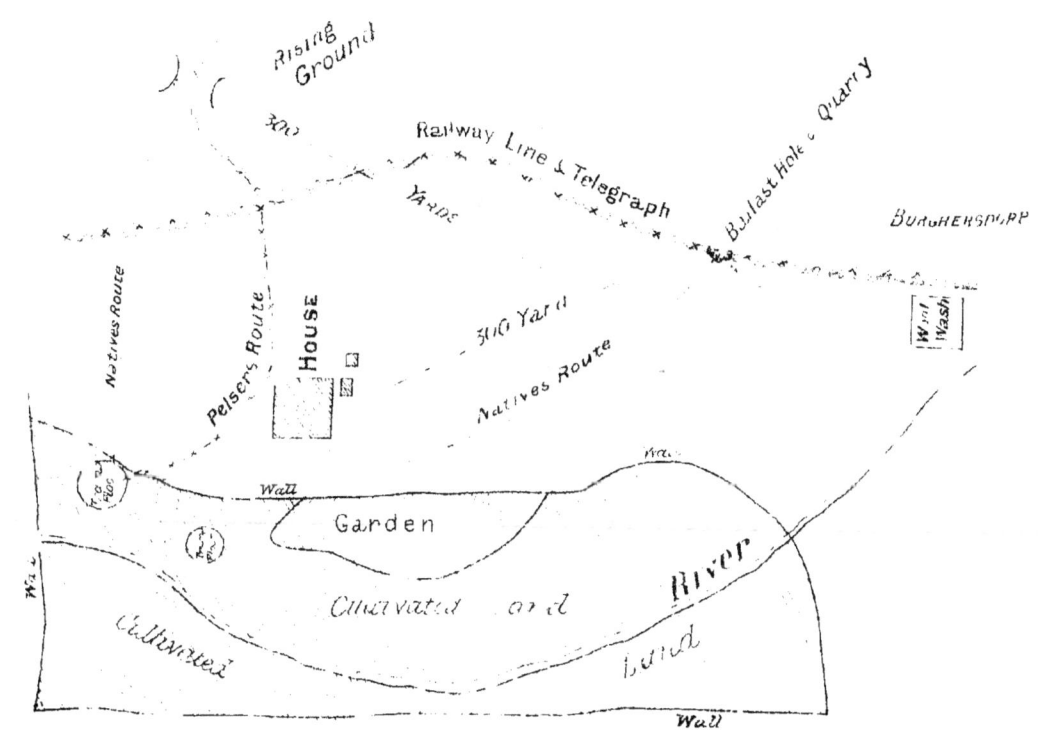

SKETCH MAP
PELSER'S FARM

Rising Ground

300

Railway Line & Telegraph

Ballast Hole & Quarry

BURGHERSDORP

Yards

Natives Route

Pelser's Route

HOUSE

300 Yard

Natives Route

Wool Wash

Wall

Garden

Wall

Cultivated and Land

River

Cultivated

Wall

REGINA *versus* DON.

REPORT OF THE TRIAL,

WITH

OPINIONS OF THE PRESS, &c

PUBLISHED BY

W. T. RANDALL, BOOKSELLER AND STATIONER, &c,

KING WILLIAM'S TOWN

SOUTH AFRICA,

1886,

CONTENTS

ERRATA

For "Hainsworth," pages 12 and 19, read, *Harmsworth*
For "Ntotyiza," page 15, read, *Ntloyiya*

INTRODUCTION.

THE interest awakened throughout the country by the late trial in the Eastern Districts' Court might, of itself, be a sufficient reason for publishing a Report of the proceedings, with Opinions of the Press, &c., in a permanent form. But, in addition to this, the whole history of the case, the circumstances out of which it arose, and the important issues connected with it, justify the present publication.

It is notorious that a year ago a species of terrorism reigned in the neighbourhood of Burghersdorp, and in other parts of the country—caused by the banding together of misguided men to promote the interests, and, if possible, enforce the views of a section of the community in the spirit of faction, not with that large-hearted regard for the interests, rights and liberties of the whole community, which is characteristic of true patriotism. Nowhere did this faction exhibit more audacity, bluster and disposition to violence than around Burghersdorp. Men of English birth or descent, and others who kept aloof from the dominant party, were ashamed of their position as subjects of the British Crown, and entitled to the privileges of freedom, but forced to cower and keep silence, and unable to count confidently on the maintenance of law and order.

Not content with local efforts to have everything their own way, this faction presumed to terrorize and threaten the Government of the country. Naturally irritated by the ruinous and alarming increase of stock thefts, for which they chose to hold the Government responsible, on the ground that a stronger police force was not provided for their protection, instead of confining themselves to petition, remonstrance, and other constitutional means, they threatened openly to take the law into their own hands   Incendiary articles and letters in a local paper fanned the flame of disaffection, till a state of things was brought about discreditable to any community existing under the broad ægis of the British Empire   W J Pelser was the writer of some of the more violent of these productions   in one of which occurs a by no means obscure foreshadowing of the deed which was laid to his charge a few weeks afterwards   It is impossible to dissociate this letter and the shooting of Zachariah, or to con-clude that the fatal act which deprived an innocent fellow-creature of his life was wholly unpremeditated and due solely to the impulse of the moment   Pelser apparently meant to challenge the Government by such an act, and he carried out his intention. These letters appeared in the *Burghersdorp Gazette*, the local Bond organ, on the 19th and 26th of December, 1884, Zachariah was killed on the 15th of January following   Translations will be found in the annexure to this pamphlet

The first notice given to the public in these parts of what was going on at Burghersdorp was contained in the following tele-gram —

Cape Town, February 12, 1885

" An *Argus* telegram from Aliwal North dated the 12th states that the Boers in this and the Albert district are buying up all guns and revolvers   At one country store fifteen applications for guns were made in one day   The occurrence is thought by some to have connection with Bechuanaland, but it is more probable to be in connection with Pelser's case, as the Boers have sworn to release him if convicted "

Attention was thus arrested, and a good deal of anxiety felt by those interested in the maintenance of law and order , especially when rumours spread of threatening demonstrations made at the Court of Burghersdorp, and it was known that the authorities had declined to prosecute Pelser   Copies of the telegrams and letters which passed between the Magistrate of Burghersdorp and the Solicitor-General will be found in the annexure

When in Burghersdorp, on the occasion of the opening of the Railway, Mr George Hay made large extracts from the record of the Preliminary Examination of Pelser before the Magistrate, and on the 24th of March an article appeared in the "Cape Mercury" embodying these extracts—an article which, with the exception of an unintentional omission and consequent erroneous statement, was held by the Judge President to represent fairly the most important parts of the Preliminary Examination

The following paragraph appeared in the *Cape Mercury* of March 26 —

The *Cape Times* says "It is most unfortunate, however, that all the rumour and menace should have preceded the refusal to prosecute , for those who threatened will inevitably take credit for having overawed the Government by their threats, while others, who resented the attempt at intimidation will find it hard to disconnect facts from facts, and so the impression of a defeat of justice will remain Where the dignity and might of the law are concerned we cannot show too sensitive a jealousy If the law were accommodated to the conciliation of any element, be it never so powerful, 'the fountain of justice' would be indeed 'poisoned at its source' "

On the 14th of April Mr Don's letter appeared, which was primarily, and essentially, not an attack upon Pelser, but a protest against the conduct of the authorities in declining to prosecute, with such evidence before them—a protest which the Court has declared that he, or any man was entitled to make in the interests of law, justice, and order The preceding narrative of events proves that there was good ground for making such a protest by one who utterly disowned political partizanship

When Parliament met, a question was asked by Mr Rose-Innes, member for Victoria East, and papers were laid on the table of the house, together with a letter from the Solicitor-General, printed in the annexure hereto, in which he assumed the sole responsibility of his conduct, but failed either to vindicate himself satisfactorily or to explain his reasons

Nothing more was done in Parliament, and it is probable that this fact led to the prosecution of Messrs Don and Hay for a criminal libel against Pelser, which was instituted upon the fiat of the Attorney-General The accused were arrested under warrant, and the Preliminary Examination was held in King William's Town on the 23rd July, 1885, when Messrs Don and Hay were committed for trial by the Magistrate

In due time the accused were indicted to appear before the Eastern Districts' Court at Grahamstown, the Solicitor-General himself prosecuting, not before the Circuit Court of King William's Town, as would have been the case, had the ordinary course been followed At the eleventh hour the Crown Prosecutor dropped the case against Mr Hay, and proceeded against Mr Don alone The trial began on the 12th of November and ended on the 16th with the acquittal of the accused

Its great importance has been widely, almost universally recognised by the Press of the Colony, as a vindication of the right of free and honest criticism of public officials, as emphasizing the sacredness of human life, and thereby increasing its security, and as a demonstration on behalf of the purity of the administration of Justice This chorus of approval is also a wholesome warning given by the law-abiding, and justice-loving part of the community to all whom it may concern, that the spirit of faction shall not be allowed to raise its head unchecked, or to force its way with impunity in a British Colony, where loyal men of different races are determined at whatever cost, to maintain their rights and privileges as British subjects and citizens

REPORT OF TRIAL.

In the Court of the Eastern Districts of the Colony of the Cape of Good Hope.

THURSDAY, NOVEMBER 12, 1885

REGINA versus DON.

This case, which has claimed much attention from the public in consequence of the peculiar circumstances connected with it, was commenced on Thursday morning, November 12th, 1885, in the Eastern Districts Court, at Graham's Town, at the holding of the quarterly Criminal Sessions

The Court was crowded with members of all professions, and a large number of clergymen were present, the gallery being occupied by ladies

Sir Jacob Dirk Barry, Judge President of the Eastern Districts Court, occupied the Bench, and the Solicitor-General, A F S Maasdorp, Esq, prosecuted on behalf of the Crown

Attorney R W Rose-Innes, of King William's Town, worked up the case on behalf of Mr Don, and Attorney Knobel, of Burghersdorp, for the Crown

The Solicitor-General opened the case at 12 10 p m, by announcing that the next case was that in which the Rev John Davidson Don was charged with the crime of Criminal Libel

Advocate Solomon I appear for the defendant, my Lord, with my learned friend, Mr Frames, and I trust you will allow Mr Don to take a seat behind me, and not compel him to go into the box

Judge It is a practice that has been initiated in cases of this description, and I think in all cases of libel it should be allowed

Mr Solomon   Thank you   The next question is that of the Jury

The Sheriff   Some of the present Jury have sat all through the session

Judge   If I consulted my own wishes I would relieve you all If the Solicitor-General and Counsel for the defence say you can be relieved I will do so, but it is not for me to say

The Registrar was proceeding to call a fresh Jury, when Mr Solomon said the indictment must first be read

The Registrar   The indictment is against Don and Hay

Solicitor-General   I amend the indictment by striking out the name Hay

The Rev Don having stood up in his place, the Registrar read the indictment, which was as follows —

"That John Davidson Don, a Minister of the Gospel, residing at King William's Town, in the District of King William's Town, is charged with the crime of publishing a Defamatory Libel, in that, whereas one Willem Jacobus Pelser, a farmer, residing at Roodeberg's Vlei, in the District of Albert, did, upon or about the Sixteenth Day of January, in the Year of Our Lord One Thousand Eight Hundred and Eighty-five, and at Roodeberg's Vlei aforesaid, in self-defence, and as he lawfully might, shoot and kill one Zachariah, in his lifetime a labourer residing at Burghersdorp, in the said District, the said John Davidson Don contriving and wrongfully, unlawfully and maliciously intending to injure, vilify, and prejudice the said Willem Jacobus Pelser, and deprive him of his good name, fame, credit and reputation, and to bring him into public contempt, scandal, infamy and disgrace, did, on or about the Fourteenth Day of April, in the Year of Our Lord One Thousand Eight Hundred and Eighty-five, and at King William's Town aforesaid, wrongfully, unlawfully and maliciously write, print and publish, and cause and procure to be written, printed and published in the *Cape Mercury* in the form of a letter purporting to be written and addressed by the said John Davidson Don to George Alexander Hay, the following false, scandalous, malicious and defamatory words, that is to say

" 'That poor man's blood' (meaning the blood of the said Zachariah) 'cries to Heaven, not merely against the wretched murderer' (meaning the said Willem Jacobus Pelser) 'but against the Government which refuses to prosecute, and the country which condones such conduct,' the said John Davidson Don meaning thereby that the said Willem Jacobus Pelser had wrongfully, unlawfully and maliciously killed and murdered the said Zachariah, and that the said Willem Jacobus Pelser was a murderer, to the great damage, scandal and disgrace of the said Willem Jacobus Pelsei, the said John Davidson Don well-knowing the said defamatory libel to be false, and thus the said John Davidson Don did commit the crime of publishing a Defamatory Libel"

In answer to the charge the accused pleaded "Not guilty"

Mr Solomon I appear with Mr Frames There are special pleas in this case, my Lord

Judge Mr Don may sit down

The Jury were then discharged, and the Registrar was on the point of calling a fresh Jury, when

Mr Solomon said he had not read the pleas He then read the following —

REGINA vs DON

PLEAS

For a special plea to the Indictment, in which the Defendant is charged with the *Crime of Publishing a Defamatory Libel* of and concerning one Willem Jacobus Pelsei, the Defendant says that our Lady the Queen ought not further to prosecute against him by reason of the matters following —

1 In or about the 20th January, 1885, a Preliminary Examination was taken before Alexander Stewart, Esq, Resident Magistrate of the District of Albert, against the said Willem Jacobus Pelsei, in that the said Willem Jacobus Pelsei did on or about the 15th January, 1885, wrongfully and unlawfully kill one Zachariah, in his lifetime a Native Labourer residing at Burghersdorp, in the District of Albert aforesaid

2 After the hearing of the evidence given at the said Preliminary Examination the said Alexander Stewart as such Magistrate as aforesaid, and acting under the directions of Her Majesty's Solicitor-General for this Colony, committed the said Willem Jacobus Pelsei for trial on the charge of Culpable Homicide, the said Alexander Stewart before getting the directions of Her Majesty's Solicitor-General as aforesaid being in doubt whether to commit the said Willem Jacobus Pelsei on the charge of Murder or Culpable Homicide

3 Her Majesty's Solicitor-General for this Colony, upon reading the evidence taken at the Preliminary Examination, and which was transmitted to him in due course on or about the 28th January, 1885, by the said Alexander Stewart, did on or about the 31st January, 1885, decide to indict the said Willem Jacobus Pelser upon the charge of Culpable Homicide

4 Her Majesty's Solicitor-General, on or about the 16th February, 1885, declined to prosecute the said Willem Jacobus Pelser upon the said charge of Culpable Homicide or upon any charge in connection with the killing of the said Zachariah

5 Before and at the time of the writing and publishing of the alleged defamatory words in the indictment set forth, public attention in this Colony had been drawn to the occurrences referred to in the preceding paragraphs and a considerable amount of public interest existed with regard to the said occurrence

6 The said defamatory words referred to in the Indictment are portions of a letter published in the issue of a newspaper, the *Cape Mercury*, bearing date the 14th April, 1885, and signed by John D Don, which said letter is hereunto annexed, and which Defendant prays may be considered as herein inserted

"SIR,—I read with painful interest an article in the *Cape Mercury* some weeks ago on the Pelser case, consisting mainly of evidence culled from the official records It was plain from that evidence, indeed it was practically confessed by Pelser himself, that a foul crime had been perpetrated, and every right-thinking person must have recognised it as a necessary consequence that Pelser should have been committed for trial It seems, however, that the man is still at large, and that the Government has declined to prosecute

"The statements in your article were such as the Government were bound to rebut and refute, or by silence be held to admit their truth and force I have been looking anxiously for such explanation or defence of the action of the Government, such as it was its duty to the country, as well as its interest to issue, if defence is possible, but none has appeared I am reluctantly compelled to come to the conclusion that your statements are true, in short, that our rulers have been influenced by political instead of such legal considerations as are alone applicable to the case It may be safely assumed that if a white man had been the victim, the murderer would not have been left untried and unpunished Indeed it may be confidently affirmed that had the same thing happened in this District the offender would have been brought to justice But it would seem that in the District of Burghersdorp, if a Dutchman shoots a Kaffir, the crime must be overlooked, Government refuses to do its duty, and the conscience of the whole community is offended I fully expected that when your article went forth through the country, especially after its statements remained unchallenged, the Press would have taken up the question and compelled the Government to break silence, if not to alter its decision But the Press, with few exceptions, has paid no attention to the case I confess I have met with nothing more disheartening for a long time than this immoral apathy in connection with such a grave business Is the matter to rest here? Is nothing more to be said or done? Is the Government to be permitted ignominiously to abdicate its functions in this fashion, and to offend the con-

sciences of all not blinded by race prejudice or party feeling?
Even were the evidence against Pelser less damning than it
seems to be he himself admits a criminal act, whether murder or
manslaughter, which ought to be dealt with in the prescribed
and proper manner, tried by a Judge and Jury in open Court,
instead of settled off-hand by Solicitor-General or Attorney-
General in a hole-and-corner fashion   Nothing less can satisfy
justice, not to speak of decency, and I trust nothing less will
satisfy the country

"I belong to no party   I am not a politician , I never was in
Burghersdorp   I know nothing of its people, and never heard of
Pelser before, but I am a member of the community which has to
bear the responsibility in the last resort of the Government's
unchallenged acts, and a Minister of a Religion which knows no
distinction of race, caste, class or colour and my conscience
refuses to put up silently with this offence   "What hast thou
done?   The voice of thy brother's blood crieth unto me from
the ground"   That poor man's blood cries to heaven, not merely
against the wretched murderer, but against the Government which
refuses to prosecute, and the country which condones such conduct   I for my part will have no share in this responsibility

"Therefore to clear my own conscience I solemnly protest, in
the name of God of Law, Justice, and order against the manner
in which this foul crime has been dealt with

"I am your obedient servant,

"(Signed)   JOHN D DON

"The Manse, King Williamstown,
    "April 11, 1885"

This is the letter referred to in the annexed pleas

R W ROSE-INNES,

Attorney for Rev J D Don

7 The said letter was and is a fair and *bona fide* comment
upon the said Preliminary Examination and upon the several
other matters hereinbefore referred to, all of which were matters
of Public Interest, and the said letter was written by the
Defendant *bona fide* and without malice, and for the benefit of
the public and not otherwise, and without any malicious intent
and motive whatever

8 It was for the Public Benefit that the said letter should be
published, inasmuch as it is to the Public Interest that all
matters affecting the administration of justice and the conduct
of the Public Officials and all facts connected with the killing of
a fellow creature under such circumstances as it was sworn to at
the said Preliminary Examination the aforesaid Zachariah was
killed should be made known and publicly enquired into

9 And for a further plea the Defendant says that the

defamatory words set forth in the Indictment are true in substance and in fact, inasmuch as the said Willem Jacobus Pelser did on or about the 15th January, 1885, wrongfully, unlawfully and maliciously shoot and kill and murder one Zachariah, in his lifetime a labourer, residing at Burghersdorp, in the District of Albert

10 It was, for the reasons alleged in the 5th and 8th paragraphs above, for the public benefit that the letter referred to in the 6th paragraph above, of which the defamatory words set forth in the Indictment form part, should be published

(Signed) R W ROSE-INNES,

Attorney for the Accused

King Williamstown, 16th Oct, 1885

The following Jury was then empanelled to hear the case — Fred Thomas Kennelly, W Carstens, E Ramsay Edgill, Henry Shea, W Keightley, Jos Oliver, Reginald S Guest, E B C Hoole, R R Smith

The Crown challenged Lawrence Harper, Geo Luke, and R W Nelson

The defence challenged Francis R Wallace, Frederick Barr and Benjamin Cinnamon

Leonard Brooks was excused with the consent of the Crown and defence in consequence of his being foreman of the *Eastern Star* printing office

R Blackburn did not answer to his name when called on, but the Solicitor General said he had been in attendance that morning

Mr Solomon said he should be there to answer to his name at once

The Registrar having sworn the jury and stated that the charge alluded to Mr Don as the prisoner at the bar

The Solicitor General said May it please your Lordship Gentlemen of the jury, you see from the indictment that the prisoner stands charged with defamatory libel in having uttered these words "That poor man's blood cries to heaven not merely against the wretched murderer but against the Government which refuses to prosecute and the country which condones such conduct" Before I go further I wish that the witnesses may be ordered out of the Court

Mr Solomon· Excepting the medical men

Solicitor-General I have no objection to the medical men remaining (The witnesses left the Court) Now, Gentlemen of the Jury, in many cases one of the difficulties the jury has to contend with in charges of this kind is to decide whether the words themselves are libellous or not In this particular case you will have no such difficulty because his Lordship will tell you that to accuse a man of murder is under such circumstances

as these libel, and it will be seen from the facts that it is such
In their special pleas in the first place they say it was a fair and
bona fide comment and entirely for the benefit of the public and
that Mr Willem Jacobus Pelser committed murder   They say
so and what is more say they are going to prove it, and that it
was a *bona fide* comment   This alleged murder has reference to
an occurrence that took place on the 16th January, 1885, in the
Burghersdorp district   Pelser has a farm or rather manages a
farm of his father's, Hendrick Pelser, who farms elsewhere
They say that at the end of this farm there was being constructed
not only a railway but a telegraph line, and you know that a
lot of labourers in connection with the work must be about the
place   In consequence of this a great deal of stock had been
stolen, and——

Mr Solomon   I shall most certainly object to evidence being
led of stock-stealing or its cause   Such statements as this are
calculated to prejudice my client in the jury's mind

Solicitor-General (laughing)   Nonsense

The Judge   Do I understand that you are going to lead all
the evidence for the prosecution at once ?

Solicitor-General   I am going to put Mr Pelser in the box
and then he will tell the story, and then my friend can examine
him   At any rate on the morning of the 16th January Mr
Pelser was at the tramp-floor with a number of other Europeans
and natives when the native Zachariah came on the farm, and
he had in his hand, according to the statement of Pelser, a rod
of iron about two feet long and rather thicker than his little
finger   In the first place he went to the kraal,

Judge   Is that so ?

Solicitor-General   Oh, yes   He went to the kraal, which was
shut at the time, and he opened the door and went in

Judge   Was this before he went to the tramp floor ?

Solicitor-General   Yes   He informed one of the boys that
he was in search of a horse   After this he went to the tramp
floor, and there Mr Pelser asked him what he was doing
there   He said that he came to look for his master's horse, on
which he was asked for a pass   I might say here that when
Mr Pelser asked him where he was going he was slow in
replying, and he spoke some Kafir words which he did not
understand and he got an interpreter to interpret   Pelser then
asked for his pass and he said he had not got one   He was
told to go and get one as Pelser had been annoyed by the people
coming on to the farm so often   The Kafir said he would not
go back, and then mumbling to himself he went off across the
veldt   After he had been away some time and got some distance
Pelser got up on the wall, enclosing the land on which the
tramp floor is, to see where he had gone to and he saw him in
the distance   He then made a remark to the men saying " I

will go and get him and fine him two shillings and you may
have it I will not take him into town " He then went to a
little elevation and saw where the Kafir had got to He had his
horse saddled and went to the house and, as is the custom on
the farm, he put on his revolver He went after him, overtook
him, and told him to go back The native made a reply in a
mixture of Dutch and English which Pelser understood to mean
that he would not He took out his pistol in order to frighten him
He turned him back and made him walk in front of the horse
When they had gone about thirty yards the Kafir turned round
and attacked him with the iron bar The first blow struck the
horse, and Pelser could not tell then how many blows he
received He was in the act of striking the last blow when Mr
Pelser fired the pistol

Mr Solomon In the act of striking ?

Solicitor-General Yes Pelser cannot tell you how the shot
took the direction it did (Mr Solomon, *sotto voce* I should
think not) He can only tell you that his horse swerved and he
fired across his horse That is a mere explanation and the only
one he can offer At any rate as soon as the man fell he at once
raced off home, told his father he had shot the man, changed his
clothes for town clothes and went to Burghersdorp and told the
Magistrate This is the account given by Pelser, and this account
is borne out by the evidence of the prosecution The defence would
say it was impossible to have taken place as he had said, but he said
his explanation was a possibility and the witnesses at the preliminary examination would bear him out The medical evidence
taken at the preliminary examination states that it would be
impossible for the wound to have been inflicted by a man riding
behind the native as indicated by those witnesses who say they
saw Pelser driving the Kafir in front of him two yards away
and that he deliberately shot him in the back The Doctor
thinks this opposed to common sense The first preliminary
examination was taken on the 20th January and the statement
Pelser made at that time was sent to the Solicitor-General's
office On the receipt of this the Magistrate was instructed to
commit Pelser for trial for culpable homicide

Judge When was that ?

Solicitor-General On the 31st January the instructions were
sent in and the Magistrate in pursuance of those instructions
took Pelser's statement and committed him for trial, He sent it
down to complete the proceedings and when I saw the statement
I decided not to indict There it would have ended (Mr Solomon
I should think so) but unfortunately we have party politics in this
country, and the opposing parties go for each other

Mr Solomon I thought my friend was going to exclude all
reference to party politics ?

Solicitor-General That's all very well There is a paper in

King Williamstown called the *Cape Mercury* which came out with a leader in it headed "Justice and Party Politics," and on this leader Mr Don bases his letter, and it is from this article that he gets his information about the case. He took no steps to get a copy of the preliminary examination to base his remarks on and find out the truth of the case, but he took it as perfectly correct and proceeded to call Pelser a murderer. I will point out one or two inaccuracies in that article. I may state that as Pelser rode after the Kafir he called to David a Kafir boy and told him to get a horse and jump upon it and call two policemen that had been about the farm that morning. The article says that there is no evidence produced in suppport of the statement alleging the sending for two policemen. That is false, for Pelser says he sent two boys, and in addition to this you have to hear what is said about the Doctor's evidence

Judge. Is there any other statement you challenge?

Solicitor-General. Yes, I am coming to it. The article says "The Doctor's evidence and the production of the revolver with one empty chamber, fully complete the chain of proof." Now the Doctor's evidence does no such thing, but the whole article will be read afterwards and you will see it is a violent attack on the Government for party reasons and alleges that Government had power to prosecute. I may tell you that the Government have as much to do with the prosecutions in the Eastern Province as you have. The prosecuting power is vested in the Solicitor-General by Legislative enactment. If the Government attempted to interfere and tried to tell the Solicitor-General what to do I should tell them to go about their own business

Mr Solomon. I must really stop my learned friend. It will be remembered that in my pleas were some paragraphs which when they were submitted to Your Lordship in chambers as it was suggested that they would give rise to a discussion of party politics, I consented to withdraw, thinking that no such element would be introduced

Judge. That is so. It was not the intention to bring up party politics in this case. I was glad that you acted as you did, and I really thought it was so decided and I am surprised to hear it introduced. I shall not stop you (Solicitor-General) but I think party politics ought not to be dragged into Court

Solicitor-General. Mr Don takes the article as a true statement, but I hold he should have seen it was a statement against the Government and should have been more careful

Judge. Are you going to put it in?

Solicitor-General. Yes

Judge. Then the argument can follow afterwards

Solicitor-General. Mr Don took it and did not get the records from my office or the Magistrate. He having thus taken it has landed himself in the difficulty as regards the letter. The evidence I shall lead at first will be evidence of publication, and after that the evidence of Pelser and perhaps others. Then the defence can examine, after which I may call fresh evidence to rebut what my friend has put up. The first witness I shall call is Mr Hay

George Alexander Hay having been sworn gave evidence as follows, examined by the Solicitor-General

You are Editor and part proprietor of the *Cape Mercury*? Yes. You produce a copy of that paper of 14th April? Yes The letter on the third page you will find signed by J. D. Don? Yes. Who is the author of that letter? The accused, Mr Don? Yes. I see he says in that letter "I read with painful interest an article in the copy of the *Mercury* some weeks ago?" Yes. That article is the one written on the 24th March? Yes Unfortunately I have only one copy of that paper (turning to Mr Solomon), "Have you an unmarked one? (witness came from the box and gave him one. (To witness) The original, have you got it there? No. Has it been destroyed? I cannot find it. What way did it come to you? It was handed in. By Mr Don? Yes

Judge. You cannot find it though you have searched for it? Yes

Mr Solomon. How long have you known Mr Don? For a number of years

Judge. Is anyone with you Mr Solomon?

Mr Solomon. Yes, Mr Frames, My Lord

Mr Solomon to witness. During the many years you have known him, have you known him take any interest in the party politics of the Colony? Not any special interest. He is not a political parson (laughter). This is the first letter I have had from him. Is it the first he has written to the paper? Yes You did not object to publish the letter? No. Why not?

Solicitor-General. It does not matter what reasons he had

Judge. Mr Solicitor, you said it was done for political purposes and having introduced it, it remains for them to show whether it was done for that purpose or not

Mr Solomon. Why did you publish it? I believed it to be a fair comment on a public act. Were you arrested with Mr Don? Yes. And the preliminary examination was taken both against Mr Don and yourself? Yes. You know that the examination was sent back to the magistrate because there was not sufficient evidence of publication? Yes. And the Crown then withdrew the charge against you so that you might give evidence? No. I see that you were jointly indicted with Mr Don? I was. Did you plead to the indictment? I did. What was your plea? That this letter was a fair comment And after serving on the Solicitor-General a copy of your pleas the indictment was withdrawn? It was. I don't suppose you asked that it should be withdrawn against you ?   I did not

Solicitor-General I must object   The letter was written and the witness and yourself can get it ?

Witness I concluded the pleas met the charge

Solicitor-General   We don't want your conclusions, we want the letter

Witness I have left the letter at home

Solicitor-General We will produce a copy of it

The Court adjourned at 1 8 p m

———

On the Court resuming at 2 4 p m , the Jurymen's names were called, and Mr Hay's examination continued

The Judge Have you got the letter?

Solicitor-General It will be here in a minute

Mr Solomon Before you read the letter to which you refer (turning to Mr Hay) had you been to Burghersdorp before writing the article referred to by Mr Don ? Yes   And the extracts from the preliminary examination which you gave in the article were taken from the preliminary examination itself ? From the records

The Judge The article may just as well be read here

Mr Solomon I see the article is headed " Justice and Party Politics " Why did you head it in that way ?

Solicitor-General The jury may form their own conclusion why it was done   We do not want Hay's opinion

Mr Solomon But why did you ?

The Judge You had better read the article

Mr Solomon then read the following article —

" JUSTICE AND PARTY POLITICS

" It was reported some short time ago that a Dutch farmer in the Burghersdorp district had shot a native in a very high-handed way , that he had been bailed out, and that there was considerable excitement amongst his fellows, who threatened to forcibly rescue him if an arrest was attempted   So much is rumour   It is a fact that Pelser was committed for trial on a charge of culpable homicide, and within the past few weeks it has been telegraphed from one end of the country to the other, that the Government declined to prosecute   There are some who hint that the reasons for restraining the usual course of law are purely political   From the official records we have taken the facts which we give, and merely ask the people of this country —the law-abiding inhabitants—what their opinion is   Let the Magistrate's record speak for itself, we do not desire to add a single word, but only explain that we give the salient parts of it, the whole being too voluminous to publish here in detail   On the 16th January, Willem J. Pelser, described as a European

c

farmer, appeared at the Court-house in Burghersdorp, and made a statement that 'He was in for a row, he had shot a nigger A Kaffir,' he said, 'came to look for a horse Upon being asked for a pass he said he had none I ordered him to go to the town The Kaffir would not, but struck my horse with an iron rod about two feet long He struck at me a second time, and I drew a revolver and shot him, and at once came to report the affair I do not know if he is dead or not' So far Pelser's own statement to the Chief Constable, who swears 'I went and found the dead body of a native, dressed, with an iron rod by his side He was lying on his back The District Surgeon examined the body, and found a wound at the back of the left shoulder-blade, the bullet having lodged in the spine The body was still warm The horse spoors were five yards away I found a pass in his bag, dated August last, for "Kleinboy"' Alfred Hanesworth, Clerk to Civil Commissioner, corroborated as to Pelser's statement, with these additions 'I told him to leave my veldt I did not allow natives to roam about there without passes I looked back and saw him still in my veldt I rode up and told him I would give him in custody of the police I sent messengers for two police who had passed my house that morning [No evidence adduced in support of this] I reined up in front when he said 'You'll not stop me' [Pelser does not understand Kafir], and struck my horse on the nose, whereupon the animal became restive The Kafir then struck at my leg I turned round and saw his arm raised to strike me again I then shot him' In cross-examination he stated that Pelser said the horse bolted, and he had difficulty in pulling it up Mr Hanesworth was not shown the horse Martinus David, a servant of Pelser's, says he was on the tramp-floor when deceased came up and asked about a black horse 'Pelser asked him for his pass, and the native said he had none Pelser told him to go for one Pelser stood on the wall of the tramp-floor watching the deceased He then jumped down and went to the house, and I saw him ride away Pelser had no revolver when on the tramp-floor I did not hear the shot' Cross-examined 'Pelser does not understand Kafir He had lost lots of stock He rode away to the town on a black horse' A Tambookie, also in the service of the Dutchman, and on the tramp-floor, interpreted for Pelser, corroborates the statement of the pass affair, and says 'Pelser went to the house, I saw him ride in the same direction as the Kafir went I did not hear the shot I thought the Kafir had a switch in his hand' Fred David, son of the before-mentioned Martinus, was herding sheep on the farm, swears that he heard a shot, that he saw the Kafir man down with his legs crossed, and beckoning with his hand, but that he was afraid to go to him He saw the man lying there a little before midday. Alfred Peters, a schoolmaster and carpenter,

working on the line, which passes close to the homestead, swears ·
' I saw Pelser overtake the Native and stand talking Pelser
was turned towards the house   I was talking when I heard the
shot fired, and, looking round, saw the native fall   Pelser stood
about three minutes, and then galloped away to the house   I
was afraid to go to the spot   It was the same man who passed
me that was shot   He had nothing in his hand   It was about
half-an-hour after he passed me that he was shot   I told my
employer about it '   Veldtschoen, who was digging holes for the
telegraph, saw the white man shoot the native, who was walking
on in front   He says ' I was looking when the shot was fired'
It was just a little before dinner time '   Nthoyoya, a labourer,
similarly engaged, swears ' I saw Pelser turn the native back'
The native had nothing in his hand   He did not have the piece
of iron produced   The native's back was towards Pelser when
he fired   I was afraid to go near because of the white man '
Breakfast saw Pelser driving a native before him and heard a
shot, but, being in a hollow, saw nothing   Canteen gave
evidence to the same effect   The doctor's evidence and the production of the revolver with one empty chamber fully completed
the chain of proof   The defence was an extraordinary arrangement, and we will briefly summarize it   Several officials and
some privates of the C M R go to the spot, and are placed at
the various points occupied by the witnesses at the time of the
occurrence   One mounted man and one dismounted go through
the performance of brandishing a small whip and a blank cartridge is fired , they then come back and the spectators of this
farce depose that from where they were (550 yards away) it was
impossible to hear the shot, though they saw the smoke , also
that they could not see the horsewhip when used to strike the
horse and rider   The Chief Constable, however, considerately
adds ' The day was windy, but that on which the native was
killed was still and warm '   This is the defence, and the Government declined to prosecute

" At Cathcart, last Circuit, Mr Filmer was charged with
shooting to frighten a native and wounding him in the hip, for
which he was fined £30, but then he had the misfortune to be
an English European farmer, and therefore had to stand his
trial

" Our duty is done   We might add to this bare statement the
gossip of railway men and others, but we are content to leave
the undisputable facts to the public   The Premier has had
much to say lately in defence of lawlessness, perhaps he knows
something of this case   We challenge the Government to publish the full text of the official record to disprove these extracts,
which have been copied from those documents "

Judge Then you say that this is the comment that is unfair ?
Solicitor-General Yes, my lord

Judge. Which is the part?

Solicitor-General In the first place it says there is no evidence in support of the sending for Policemen, and then says that the production of the revolver with one chamber empty and the Doctor's evidence completes the chain of evidence

Judge What evidence is there in the preliminary examination about sending for the Police?

Solicitor-General I will refer to it in cross-examination

Judge to Witness The extracts are from the preliminary examination? From the examination itself When were you at Burghersdorp? At the opening of the railway

Mr Solomon Before writing this article did you consult any medical men about the wound? Yes And I suppose you are quite willing that your statement of facts in this article in all its important bearings should be compared with the preliminary examination? Quite I see there is no heading to the letter written by Mr Don in your paper Is it simply correspondence? Yes Is this the letter you received from the Solicitor-General

"[No 475] Office of the Solicitor-General,

Grahamstown, 3rd November, 1885

THE QUEEN *vs* HAY AND DON

Sir,—In answer to your letter of the 24th ultimo, I beg to inform you that, in consequence of the difference between your pleas and those of the Reverend Don, I have come to the conclusion that the two cases cannot be fairly tried together Under these circumstances, and upon a mature reconsideration of the case, I have come to the conclusion that the ends of justice will be sufficiently met by proceeding against the Reverend Don alone You will therefore take notice that the indictment served upon you in the above matter is withdrawn as far as you are concerned and will be no further proceeded with

I have the honour to be, Sir,

Your obedient servant

A F MAASDORP,
Solicitor-General

G A HAY, Esq.,
Cape Mercury Office, King Williamstown "

Yes, that is it.

Solicitor-General. Shortly after you received the letter you had a subpoena served on you to give evidence in this case? I had

The Judge. For the Crown? Yes

Solicitor-General You say that at the preliminary examination there was some difficulty in proving the authorship of

Don's letter   Do you know that a Mr Daly was called and I believe he has absconded, and he gave evidence?   I have not heard so   You say that article is a fair comment after seeing the preliminary examination?   Yes?   You say there is no evidence of sending for the Police?   That is an error   Oh, that is an error?   Yes, it is the only error   Now at the preliminary examination the witness Martinus was examined and gave this evidence "I had seen two Policemen at the house on foot They came towards Burghersdorp   I saw prisoner mount a horse and ride away   When he passed the tramp floor he shouted to me to go and get the Police"   He went to get the Police   You leave out the whole of that in your article.   What made you do it?   I did not make a complete transcript of the records and I evidently omitted that   Oh yes, of course you omitted everything favourable to Pelser   I unintentionally omitted it   Oh, of course you did   Then Martinus David says "I heard him call out as he rode away, but I could not hear what he said, as he was too far off"   Why did you not mention this?   It was not an intentional suppression   Abo also says he called out as he rode away   Why omit this?   I was pressed at the time and I thought I took extracts of all   There was no object in the suppression   Then you say the production of the revolver with an empty chamber and the Doctor's evidence completed the chain of proof, but the Doctor's evidence says "It is impossible that the wound could have been made with the man right behind in the way indicated by the witnesses?"   The Doctor's evidence as it appears simply proved the man was dead If you take the statement of the Doctor's examination of the wound and compare it with the statement as made by witnesses you will find that the wound could have been inflicted as said by them   Well I will read what the Doctor says, "I heard the witness say that the black man was close to the horse's head with his back towards the horse   Had a pistol shot been fired then it would have gone straight into the back and would not have caused the wound from which the deceased died"   How do you make that tally with the evidence of the witnesses? Because the witnesses do not say that the man was with his face turned away from the prisoner   They say he was in front of the prisoner, and it would be quite possible to be in front of the prisoner and shoot in the way described by the Doctor   You say that the evidence of Ntotyiza, when he said "I saw the white man shoot him   He was about two yards from the native The native's back was turned towards the white man's horse The native fell when he was shot"   You say that this contradicts what the Doctor says?   No, I do not   Well, we will see what the jury say about it

Mr Solomon   This matter might have been brought in if Mr Hay had been indicted, we are here to defend Mr Don's letter and it does not matter if one thousand omissions appear in the article, it does not affect Mr Don

Judge This all goes to show that in your opinion Mr Hay should have remained where he was

Mr Hay I wish I had (laughter)

Solicitor-General At any rate you did not think it worth while to mention that the Doctor had given some evidence in favour of Pelser? I did not read the Doctor's evidence as favourable to Pelser in that part

Willem Jacobus Pelser was next called and examined by the Solicitor-General Do you speak English? Yes Your name is Willem Jacobus Pelser? Yes And you are a farmer? Yes You reside at Roodesbergsvlei in the district of Albert, and the farm is a little more than two miles from the town of Burghersdorp You are managing it for your father? Yes Towards the end of last year or the beginning of this the railway and telegraph lines were being constructed across your farm? Yes And a number of natives used to cross your farm? Yes You remember the morning of the 16th January a Kafir came to your place? Yes And afterwards he turned out to be a Kafir named Zacharias? Yes You were working at the tramp floor? Yes Can you tell us who you all were at the time? Yes Abo, a native, Marthinus David, old Marthinus, Willem Pelser my cousin, and Abraham de Klerk, a white man in my employ What happened when the Kafir came there? The Kafir came and I asked him where he was going Had the Kafir anything in his hand? Yes, an iron rod which he was holding like this across his shoulders (witness indicated that the native held the bar at each end over his shoulders) I cannot say exactly how he was holding it when he was coming up only when he came up he had it across his shoulders Was this the sort of implement he had? (exhibited a small half-inch iron bar square with small hammer-head and a worm for a bolt at the end about 2 feet in length) Yes, that is something like it (handed to jury) Later on this rod was found lying near the body of the man When I asked him where he was going to I received no answer

Judge In what language did you speak?—I spoke in Dutch and received no answer and thereupon I asked Abo to interpret I asked him to ask where the native was going He answered that he was looking for some horses

Solicitor-General Did he say a horse or horses? I am not sure Then I asked him whether he had a pass and he said no, he had not I then told him to go and get a pass as I did not allow any native or anyone to walk on my veldt without a pass Then he replied he wouldn't go and get a pass

Judge This was all through Abo?—Yes

By Solicitor-General He said he would not go as it was not

his horse or horses (I cannot say which)   Then I told him I would not allow him to go across but if he goes and gets a pass from his master I would allow him   Thereupon he turned away and walked into my veldt —Did he say anything as he walked away ?—Yes, in Kafir   I don't understand it and Abo did not interpret it for me —Had you any special reason for stopping people going across your veldt ?—Yes

Mr Solomon   I object to these special reasons being given I think it would have an undue effect on the Jury   The Crown have alleged that the man Pelser shot a native in self-defence and we want his evidence on that point

Solicitor-General   Very well, I admit that   (To Pelser) You had special reasons ?   Yes —He then went and you went to the tramp floor wall afterwards ?—Yes   The tramp floor is within the wall which surrounds the lands and you had to go to it to get to the house ?   Yes — And then ?—While I sat on the wall I said it is rather a trouble to go after that native

Judge   Was anyone near you ?   Yes, my boys could hear me. I said I will take him back and fine him 2s , that will save me the trouble of taking him into town   And then I went off to the house   I said I would give the money to my boys

Judge   This is not strictly evidence

Solicitor-General   You went afterwards to the horses ?   I have two stables on my farm   There is a little height from which I am able to see a great deal of my land   I went up on it as it was on my way   It is in a line with the second stable and I saw the man walking a great distance away in the veldt I went through the house and took my revolver which was not unusual as it was the custom more or less to carry a revolver when we go into the veldt   I then walked to the stable Between the house and the stable is a fountain where my father was working at a tank

Before we go further, that morning had there been any policemen at the farm ?   Yes two

You had some conversation with your father before you went on to the stable ?   Yes   And you went on and got your horse ? Yes   And rode off ?   Yes   I had the revolver slung round my shoulder   That is the pistol produced (regulation six-chambered revolver put in)   I then rode off in the direction of the man In doing so I had to pass near the tramp floor about 150 yards from it, and the men were still working there   I called out to Martinus to take my younger brother's horse which was grazing near by, and make haste and go and get the police, and thereupon I rode off to bring the man back who I could see in the veldt from where I called out to Martinus

Judge   Could you see whether he was the same man as had been there ?   No, I could not see that   Did you think so ?   Yes, I thought it was, but whether it was or not I went to see

By Solicitor-General It was a little past nine when he came, and it must have been a little before ten when I passed from the house in pursuit, and it must have been a little before ten when I came up to him as it is not very far from the house to the spot where I overtook him

Judge How far? About 2,000 yards, but I cannot say for certain

I did not notice any natives working on the telegraph line, but they may have been there but I did not see them as I know they were constructing the line The natives are continually coming about there and they may have been about without my taking notice When I overtook the native I stopped him and I asked him why he went into my veldt as I had told him not to go Then he said he was going to look for a horse

The Judge In what language did he speak? In English and Dutch mixed Can you say his words? That I cannot, your Lordship, but I understood him to say he was looking for a horse and I told him to go back as I wouldn't allow it

Solicitor-General You said to him " You are my prisoner now?" Yes, and that I had sent for the police to take him to town He answered that he would not go at first and afterwards

Judge Did he make any reply? Yes, he said I am going to look for my horses, and he said he would'nt go back at first Did he say he would not go, or that he would go and look for his horse? No, he did not say that exactly He persisted in saying he would go and look for his horses

Solicitor-General He would not go? He stood still at first and I pushed up my horse towards him I had my revolver out to frighten him

Judge When did you take out your revolver? A little before then when he resisted I took it out when I pushed my horse up towards him

Solicitor-General You took it out to frighten him and he moved? He moved a short distance towards the house He was walking very slowly, very slowly in front of my horse, and I told him to go on a little quicker and I pushed my horse a little nearer with my legs

Judge Against him? I cannot say against him—towards him He suddenly turned round and struck at the nose of my horse with the iron He struck several times at me How many times? I did not count I think it was about three times In addition to striking at the horse? Yes I was very excited then as I did not expect him to strike at me as he did He took me unawares The horse gave way while he was striking the first time, and then I pulled the horse up and he again struck at me in such a frightful way that I knew my life to be in danger Each time he struck the horse gave way, he swerved and would not stand still,

Solicitor-General It swerved to the left and he had come at you from the right? Yes I could clearly see my life was in danger As he struck the last time the horse gave way and the revolver went off You were prepared to use it? Yes Did it go off accidentally? Not exactly, but as the horse swerved it went off sooner than I meant it to do, that was caused by the horse giving way It went off and struck the deceased He fell? Yes You afterwards saw the corpse, and saw where the bullet had entered, and the course of the bullet? Yes Can you explain to the jury how it was that the bullet took that particular course

Judge With which hand did he strike you? I think with the right If he struck at you so often you must have known? As far as I can remember it must have been with the right As the horse gave way the last time he must have come a little forward He was just standing in this way (witness held the bar in his right hand above his head in striking attitude)

Solicitor-General Suppose I am the Kafir (laughter) in what position was he? He was slightly to the right and I was facing him and the horse was slanting and my face turned towards him

Judge Don't be in a hurry

Solicitor-General Now I strike at you (struck with right arm and brought his left shoulder round slightly away from Pelser and bent his head) How could the bullet strike him? The horse swerved and he must have come forward and the bullet entered his back

Solicitor-General This is merely a suggestion? Yes, because I cannot tell you exactly The man then dropped and I went to the house and left him there

Judge You did not stop to see? No, I did not stop to see whether he was alive or dead I rode off as quick as I could go and the first one I saw was my mother and I told her

Mr Solomon Now, now, now!

Solicitor-General Never mind what you said You saw your mother? Yes, and we sent for my father I took off my clothes and put on my town clothes My father came after I was dressed and we had a conversation and I rode off to town This was between eleven and twelve o'clock I reported the matter to Mr Hainsworth

Judge Was he the first man you saw? Yes He is the Civil Commissioner's Clerk

Solicitor-General Did you tell him the same story as you do to-day? Yes, though not in the same words I was very excited and may not have told all the details I did not report to any one else nor did I see the Chief Constable present when I spoke to Hainsworth though he might have come in whilst I was speaking I did not report to the Chief Constable (Williams) first and he must have heard it from Hainsworth I then went

D

back to the farm with the Chief Constable Williams and Dr
Paul and showed them the place where the body was   This was
after dinner   We found the man was dead   It was about 3
o'clock when we got there, but I cannot say exactly   The body
was lying on its back with its head towards the East in the
direction of the homestead   The iron bar was there lying about
a few yards from the body   The Chief Constable picked it up
The preliminary examination took place on the 20th I think but
I don't know exactly   I did not make a statement at the
examination

Solicitor-General   I believe the papers were sent to the
Solicitor-General ?

Mr Solomon   How does he know ?

Solicitor-General   I will show that he knew   (To witness)
You were re-examined and you were told that the papers would
be forwarded to the Solicitor-General ?   Yes

Judge   There was another examination after that ?

Solicitor-General   No   It appears the evidence was taken
upon two separate days the 20th and 27th and he was told on
the 27th

Witness   On the 11th February I made a statement as
follows —

I am not guilty   Latterly we have lost sheep day and night
in great numbers   When the deceased came to me I asked him
for a pass, as we did not allow anyone to go into our veldt
without a pass   Deceased was determined to go into our veldt
Upon this I went to fetch him back   When I got to him he
would not come back   At last he did go a few yards in the
direction of the house, but he suddenly turned back and struck
at me three times, in such a way as to show me my life was in
danger   I had already my revolver out for the purpose of
frightening him   The horse got restless, and when the horse
gave way for the deceased, the revolver went off and hit the
deceased   I thereupon went to the house and told my father,
and requested him at once to see about the man I had shot   I
am very sorry that such an occurrence should have taken place
as I had not the slightest intention to exercise malice

                                              W J PELSER

Did you ever confess that a crime had been committed ?
Never in my life   Then the statement in the letter is false ·

Mr Solomon   That is a matter of argument and we shall
endeavour to show it is not

Cross-examined by Mr Solomon   You do not know Mr
Don ?—No   The first time I saw him was at the preliminary
examination taken against him at King Williamstown   To my
knowledge he has never been in Burghersdorp

Judge   Don't use the words "To my knowledge," say "As
far as I know"   To my knowledge means that you know

Mr Solomon As far as you know he was never there ?—No
When the examination was taken against you, you were put in
the dock ?—No You were not ?—No ! At all events that was
not the first time that a charge—

Solicitor-General I must object —It is not evidence If he
was on his trial for murder you could not ask him such questions

Mr Solomon Of course I can What, not test his credibility ?

Judge I cannot have the matter disposed of in this off-hand
way I should like to have it argued Will it affect his credibility ?

Solicitor-General Certainly not, my Lord I do not know
whether it is true or not

Witness did not answer the question

Solicitor-General You can do so,

Witness The only time I was summoned before a Magistrate
the native who brought the charge did not appear

Mr Solomon Do you not remember that you and a man
named Abram de Klerk were charged with assaulting Klemboy ?
Yes And you pleaded guilty to that ? No, I did not ! Are
you certain ? You had better be careful Who said it ?

Mr Solomon I will tell you You were charged with striking
him with your fist—throwing him on the ground and kicking
him and then tying him to a waggon with a rem and beating
him with a stirrup leather Were you charged with that ?
(hesitation)

Judge Were you charged with it ?

Witness Yes, I was charged with it

Mr Solomon And you pleaded guilty to the charge ? I did
not I have the original here

Judge (smiling) Now Mr Solomon, don't excite yourself
(laughter)

Mr Solomon Can't you remember ? It is so long ago
Only 83 Yes but it is now 85 This is the only charge you
have against you ? I think Mr Edye was Magistrate This is
before Mr Andrews

Witness No, then I was not I was never before Mr Andrews

Judge Not on any charge ? No

Mr Solomon Then the official records are wrong It might
be another W Pelser I was before Mr Edye What for ?
For assault on Klemboy How long ago ? It must be that
(pointed to record in Mr Solomon's hand) You and de Klerk
were together ? Yes

Judge It may have been taken before Mr Edye and sent up
for signature to Mr Andrews

Mr Solomon The records say Pelser pleaded guilty, de Klerk
not guilty, and the prosecutor did not appear and case dismissed

Witness Then it must be wrong I never pleaded guilty to

the charge, it was just the reverse (record taken by Solicitor-General)

Solicitor-General This is not a record It is not signed You cannot put in a blank piece of paper

Mr Solomon We will prove it To witness Then again in May, 1884, you were charged with assault on a native named Jantjie Jonas? I do not know

Judge Do you know him? Where is he? (sharply) Do you know a Jantjie Jonas?

Witness Your Lordship, I have been charged several times, I will come up clearly

Mr Solomon You have been charged several times with assaults on natives? Yes And of course they were perfectly groundless? Yes (laughter), being charged and found guilty is different Do you know the case of Jantjie Jonas? If you explain the case I may know it

Judge Do you know of it? It might have been

Mr Solomon I will refresh your memory

Solicitor-General I hope this is a signed record

Mr Solomon This is it Jonas says he was on your farm, and you were coming up with a gun in your hand, and asked him what he was doing He replied, "I am going home" You said, "Go on," and at the same time struck him a blow on the back with the butt end of the gun You pushed him with the gun and told him to go on You then fired the gun He cannot say whether you fired at him as he was behind you The bullet went across his head

The Judge You say Jonas said this, and there is not a word of truth in it?

Witness No truth at all If you like I will tell you the story (laughter)

Mr Solomon Haven't natives brought charges against you several times? How many is this (laughter)? You said charges of assault had been brought against you several times? Yes That is true, I suppose, or you would not have said it? Yes How many can you remember? Two Two is not several? I can only remember those at present Jantjie Jonas disappeared, but I did not see him afterwards, and I do not know what became of him

Mr Solomon Abo and Marthinus David are in your employ? In my father's And David has been there for twenty years? I am only twenty-six, I can't say As long as I can remember he has been off and on there He stays away for a month, two months or so, and then comes back Abo has been likewise a long time I cannot say exactly where I was standing on the tramp-floor when Zacharias came up, it must have been with the boys I was about eight or ten yards from him I cannot say whether Abo or myself was nearest to him What he said was interpreted by Abo, as he spoke in Kaffir, which I do not understand, and my answers to him were interpreted by Abo   I spoke in Dutch, and I inferred Zacharias could not understand Dutch   You say he was standing about eight yards from you, and had an iron bar like this (held up bar) across his shoulders , you could not see it all?   Yes   Did you take particular notice of what he had behind him when he came up to you?   No , I noticed that he had something in his hand   it might have been a stick   It is not usual for a native to walk about with a thing like this?   It is usual, and I have seen it often , they use it for digging holes to get out roots   As it is usual to carry them will you tell us what it is used for?   Oh, yes , it is sometimes used for screwing beams together on the arms of ploughs   Is there any likelihood of picking up a piece of iron like this on your farm?   No , if I saw piece of iron like that on my farm I would pick it up and put it away in case I might require it   The native was standing about ten yards away   and I could tell it was iron he had across his shoulders   At the time he came to the tramp-floor did you settle the question in your mind that the rod was two feet long?   Yes, but I think—   You know English perfectly well   I want to know if you knew the length of the iron when he was at the tramp-floor?   No, I did not know   I suppose the Kafir spoke civilly?   No, I don't think so   Oh but you have such lordly ideas, you know, Mr Pelser   Please look at the Jury   It is rather difficult to answer you and look at the Jury at the same time

Judge   Try to do so

Mr Solomon   What else did he do?   He mumbled and from the way he acted showed that he did not like to go and get a pass   Is that all?   Yes   Up to that time he had been perfectly civil in his demeanour?   Yes   He told you he was looking for his master's horse?   I can't say exactly   Let me try and bring it to your recollection

Judge   Did Abo interpret "my master's horse"?

Witness   He may have said so but I did not understand Abo to interpret it

Judge   At the time you did not think he mentioned "master's horse"?   No   After that I heard the boys saying that he was looking for his master's horse

Mr Solomon   And when he told you he was looking for his horse you said nothing in reply?   I told him he must not go as I could not allow him   I understood that he was looking for his own horse and if he went to get a pass I would let him

Mr Solomon   What were his last words?   He spoke in Kafir I told Abo to say he should not go into my veltd

Judge   Did Abo interpret that?   He spoke to him in Kafir I believe he said so

Mr Solomon   And when you saw him go off you were very

indignant? No, not at all Oh, you did not mind it? No, I thought it was my duty to go and bring him back And you made a remark on leaving that you would fine him 2s? Yes Did you say when he went "Oh, let him go, I'll show him I'll make him pay me 15s for this"? No What did you say? I said it is a trouble to go and get that boy back and to bring him to town as we have so much to do I'll fine him 2s and let him off Then your intention in going after him was to fine him 2s and let him go after the horse? No If he had done it I would have sent him off

Judge Would you have let him off? I do not know what I should have done

Mr Solomon If he had paid you you would have brought him back and taken him to town? Yes What would you have done if he had not paid you the 2s? I may have granted him a pass I do not know what should I have done What do you think you would have done if you had taken him to town? Don't evade my question I should have given him over to the police for trespass And to save yourself the trouble you would have fined him 2s? I said it in a joke Now, now Mr Pelser don't say that I was not angry about it Then the impertinence and incivility were nothing? No I laughed You thought you would have had no difficulty in getting the 2s from him? I can't say Did you go after that native with the determination to bring him back at all risks? It is an easy question No I never thought about anything of the kind Then what did you go after him for? I went to bring him back I did not think he would resist If you thought there would be no difficulty to bring him back why did you go into the house and get your revolver? It is mere custom Oh! Yes, it is mere custom It was such a custom with you to carry a revolver that you simply and involuntarily put it on? Yes Was it loaded? It is always loaded, at this time I did not look The horse you rode on this occasion, was it a black one? Yes A quiet horse? Yes In fact so quiet that the children on the farm rode it? Yes I believe the native boys ride it with what you call a reim in its mouth? Yes Had you spurs on? No Is it a lazy horse? Not exactly so Had you anything in your hand? Yes, I had a switch—a little sjambok You had not a rod of iron? No Are you quite certain? Yes, certain Zachariah, what was his height? A little more than five feet Not a little more, say about my height? He was about five feet or so Oh, hang it, I'm a little more than that (laughter) He was a moderately sized man When you went up to him did you speak? Yes In what language? I spoke in English and Dutch first

Judge What did he say? It is difficult for me to say Not if you heard his words? I cannot remember his words

Mr Solomon When you came up to him did you ask him for the 2s ? No Then you soon gave up that idea ? Yes, when I went to the house I was joking Then you took out your pistol ? He saw you had the pistol out ? Yes How high is the horse—13 or 14 hands ? Between 13 and 14 hands Now, now, was it big or little It wasn't a donkey was it ? It was 14 hands When you took out the pistol was he frightened ? No He did not seem so You made him turn round ? I said you must go on You brought the horse right up to his heels ? I won't be sure

Judge How did you do it ? I pushed the horse towards him to make him go on

Mr Solomon And you got very angry because he would not go on ? I was—not very

The Judge The question is were you angry ? Yes, I was angry

Mr Solomon I want to know how far you were when he turned round ? My horse's nose was almost touching him And he knew you had the pistol out ? Yes He must have seen it as I had it in my hand When he turned he simply suddenly turned round and made a blow—did he hit the horse ? I do not know whether he hit it or not The horse swerved and it had a halter on I want you to go through your performance again Did he strike the horse or strike at the horse ? I should say that he struck the horse Do you mean to say you could not tell being so close to him ? I didn't expect him He struck at the horse, then the horse gave way Was he still facing you ? Yes He saw I had the revolver out He struck at me several times How many ? Three times Why can you say three times

Judge Besides one at the horse ? Yes

Mr Solomon Did he hit you ? No It was at the last time that the revolver——I want to know how you were ? I cannot tell exactly It is so difficult You were quite close ? I was a little distance

Judge How was it ? It is so difficult Yes, but you must get over those difficulties ? He struck at me three times Was the horse facing the native, or how ? If you explained it to the authorities as you do now I cannot see how they understood you The horse was facing round I was sitting on the horse facing the native If you did not explain it better to Dr Paul I do not see how he could come to any intelligent decision (witness smiled) This is no laughing matter, I can assure you The native stood on the right side and as he struck with his right hand he bent forward and the bullet went into his left shoulder

Mr Solomon How did he do it ? The horse swerved a little on one side When the revolver went off was he in the act of striking, or had the revolver already gone off? He was in the act of striking

Solicitor-General Just happened then? Yes

Mr Solomon At all events he was facing you? He was facing me with his left shoulder a little forward On which side were you? I was on the left side Look at this coat (Zacharias' coat produced) You see where the bullet hole is—how far from the middle seam? Three fingers I am going to put the coat on a man

Judge What for?

Mr Solomon To show where the bullet wound is

Solicitor-General Surely this is explained by the Doctor

Judge But if it was not explained in a more intelligent way than it is now I cannot see how he could decide

Mr Solomon You were present when the doctor made a *post mortem*? Yes And you saw the bullet had penetrated the spinal marrow? I don't know

Judge You know what the spine is? Yes I saw him take it out of the spine And if it had gone on it would have come out where? I think it would have come out at the right side of the back below the right arm (man put coat on and stood facing witness)

Mr Solomon Now the coat is on I want you to explain how when in firing the bullet could have lodged there? By his raising his right hand and by turning his—(man rose his right hand and turned as if in act of striking, but his left shoulder turned naturally from witness) I do not see any difficulty (native put through it again and bent forward as directed) It is strange that the wound did come there

Judge I can understand it It is a question for the Jury Cannot you call Dr Paul when this witness could show how it was done?

Mr Solomon You are quite sure you were not behind him? Yes The man was facing you? Yes And facing you when he struck? Yes I do not mean with his whole body He was facing you and struck you? Yes Did you take up the revolver or did it go off by accident? I had to pull up the horse Did you intend to pull the trigger? Yes, but it went off sooner than I expected it I was pulling up the horse You intentionally shot the man because you thought your life in danger? Is that so?

Judge Would you have shot to protect yourself? Did you consider your life in danger? I shot to disable him not to kill him

Mr Solomon You did not come down from your horse to see if he was killed or not? No You didn't get down to see if he was disabled? No I was very excited Then you think that if you had shot at him in self-defence your first duty would have been to get off your horse and see what you could do for him? Yes Is it natural Yes, it would have been my duty Instead of that you galloped off to Burghersdorp to protect yourself? No I first went off to the house and told my father I don't want that You went to Burghersdorp to protect yourself and you saw Mr Harmsworth and said " I am in for a row, I have shot a Kafir " I don't remember what words This is an important thing Surely you can remember what you said

Judge (sharply) Did you say it? I may have said it but I think Mr Harmsworth has turned it, (read following statement made by witness to Mr Harmsworth)

" I am in for a row I have shot a Kafir It occured this way I was riding on my farm when I saw a Kafir going through the veldt I rode up to him and asked him what he wanted there, he answered ' I have come to look for a horse ' I then demanded to see his pass, but he said he had none I told him to leave my veldt as I did not allow natives to roam about there without passes I then went away some little distance, and on looking back saw the Kafir still in my veldt I thereupon rode up to him and told him that as he did not choose to leave I would give him into custody of the Police, and I then sent for two Policemen who had passed me previously I reined my horse in front of the Kafir, and he then said, ' You'll not stop me ' He had a bar of iron in his hand, and with this he struck my horse a blow on the nose My horse thereupon became restive and unmanageable, and the Kafir then struck at my leg with the iron I turned the horse round and as I did so I saw his arm raised again to strike me, and I thereupon shot him "

Witness I did not say to Harmsworth " I went some little distance and on looking back saw the Kafir in my veldt " I did not say I rode up to Zacharias and told him if he did not choose to leave I would give him into the custody of the Police " I told Harmsworth that I sent for the Police before I went It is all correct but Mr Harmsworth just turned it

Mr Solomon How do you mean? He has mixed it up I did not tell Mr Harmsworth that I reined my horse up in front of the Kafir and he then said " You will not stop me " I did not say to Mr Harmsworth that I turned the horse round and as I did so I saw his arm raised again to strike me and I thereupon shot him " Did you on that occasion tell Harmsworth that the pistol went off sooner than you expected No, I don't think so You did not No And do you mean to say that you did not tell him that you shot the Kafir as he raised his hand to strike you? No I said while he was striking

Solicitor-General Did you say anything? I said whilst striking at me

E

Judge   What did you do then ?   I shot the Kafir

Mr Solomon   You had an Attorney watching the case had you not ?   Yes, Mr Knobel   And he cross-examined Mr Harmsworth ?   Can you explain why when Harmsworth said you told him that you shot the Kafir while he was striking that there is no cross-examination upon it ?   No I cannot   Was anyone present when you made the statement to Harmsworth ?   I cannot swear positively   I think Mr Williams came in just at the end of it   And you made a separate statement to Williams ?   I don't know, I may have done   To tell the truth they came up rushing to me   One asked me this and one that

Judge   No, no   Do you not know if you made a statement ?   I don't know, I might have done so

Mr Solomon   Did you not tell Williams that you shot a Kafir on your farm ?   I may have told him   And he asked you under what circumstances ?   Williams may have asked me for an explanation   And you replied that the Kafir said he came on to the farm to look for a horse ?   I may have said so   You then said, " I asked the Kafir if he had a pass, and the Kafir replied he had no pass ? '   Yes   " I then ordered him back to get a pass "   I may have said that, I cannot say   ' I insisted on his going back, but the Kafir would not do so "   I may have said that   " I then rode up to the Kafir to tell him to go back "   Did you say that ?   Yes   ' The Kafir turned round and struck at my horse with an iron bar about two feet long "   I may have said it,   Did you tell him that the Kafir struck a second blow at you and you then drew the revolver and shot him ?   I may have said that   You went out with Williams to the body ?   Yes

Judge   Did you say he struck three blows ?   It may be   I cannot say that I made this statement

Mr Solomon   You heard Williams give his evidence at the preliminary examination ?   Yes   And you told us you had an Attorney ?   Yes   And you did not challenge the statements made by him, and you did not get him to cross-examine when you heard him say you shot him when he struck the second blow ?   No   Williams went out with you to the spot where the body was found ?   Yes   And you told Williams he would find the wound on the man's head ?   Yes   In the front of the head ?   I can't say that   On the right side of the head ?   No

Judge   Didn't you point out on the corpse and say the right side of the head, that is what Williams said ?   No   When I saw a mark on the side of the face I thought that to be the bullet wound   I thought it might possibly be the mark   The Doctor saw it before I saw it

Mr Solomon   You have told us that as the man was striking at you the man bent down his shoulder and that is how he got the wound

Solicitor-General No He said he could not say It was merely his opinion I distinctly asked him the question in his evidence in chief, and that is the explanation he gave

Mr Solomon When the man struck at you did you or did you not see the man bring his shoulder forward ? I did not look at him so particularly Do you wish us to believe that you on horseback with a loaded revolver and the man on foot that you could do nothing but shoot him ? You could not have ridden away ? There were two ways, I had to defend myself or die the death of a coward (sensation, during which the Messenger's stentorian voice proclaimed "Silence")

Judge If he had hit you and you had ridden away, what position would you have been in ? My life would have been in danger

Judge Then you should have ridden away, and it is as well that you should know what you should have done

Mr Solomon It was only a black man You had no respect for the sacredness of human life Did you assist to look for the body ? Yes, I was under arrest, and sent for on the 16th

Judge After you made a report to the Police you came out with them ? Yes I went into town twice on the 16th You went in to tell Harmsworth and then they took you back again ? Yes

Mr Solomon Did you only show the body ? No, I showed some spoors Did you see the spoors of the horse where the man was lying ? Yes Did you show them to Williams ? I cannot say, because it was grassy, and I won't swear it was five yards

Judge How far ? A little more than two

Mr Solomon You heard Williams swear at the cross-examination that the horse's spoors were five yards away from the body ? I was there, but I did not hear him Now, you are an intelligent man, and if he did say that it must have struck you that it was a very strong point against you I do not understand law Oh that will do ! I did not care much about Harmsworth or Williams' statements, because I didn't think they contained anything against me

Judge Did you think that when you made your statements before the Magistrate did you then think they would go to help you ? No, I cannot say Then why did you make them ? You say you thought nothing about Harmsworth and Williams, then why did you make a statement ? (hesitation) There were two statements one on the 20th and another on the 27th Harmsworth and Williams both gave evidence and you do not cross-examine though on the 11th February you make a statement ? They did not say exactly what I said

Mr Solomon Why did you not cross-examine them ? I had an Attorney. But you should have instructed your Attorney Did you show Williams the spoors on the 16th that is the indications ?   I could not show him all the spoors as there was some grass   There were indications of a struggle

Judge   Be careful   Was there a struggle ?

Mr Solomon   There must have been—the man striking and the horse jumping about

Judge   That does not exactly constitute a struggle, Mr Solomon

Mr Solomon   Why did you say on the 11th February that the revolver went off because the horse was restive ?   By that I mean it went off before I meant to pull it off   You say it was an accident and now you say it went off before you intended pulling the trigger

Judge   How is it consistent with what you stated to Williams —on hearing him say it why did you allow it to pass (revolver handed to witness) ?   You see it can go off easily

Mr Solomon   You knew that when you pulled the trigger that it would not miss the man ?   No, I did not   It might have done so   Then why did you say a little while ago that you intended to disable him ?   Yes, I wanted to do so before   I intended to shoot him, but it went off before—when I was preparing   Now, it is only a while ago that you said it was only when the arm was raised you shot him ?   I had the revolver out all the time, and he turned, and as I was putting my revolver in aim all this happened   Then the only explanation you can give for the course of the bullet is that the man lent slightly forward ?   I was not in front of him   I'll be the native, and you come about two yards from me

Judge   Do you understand it ?   Yes   Witness took pistol and Mr Solomon turned his back and went through the performance of turning round to witness, and pretending to strike with the iron bar

Witness   I was facing him and stood to the right hand and as he struck I was a little excited and the revolver went off

Mr Solomon   Do you know that the bullet went into the spinal marrow ?   Yes

Solicitor-General   I understand that as you were on the horse the native leant forward and the bullet went diagonally across his back   This is only an explanation, it is not the actual one only a possible one ?   Yes   And you are certain that you did not shoot this man when he was walking in front of the horse ?   I am certain of that   I would not do a thing like that   This happened close to the railway line where people were passing backwards and forwards continually ?   Yes

Judge   How close to the railway line ?   About five or eight hundred yards

Solicitor-General   It is about 560 yards, my Lord   You mentioned to Williams that he would probably find the bullet in the head ?   Yes, I may have done so.   You say the pistol having gone off before you actually intended to shoot you did not know where he had been struck? Yes The horse you rode is quiet, but would object to be struck over the head? Yes He is a "kopspeiller," and you must have something in your hand to make him go on (laughter) You did not use a bar like this (held bar up)? No Now about these charges You say several have been brought against you. Klemboy never appeared and Jantjie Jonas You say you never heard anything more about the case? Yes

Judge There were such men as Jantjie and Klemboy, you saw them, and something happened, but you did not assault them? Yes And they lodged a complaint against you? Yes, and did not appear And then charges are not a correct version of what happened? No, my Lord You say you did not know whether you were struck? No But you say you were going to disable him Where were you going to shoot? At his arm Then why did you point to the head to Williams and say he would find it there? (hesitation) If you did not know where it struck why did you tell him to look on the head? I wanted to shoot his arm, and I did not know where I had struck him Did you ever tell anyone that you shot at his arm before to-day? No

Solicitor-General You mean officials, I suppose

Judge No, no, to anyone Did you ever say it to anyone? I don't think so

Solicitor-General I should like to ask him through you, my Lord, did he tell me so?

Mr Solomon In consultation?

Solicitor-General Yes

Judge Did you ever tell anyone so? I might have told them so but I will not swear to it

Solicitor-General That will finish the evidence for the prosecution so far

Mr Solomon Won't my learned friend bring the Doctor?

Solicitor-General That will do afterwards

Judge I do not wish to throw out anything After leading this evidence I should like you to go to the authorities and see whether you can go on with the evidence Whether you are debarred from leading rebutting evidence of the same character

Solicitor-General It is merely whether I go on with it or not

Judge The question is if after they have led evidence to rebut the evidence whether you can lead evidence afterwards to confirm this evidence Will you look up authority

The Court adjourned at 5 45 p m to Friday morning

FRIDAY, NOVEMBER 13 1885

The Court resumed at 10 10 a m

The Jury having responded to their names the Judge asked the Solicitor-General if he had looked into the matter alluded to, on the previous evening

Solicitor-General   I have decided to go on with the case

Judge   You will find the authorities as clear as possible on the point

Solicitor-General   I will go on   The next witness is Dr Paul

Dr Paul on being sworn was examined as follows by the Solicitor-General —Your name is Ferdinand Paul, and you are a Doctor of Medicine?   Yes   You are District Surgeon of Albert?   Yes   You recollect on the 16th January last going out to an inspection in company with Pelser?   Yes   You went to the farm Roodebergsvlei where he was living?   Yes   What time was it?   About 2 o'clock   You found the body of a native?   Yes   Dead?   Yes

Judge   In the veldt?   Yes, about half a mile from the house

Solicitor-General   Now, how was it lying?   It was lying with its head North-east, on its back   What further did you find?   I found above the left shoulder blade about an inch and a half to two inches from the spine an oval puncture

Judge   What you call a gunshot wound?   A bullet wound I further examined and I found that a bullet had travelled in an oblique direction towards the spine, fracturing the second vertebra of the spine   I found a bullet embedded in the second vertebra compressing the spinal marrow

Solicitor-General   Was the spinal marrow injured?   It was compressed   Merely compressed not broken?   No, not broken There were no external signs of any injury and on internal examination I found all the organs in a healthy state   To cut short the wound was the cause of death?   Yes   How did the bullet go in?   It went in horizontally

Judge   Not downwards or upwards?   No   There was no deflection   Could you see where it was?   No, I could not

Solicitor-General   From such a wound as you found there would a man drop at once?   He might   You found the marrow so far compressed that it would produce an immediate collapse? Yes   You say the wound was an oval one?   Yes   What does this show?   That the shot was not fired in direct from the back but sidewards   That it was not fired direct into the back but in a slanting way?   Yes

Judge   You mean not direct from the back?   Yes   Did it touch any bone before it lodged in the spine?   No, the wound was a flesh wound before it struck the vertebræ   Being a flesh wound you think the bullet kept its course as it had been fired? Yes

Solicitor-General You heard Pelser give his evidence yesterday? Yes You heard him say he was struck three times, or rather the horse was struck on the head and he was struck three times? Yes

Mr Solomon No he did not say that

Solicitor-General Well, he was struck at, and three blows were made at himself? Yes You heard him say that he was being attacked and that each time a blow was being struck the horse swerved away? Yes He has given a possible explanation of how the wound was caused? There are a great many explanations of how it could be caused

Judge Give us every possible explanation how it could be caused? There are many ways possible First, if he was riding alongside the man, the man being right close to the horse's head on the right

Solicitor-General Not in front of the horse? No Then he might have been walking right in front of the horse's head and turned round slightly to the left and he may have then received the wound from Pelser on his horse

Judge From behind? Yes What is the third? The native in the act of striking

Solicitor-General Place the native

Witness On the left side of the horse striking at the horse and the horse swerved to the left of the deceased and Pelser had then fired it might have been caused

Solicitor-General The next? I heard Pelser say that he was standing to the right side of the horse and the native was striking at its head and the horse swerved backwards so as to come to the left side of the native and that then the pistol went off If so that wound may so have been caused You heard the native witnesses examined before the Magistrate at the preliminary examination? Yes You heard Veldshoen say "The man was walking in front of the horse which the Dutchman was riding The horse's head could touch the man as he walked?"

Judge Does he not say he saw the shooting?

Solicitor-General Yes, my Lord, in the first part of his evidence he says "I saw the white man shoot him and then gallop towards the house" He says the man fell at the time he was walking

Judge This is a matter for argument

Solicitor-General Supposing if a man had been walking in front of the horse and Pelser had then fired at him? It would then have been a round wound—the bullet would have entered straight

Judge Supposing if he had shot and the bullet had travelled on Where would it have come out? It would have come out on the left breast Not straight through? No Would it have met a resistance? Most likely What bone? One of the ribs on the right And so be deflected? I wish to correct myself, if the bullet had gone straight through though it would have had its exit on the left breast near the nipple

Solicitor-General Well you heard the men Canteen and Ntloyiya give evidence? Yes You heard the latter say "I saw the white man shoot him He was about two yards from the native The native's back was turned towards the white man's horse The native fell when he was shot?" Yes If the native had been in front of Pelser about two yards with his back to the horse, could the shot have been fired then? No

Mr Solomon Did you make any measurements when you found the body of the deceased? No I mean did you measure the distance from the wound to the spine? No Why do you say it is one and a half inches—it is very important You ought to have measured it, Doctor I should say nearer two inches And what depth was it embedded I found the bullet embedded in the cavity of the spine What depth is that? About two inches from the back I don't mean how far it travelled in an oblique direction How far was it in the back? About two inches Then if that is the case, then the wound in the body being about two inches from the middle of the back and the bullet embedded about two inches deep in the spine the shot must have been fired at an angle of about forty degrees? Yes I don't quite understand your question

Judge The bullet you found lodged in the spinal cavity and it would have come out about the nipple of the right breast

Solicitor-General No, he did not say that

Mr Solomon I want you to illustrate on this Kafir (Kafir produced) so as to be made clear to the jury

Witness The bullet if it had pursued its course from the wound would have found its exit at the right breast, but if deflected may have come out under the armpit

Mr Solomon According to you it must have been fired at an angle of 45 degrees You have to draw a line from a vertical point? Yes You have given a great many explanations of this I want to ask you as an intelligent man, and as a man of common sense, how you think the wound could have been inflicted? My conclusion is that if I had seen the body and examined the wound without reference to any of the stated circumstances I should have said that the shot had been fired sidewards (Mr Solomon put the native in front of him to the right, at an angle of about 45 degrees)

Witness You must be higher than the native

Mr Solomon I will be the native and you be Pelser (Position taken up) If I were walking in front of you and I slightly turned my head like this (head turned half way, accompanied by movement of body to the left) could the wound have been inflicted ? Yes That being the case why did you say that the native's evidence was entirely inconsistent with the nature of the wound ?

Judge I suggest that the preliminary examination be read to the Jury

Mr Solomon It will be read when our case commences It is part of our case (To witness) You will admit that at a distance of 400 yards it would be impossible for a native to see whether Pelser was immediately behind the native or slightly on one side ? Yes And if this native had said that Pelser was slightly at the side of Zachariah then his evidence would have been perfectly consistent with the course the bullet took ? Yes Supposing a man had been immediately behind the native and he had given the slightest twist to his back, could the wound have been caused in that way ? Yes I mean swaggering ? Yes If Pelser had fired at the man—

Judge This makes the sixth

Mr Solomon If Zachariah was in the act of striking and facing Pelser and—

Witness If deceased had struck at Pelser facing him in front and then Pelser shot, the wound could not possibly have been where you see the wound And if Pelser had been slightly on one side—to the side of him—and the native in the act of striking at him (Mr Solomon put himself in the position of the native with Dr Paul standing with his head turned towards him) could the wound be inflicted ? Not without you expose your left shoulder more I cannot do so, as I strike you with my right the left recedes Is it possible supposing I am striking at you, to bring my left shoulder forward whilst I strike with my right? It is impossible, the muscles are so formed to operate in that way

Judge Do it slowly Mr Solomon

Mr Solomon There, now I strike with my right hand the left one must recede

Witness Yes, he cannot do it

Judge Supposing instead of striking—whilst striking Mr Solomon fell, wouldn't the left shoulder still be deflected back ? Yes Then how could you get at the left shoulder? You could not The shot would have gone downwards It would not have taken a horizontal direction ? No If he had missed his blow and fallen and the horse backed when he fell, you say the shot would not have been horizontal but would have gone down ? Yes —Just listen again, Doctor If the deceased fell whilst striking at Pelser with his right arm, Pelser being in front of him and slightly to his left and the pistol then went off, would the wound on the body be inflicted ? It would have had a different direction and not a horizontal

Mr Solomon Then I say your opinion as a medical man is

F

this, that Pelser must have been behind the Kafir and slightly to his left? Yes If the native was on the left and the horse swerved he might have got the wound? Well, that is, the horse would have had to describe almost a semi-circle

Judge Then the native must have been standing because of the horizontal nature of the wound? Yes

Mr Solomon Pelser said yesterday that the native was on the right when he struck at him Can you conceive how the horse swerved all the way round when he struck? No

Solicitor-General Pelser never said anything of the kind He said he was on the side of him and the horse swerved and backed

Judge What he said was that the native was more to his right

Solicitor-General Pelser says that the horse swerved and he pulled him back and then his pistol went off

Judge He says the horse became restless He swerved and backed and I pulled him up (to witness) If the native struck at Pelser in front of him or at his right and the horse gave way, would the wound have then been caused? It might though he must have swerved round to the back

Mr Solomon As a man of common sense you think that very improbable?

Solicitor-General That is a question for the Jury

Judge Is it so?

Witness It is possible but not probable

Mr Solomon From the examination of the wound, could you say what distance he was off when the shot was fired? I cannot rightly say, at least two yards The effect of compressing the spinal marrow would be to paralyze the lower limbs altogether? Yes And that would cause the native to drop where he was shot? Yes You did not notice if there were any powder marks on the coat? No I saw none Wouldn't you infer from that that he was more than two yards off when he fired? It is a small revolver and a small charge of powder There was nothing in the wound inconsistent with the shot being fired at a distance of five yards? No

Solicitor-General You say that the man most probably dropped when he was shot? Yes If he was two yards away from the horse when he was shot do you expect to see hoof marks there? Yes Did you actually see any spoors? I left the examination of the ground to the Chief Constable Was the wound caused in any other way? It may have been caused if deceased's back was slightly bent If the horse had swerved when struck at and then backed some short distance so as to come behind the native, then the wound might have been caused if the deceased was standing to the left, and I also think the deceased's back had been slightly bent at the time,

Mr Solomon   Mr Pelser must have been riding a circus-horse considering the extraordinary gyrations

Judge   You may amuse yourself some other time, Mr Solomon   This is a serious question

The Doctor was thanked and left the Box

Abo, a Kafir was next called and stated, in reply to the Solicitor-General, that he was in the employ of Mr Pelser On the 16th January I was riding corn to the tramp floor from the lands   Whilst I was there I recollect a native came there When he came to the tramp floor there were present Marthinus David, old Master Willem, Abram de Klerk Willem Jacobus Pelser and Marthinus David the younger   I was upon the wagon when the native came, throwing down the corn on to the tramp floor   I saw the man   He came there and after greeting us he asked me about a horse   He was then standing on the other side of the wall against the ridge   There is a wall there The tramp floor is inside the wall   He was standing outside the tramp floor when he asked about the horse   I said I had not seen such a horse   We both spoke Kafir   Then he asked me to enquire of the old man Marthinus David if he had seen anything of it   He said no   He described the horse and said it was a black one   I spoke to Marthinus in Dutch   The master asked me what the man wanted   I said He is in search of a horse   Then the master asked him if he had a pass   and I said I did not know   Then the master said "Ask him"   I did so and the man said 'No"   The master then told me to tell him to return immediately   Everything he said I interpreted to the master   The man then said "I cannot go for a pass because the horse does not belong to me," and then with that he went

Solicitor-General   Mr Pelser said that as he was going away he was talking something

Judge   When he was going away what did he do?   He did not do anything   Did he say anything?   No nothing special How do you mean?   He only said he could not go for a pass He did not mumble or speak low in my hearing   When he left he went in the direction of the ridge which is away from the homestead going in the veldt   My master then went and stood upon the wall looking where the man was going   Then Marthinus David asked the master where the man was   and the master replied ' There he goes"   He also added 'Let him go, I will make him pay 15s"   With that he came down from the wall I did not hear him say what he would do with the money

Solicitor-General   Now when the Kafir came there that morning had he anything in his hand?   Yes   Can you say what it was, did you notice at that time what it was?   It appeared to me to be a switch—a laatjie   How thick was it? About the thickness of my small finger   How did he carry it? Across his shoulders with his hands at each end, and I could see

it was a switch because it was pliable Did you take particular
notice of this? I didn't notice particularly though I could see
it What length was it, was it as long as this (holding up bar)?
No Longer than that Before the magistrate you said it was
the same length? I did not say so I will read what you said
' I noticed that the Kafir had something in his hand I
thought it was a switch It was the same length as the piece of
iron now produced" I don't know those words You said you
thought it was a switch? I didn't think it was a switch I
said it was And he kept this switch or whatever it was—on
his shoulders till he went away? Yes He did not remain
long speaking

Judge And when he left had he still got it? Yes, he turned
and went into the veldt

Solicitor-General Since you gave the evidence before the
Magistrate you have been twice in King William's Town? Yes
You went to see the Attorney (Mr Innes) for Mr Don? Yes

Mr Solomon I should like to know why these insinuations
are thrown out

Solicitor-General I have not thrown out any insinuations

Judge I don't think that, Mr Solomon It is quite clear
the man has altered his evidence, and I do not think the
Solicitor-General meant to insinuate anything

Abo continuing After my master came down from the wall he
remained standing there for a little while Without saying a word
he walked towards the house He went in and then we saw him
go towards a spot where there are two poles planted on a little
height It is a seat made for the old master upon a rise and
you can see a large part of the farm from it There I saw him
looking through a telescope in the direction the Kafir had gone
He came down and went again to the house Then we saw him
pass on horseback He was some distance from us He pulled
up and called for Marthinus and said "Catch Kenning's horse
and ride down to call the Police down below at the cottage" It
is a railway cottage I did not know there were Police there I
did not see Police that morning I had been in the lands and
had not seen them though I heard of them being there Marthinus
got the horse and rode away to the cottage When master had
given the order he rode on and went in the direction of the line
The next thing I saw was when master was returning from the
man

Solicitor-General When you saw the master returning from
the veldt, was Marthinus back already? No When the
master came back how was he coming, was he in a hurry or not?
He came galloping And went straight to the house? Yes
Then we saw people coming out of the house and examine the
horse and turn him about Then the people went into the house,
and Nettie Pelser ran to the fountain where the old master was

Then we saw him coming up to the house and he entered We remained at work Then after that we saw Pelser come out of the house, mount his horse, and race away towards town

Judge And as he was racing towards town did he meet Marthinus? Yes Just as he got past the kraal where there is a sluit he met him

Solicitor-General It is a short distance from the house? Yes So he met him just as he had started? Yes

Judge Did he stop? No he simply rode past him Were you near enough to hear? No

Solicitor-General You do not know if he spoke to him? No From the time the master went away till he came back how long was it? It was not so long

Cross-examined by Mr Solomon When Zachariah came to the tramp floor who was the nearest to him? I was And how far were you off from him? About fifteen yards Where was young Mr Pelser? He was in the tramp floor How far away? He was about twelve yards from me You say Zachariah was perfectly civil? Yes How far was Pelser from him? About twenty-five yards

Judge Was he ever nearer than that to the Kafir? No, not while he was talking Was he nearer at any time at all? No You were nearest to Zachariah all the time? Yes

Mr Solomon What was the first remark the Kafir made when he came up How did he greet you? He greeted us in a friendly way All the time he was there, was he speaking in a friendly way? Yes, he spoke so Now when the Kafir said he could not go back for a pass as he was looking for his master's horse and not his own did you interpret it to Pelser? And did Pelser make any reply to that? Yes, he said he must go home and get a pass

Judge And what did the man say? He said I cannot go Did not Pelser say, Tell the man he must get a pass whether it is his master's horse or not? Yes He only once said he must get a pass

Mr Solomon He told you it was a black horse? Yes Did he give you any other description? Yes, he said it was a gelding You say you thought it was a switch in his hand? I did not think so because I said it was Why did you say so? Because I could see that it bent When you saw the people examining the black horse at the house—did you go too? I didn't go immediately Did you during the day? That evening I did And did you see anything the matter with it? No nothing special What you mean by "special" Did you see the mark? No, nothing that was broken

Judge Did you look at its head? Were there any marks? Nothing that I saw

Solicitor-General The horse had a halter on? That evening it had one on

Judge Can you say it had one on when it came back from the veldt? That I cannot say

Mr Solomon One or two questions arise out of this examination which go to test the credibility of witness This witness said to-day that he did not see the Policemen Before the Magistrate he said " I saw Marthinus ride away in the direction the Police had taken "

Judge Put that to him

Witness I did not say this

Judge What did you say about the Police? I did not speak of the Policemen How did the Magistrate imagine it? I can't say

Solicitor-General And you did not say that Marthinus rode in the same direction the Police had taken? That is what they told me Who told you? Marthinus

Judge Why did you tell the Magistrate that Marthinus rode after the Police How did you know it? We heard our master call out and say he must ride after the Police Just look at that (iron bar handed to witness) Now put it behind your back Did you go to the body? No When did you first see that rod? In this office, Did you ever see such a rod on your master's place? No When the master came from the veldt you say he dressed and raced off to town? Yes Did he change his jacket? I didn't notice After the master came back did you see anyone going to the veldt where the Kafir was after the master had gone to town? Yes Whom did you see? I saw the old master (Mr Pelser, sen) Go towards where the Kafir had gone? Yes he first came to us On foot? Yes At the tramp floor? Yes He then asked us if we had seen a man that had been there and we said yes You cannot say what he said (turning to Counsel) If neither of you object I should like to ask him a question but I cannot do so if you object

Solicitor-General I object to a question on the conversation Not that there is anything in it, but,

Judge Oh, very well I will not put it (to witness) He spoke to you? Yes, and he left and went through the gate in the direction which the man had taken We then went over the wall with a view of standing on the ridge to see where he went This was in consequence of what he had said Then we saw him speak to some people at work—it was the natives at work on the telegraph line He then came back to the house and then we went to our work Where was Marthinus at that time? He was also upon the floor Where was Frederick David? He was behind at the stock in the field He had not been at work at the tramp floor Did you see in which direction he had gone with the stock? No Then you cannot say where he was relative to the direction the deceased had taken? No When the old master came to you had he anything in his hand? Yes What? A stick Does he always have it? Yes He walks with it Had he anything else? No Now when your master went to the veldt on horseback had he anything with him? Yes What? A revolver I did not see anything else When did you first see the dead body? I did not see it at all

Mr Solomon Will your Lordship ask one question How far was he from Pelser when he rode up from the veldt and met Marthinus? [question put] I was as far as to Page's store (about 200 yards)

Judge You saw the pistol? Yes Where was it? I saw the belt over the shoulders And could you see if he had anything in his hand? No If he had anything could you have seen it? No You cannot say if he had anything in his hand? No, that I cannot Now you have seen the master ride the horse before? Yes Now when he rode the horse did he generally have anything in his hand? Nothing but a laatpe Was it a sjambok? No Have you seen him ride the horse with a sjambok? Yes, sometimes He may have had one on this occasion—you cannot tell? Not that day

Abram de Klerk was called

Solicitor-General You were at the tramp floor? Yes When the master came there? Yes I was driving How did you drive them? With a whip I stood inside and the horses go round me Where was the Kaffir when you first saw him? Approaching from the house He came to the floor and he was carrying an iron on his back on his shoulders in this way (intimated by holding hands up level with his shoulders) it was about two feet or two-and-a-half long and one hand was on each end You noticed it was a bar of iron? Yes Something like this (bar produced)? Yes You could not see the ends of the iron? Tell us what happened He stood outside the wall

Judge Where was Abo? He was in the floor What part of it? On the floor What doing? He was working with the corn

Solicitor-General As he came to the wall he dropped it down by his side perpendicularly and pressed one end on the ground? Yes At any rate you could not see it all as you were standing behind the wall It seemed to you that he was pressing upon it?

Mr Solomon Don't lead him He has said that

Solicitor-General Well go on! He did not speak at first and Pelser asked him where he was going in Dutch He did not get a reply Then Pelser spoke through Abo Then Abo asked him where he was going He said he was in search of a horse belonging to his master Then Pelser asked him whether he had a pass and he said "No" Then Pelser said he was to return to his master and get a pass Then he turned and left What was the last thing he said when he left? He said he had no need to carry a pass

Judge In what language? Kafir

Solicitor-General Did Abo interpret that? Yes

Judge You cannot understand Kafir? No

Solicitor-General What were the last words Abo interpreted? That was the last thing, but as the Kafir walked away he went speaking and Abo could not understand, no more could we Then Pelser went towards the house and stood upon the wall, and he said he would make the Kafir pay 2s He thought the Kafir had been impertinent and he would make him pay 2s And did he say he would go and get him when the policemen came? Yes, and then he went to the house How did he go to the house? In what direction? He went straight from the floor to the house Is there a gate? Yes But he got from the floor on to the wall and got down and over the gate? He was standing on the wall and he went straight to the house and not through the gate We remained at work Then he saddled his horse and passed us

Judge Did you not see him up-saddle? No He then went in the direction the Kafir had taken As he passed the floor he shouted to Marthinus 'Saddle up the horse and go at once for the police" He went and we did not see him again What do you mean? Marthinus saddled the horse immediately and went in the direction of the railway cottage Had there been any police there that morning? Yes, they were in front of the door

Judge Had you seen them? Yes

Solicitor-General Did you see them speak to anyone? No, I did not

Judge Did they go into the house? I cannot say I did not notice Did you see them leave? No

Solicitor-General It is usual for the police to call at the farm houses to see if there are any complaints? Yes Well what next? I saw Pelser return I was still on the floor, He pulled up in front of the house and I saw him ride away from the house into the town road

Judge Did you see him meet anyone? No Where was Marthinus? He had already come on towards the door Who had come on? He came out the same time Pelser returned Who came first? I cannot say It was about the same time Marthinus must have come with Pelser? Yes I cannot say when they returned

Solicitor-General Pelser did not stop long in the house? No I saw him ride towards the town When Pelser left to follow did he go away in a rage? No, he went away as I generally knew him "good" He remained there, Abo says, some time after the native had left? Yes, he did remain a little while What did he do during the time he was on the floor? He stood by us He first went by you and then went to the wall? Yes And then went into the house? Yes And the only thing he said about the Kafir that time was that he would make him pay 2s? Yes For being impertinent, and that he would go when the Police came? Yes And that is all he said? Yes Did he say this in an angry way or calmly? No, not at all—good

Mr Solomon I suppose you live on Pelser's farm? Yes The old master has taken me as a child I have been there ten years You live in the same house? Yes Are you related to him at all? My brother is married to the daughter of old Pelser Now when the Kafir came up, how far away were you? About ten yards And you very carefully noticed what he had in his hand? Yes Why did you notice it so well? Well I noticed because he was carrying it behind his back What is peculiar in that? Nothing I saw it was an iron Was it an uncommon thing for a Kafir to carry an iron? Yes It is not the custom You have never seen it before? I have often seen them carrying kerries, but not iron

Judge Is it common for a Kafir to carry a stick in that manner? Yes

Mr Solomon Then you do not agree with your friend Mr Pelser that it is a very common thing in that part of the country for Kafirs to carry a piece of iron like this? No I never see it What was the height of the Kafir? A little over five feet Then what do you mean by saying before the Magistrate that the Kafir who came to the floor was a tall man? I did not say he was a long man I said he was about my height or a little less You say he did not stand with the iron across his shoulders? No But he stood with it by his side pressing it on the ground with one hand? Yes, the right hand He showed his civility by doing that? He was not impertinent then Of course you could not see the iron bar when he had it on the ground? Yes What through the wall? No, but the wall is low and the ridge is highish and as he stood I could see a little of the iron Then you could see if he had the iron on the ground? I could not see so low as that How much could you see? About a foot of it And are you prepared to swear to the iron produced in the Magistrate's Court as the identical iron he had in his hand? Yes By what do you identify it? Why can you swear so positively? I noticed that he had this iron When he came first he had it across his shoulders How much could you see of it? As much as you can now (Mr Solomon held it across his shoulders in the way Zachariah is alleged to have held it)? Yes. I could not see the ends as he

had his hands on them   And that being all that you could see
you are prepared to swear it is the identical iron ?   Yes, that is
the iron (laughter)

Judge   What sort of iron is that—does it belong to a plough ?
We have such iron belonging to ploughs and also bolts which
are used   Where were you when Pelser went to town ?   On the
floor   Yes, and did old Mr Pelser come to the floor after young
Mr Pelser had gone to town ?   Yes   He came from the house
to the floor and he said——   No, you cannot say what he said,
that has been objected to   Where did he go to ?   He went over
the rise   Could you see where to ?   He went upon the ridge
But you could not see ?   No   You saw him go—where did you
lose sight of him ?   I saw him go on to the railway line   And
you saw him go to the telegraph people ?   No, I did not see
that but I returned again to the floor   When did you see him
again next ?   Some considerable time after that   (To the
Solicitor-General) Is old Mr Pelser here ?

Solicitor-General   Yes, my Lord

Court adjourned at 1 30 p m and resumed at 2 30 p m

Solicitor-General   There are one or two questions I wish to
ask Dr Paul   My learned friend can cross-examine him again
They are questions that have not been asked

Dr Paul was recalled

Solicitor-General   Will you tell us this   When you found
the body it was lying on its back with its head in a north-east
direction ?   Yes   In which direction was the homestead from
the body ?   Due east   Then if the man was walking and got a
shot into the spine would you expect him to fall forwards or
backwards as he was in the act of walking ?   In injury to the
spine I would expect a man to fall backwards   In the act of
walking you would expect him to fall forward—the act of
walking would give the body some momentum ?   I should
expect him to fall backwards

A Juryman (Smith)   If the man was two yards in front do
you not think the bullet would have gone right through the
man ?   It depends how the revolver was aimed at the man   If
it was aimed straight and met with no resistance it might

Solicitor-General   I understand the Jury to ask whether if
the shot was fired directly behind it would go right through ?

Juryman   I want to ask this   If it would not go through
everything at two yards distance ?   It would depend on the
charge   (Revolver handed to Jury and proved to be of regulation pattern)

Judge   Do you know anything about pistols ?

Solicitor-General   (laughing) No, my Lord

The Judge   We must leave that point for someone

Dr Paul asked for leave to return home   There being no
objection it was granted

Willem Jacobus Pelser was next called

Solicitor-General You are a cousin to this Mr Pelser?
Yes His father is your uncle? Yes You were on the tramp
floor on the day when the Kafir came up? Yes Just tell us
what happened? I was standing on the tramp floor working
untying the sheaves I saw the Kafir come He was just
opposite to us on the outside of the wall Did you see if he
had anything in his hand? He came with his hands in this
position (raised on a level with his shoulders) As if he had
something in his hand—say if you do not know?

He had an iron in his hand How long do you think it was?
I cannot say but it was not a long one You say he held it
like this—did the ends project from his two hands? How far?

Judge Did they do so at all? I did not notice it

Solicitor-General What length did it strike you that this
piece of iron was? This iron handed to me looks like it Did
you commence to tramp the corn? No Were the horses in
the tramp floor? No The horses were not in Where were
they? They were in the kraal Can you tell us who brought
the horses to the tramp floor—one of the boys? Abram de
Klerk went and I do not know which boy was with him

Judge Were the horses brought to the kraal before the Kafir
came? Yes Were they in the tramp floor? No

Solicitor-General When did they come into the tramp floor?
When we had got the corn ready—the Kafir had already arrived
You were all very busy? And whilst busy the Kafir came
there? Yes Tell us what took place? Pelser asked him
where he was going In what language? In Dutch The
Kafir made no reply and then Pelser told Abo to ask him where
he was going and he said he was in search of a horse, and then
Pelser asked him if he had a pass Then he said " No " and
Pelser said to him ' Go back and get a pass from your master,
and then you can come and seek the horse ' He immediately
turned

Judge Was there any reply from the Kafir after that? No
He went over the ridge

Solicitor-General It was not interpreted? No And you did
not understand Kafir? No After the Kafir went off what
did Pelser do? He remained for a little while and then went to
the house Before going to the house did he do anything? Not
that I know of He remained there with us at the floor and I
did not notice anything special Did you not notice that he got
up on the wall? I noticed that when he was going to the house
that he went over the wall Did he say anything in getting over
the wall? Nothing that I heard You say you saw him going
to the house ? Yes, and after that I saw him ride right past us
I heard him call to one of the servants Marthinus as he went
away I could not hear what he said And after that you saw

Marthinus doing what? Marthinus passed me and I spoke When Pelser shouted to Marthinus how far was he from the tramp floor? About 150 paces Marthinus went and got a horse, and when he was passing me I asked him where he was going In which direction did he go? Towards the house

Judge Is that the way to the railway cottage?

Solicitor-General You saw him go to the house? Yes You do not know what became of him afterwards? Yes, he told me You cannot tell us what he told you

Mr Solomon How far were you from the Kafir when he came to the tramp floor and talked? About 40 to 50 yards

Solicitor-General What was that? Let it be put again

Mr Solomon From the distance where you were standing to where Zachariah and the native were talking, how far was it? About 30 yards And they did not come nearer than that? Yes You were very busy that morning? Yes And you would not have had time to notice particularly what the Kafir was doing I suppose? When Pelser was speaking to him I stood looking on So the Kafir stood like this (old position) all the time he was standing talking to Abo? No, when he came up he dropped one end And how much of it could you see then? About a foot of it You say that Abram de Klerk came to the tramp floor with the horses? He brought them to the kraal and turned them into it He came to the tramp floor before the Kafir arrived? Yes Who was nearest the Kafir, he or you? I cannot say We were all occupied with the wheat And Abo was nearer—was he not on the wagon when the Kafir arrived? It is possible, but I cannot say so We were all in the tramp floor

Judge Was there a wagon there? Yes Was it driven between the wall and the tramp floor, and was the wall where the Kafir stood between the wagon and the tramp floor? The Kafir was on the side of the wall, and the wagon was between the wall and the tramp floor

Solicitor-General The wagon was not standing between you and the Kafir You could see him? Yes And you say from where he stood to where you stood was about thirty yards? Yes Could you say what is the width of the tramp floor—I mean width across? About fiften or sixteen yards

Judge What part of the tramp floor were you standing on? About the middle

Marthinus David (the younger) was next called

Solicitor-General There is another man named Marthinus It is a brother We will call this man Marthinus, and the other Marthinus David You are a son of Marthinus David? Yes You live at Roodebergsvlei? Yes I recollect the morning in January when a Kafir was shot He first came to the tramp floor where I was working with others Before he came to the tramp floor had you seen him anywhere else? He was at the kraal by me When he came there the horses were in it? Yes

Judge Is the kraal near the tramp floor? Yes

Solicitor-General Was the kraal open or shut? The gate was closed Abram de Klerk brought the horses in When the Kafir came he asked if I had seen a horse, and with that he entered the kraal I did not say anything because I could not understand, because he was speaking Kafir

Judge How do you know he enquired for a black horse? He said something but I did not understand it You did not reply, and he then went into the kraal? Yes

Solicitor-General And looked about amongst the horses? Yes He did not ask you if he might go in but went in? Yes And then he came out? Yes, and at that time I had left Where did you go to? To the tramp floor He came there and Abo was the interpreter He asked if we had seen such a horse Abo asked the master who said "Without an order from your master you cannot walk about my veldt" and then the man left When he came to the tramp floor what were you doing? I was working with the corn Doing what with it? Getting the sheaves loose for the purpose of threshing Is that all you could recollect that passed between them? Yes When the Kafir left, the master went and stood upon the wall and looked In what direction—for what purpose? Towards the line, the direction the Kafir had taken, and then the master went out again to the floor and said to us he would make him pay 2s Did he say what he would do with the 2s? He said he would give it to the servants Did he say how he would get the 2s from the man? He said he would catch him because he was walking about in the veldt Catch him and do what with him? I don't remember that Then after that the master went to the House

Judge How did he go? From the floor down towards the house How did he go—over the wall or through the gate? Over the wall

Solicitor-General After that? Then he rode away to catch the man He rode away in the direction the man had taken? Yes Did anything take place as he rode off? Yes As he passed the floor he called out to me and said I must ride down for the Police at the cottage

Judge Had you seen these Policemen before? No Did you know they were there before the master told you to go? No

Solicitor-General You say you did not see any Police about that morning? No You got the horse and rode in the direction he told you? Yes You did not find the Police, and you turned back? Yes When you came home was the master there already? Yes Now you recollect giving evidence before the Magistrate? Yes Did you or did you not—

Mr Solomon I do not know whether my friend can cross-examine his own witnesses, especially as this one is not hostile

Solicitor-General I have not seen the original preliminary examination, mine is only a copy therefore I must examine on it

Judge When the original is put in it will be well to compare them

Solicitor-General Yes it would He said at the preliminary "I had seen two Policemen at the house They came towards Burghersdorp"

Judge Did you say to the Magistrate that you had seen two Policemen at the house on foot? No And that they came towards Burgherdorp? No You say you could not have said so because you did not know anything about them? Yes But you had heard before you had given evidence that they had been there? Yes You may have told the Magistrate that? Yes

Solicitor-General And you heard your master shout to you? Yes That was the first time you had heard the police had been there? No Who told you? I heard from Abo Was that before your master had shouted to you? Yes Abo said that he had seen the two policemen at the house that morning When he came to the tramp-floor had he anything in his hand? Yes In the first place let us go to the kraal had he then? Yes What was it? A small iron You saw he carried it at the kraal when he came up to you? He had an iron his right hand pressing upon it, leaning upon it standing at the kraal And when he came to the tramp-floor had he still the iron? Yes In what way was he carrying it? Then he had it across his shoulders I can swear it was a bar of iron, You are certain what he had in his hands was not a switch? Yes It was just such a bar as this (bar produced)

Mr Solomon Just stand as the Kafir was when he came to the kraal resting on the iron - oh no, I can't give you the rod Do it without it (witness stood up, dropped his right hand to his side and slightly bent his right shoulder as in the position of resting upon the iron) Was he pressing on it? Yes Were you close to him? About three or four yards away How far is the tramp floor from the kraal? About as far as the other side of the street (100 yards) Could the people at the tramp floor see what was going on at the kraal? No How is it that you said nothing whatever before the Magistrate about the Kafir coming to the kraal and seeing something in his hand? I gave that declaration and it could not have been put down Then you mean to say that you told him and he did not put it down? Yes You forgot such an important piece of evidence as that? Yes You were cross-examined by Mr Knobel? Yes And did it not come out? You forgot to give that evidence on that occasion? Yes. And he stood with the iron in his hand, and across the shoulder all the time till he left? Yes. When he went into the kraal was he impertinent? No, but I went to the master and mentioned it to him. And the master did not go to the kraal? No. When I went to the tramp floor I said this is the man who was in the kraal. Did he say anything to him for being in the kraal? No. Your master objects to Kafirs coming on his farm but he does not object to them going into his kraal? I don't know about that.

Judge. You told your master that that was the man who came to the kraal to seek a horse? Yes.

Solicitor-General. That is the case for the Crown, except the evidence that I spoke of to impeach the credit of their witnesses.

The prosecution closed at 3.40 p.m.

Mr. Solomon. I shall begin the defence by reading the preliminary examination to the Jury. Will you read it Mr. Frames.

Mr. Frames read as follows :—

At Burghersdorp on this Tuesday, the 20th day of January, 1885, before me, Alexander Stewart, Resident Magistrate of the district of Albert and in presence and hearing of the prisoner, Willem Jacobus Pelser who was in his sound and sober senses, appeared.

Edward Williams, who being duly sworn states :—I am Chief Constable of this district. I know the prisoner. On the forenoon of the 15th instant I heard him make a statement in the office of the Resident Magistrate's Clerk. He said he had come in to report that he had shot a Kafir on his farm. I asked him under what circumstances, and he replied that the Kafir had said that he had come on to his farm to look for a horse. He asked the Kafir if he had a pass and the Kafir replied that he had no pass. He then ordered him back to town to get a pass. He insisted on his going back, but the Kafir would not do so. He then rode up to the Kafir to compel him to go back. The Kafir turned round and struck at his horse with an iron rod about two feet in length. He then struck a second blow at him (Pelser) and he then drew his revolver and shot the Kafir, and then came to town to report having done so. He said he did not know whether the Kafir was dead or not. Under instruction from the Magistrate I then went to the spot with the District Surgeon accompanied by the prisoner. On arriving at the spot, I found the dead body of a native man. He had on a jacket, shirt and trowsers and his hat lay a little distance off. I also found the piece of iron now produced, lying alongside the body, within about a yard from it. I think it was on the right side of the body. Prisoner showed us the body. The District Surgeon examined the body to find where the wound was. Whilst doing so the prisoner said that the deceased must have been shot on the right side of the head. The District Surgeon and I both examined the head, but found no marks. The District Surgeon afterwards discovered the wound at the back part above the shoulder blade. I saw the wound myself. The bullet had lodged in the spine and had gone from left to right. The District Surgeon found the bullet lodged in the spine. The deceased had not bled much. The body was still quite warm There was no other wound on the body that I saw I saw foot-prints about the spot, but they were indistinct I saw spoors of a horse about five yards from the body I could not see which way the spoors went as our horses stood on the same spot Prisoner pointed out the spoor to us The body was lying with its head towards prisoner's house, on its back Searched the deceased man and found on him the small bag now produced, in which I found some silver amounting to 3s 9d and two pennies I also found in it the pass produced, dated August last, for one Kleinbooy I also found the receipt for 15s dated December last granted to Zachariah, and the table book with the name Zachariah Gqischela I took the shirt now produced from the body containing the mark made by the bullet as also the jacket produced I produce the bullet found in the body It is a revolver bullet The point is slightly blunted

Cross-examined by Mr Knobel who appears for the prisoner Prisoner did not mention the length of the iron with which deceased had struck him I found subsequently that it was about two feet in length He spoke in English He might have said that he went after deceased for the purpose of bringing him back I understood him to say that he went for the purpose of compelling him to return He did not tell me that he had taken out his revolver for the purpose of intimidating the deceased The prisoner did not tell me whether it was after the first or second blow that he drew his revolver, or whether he had drawn it long before Prisoner pointed to the right side of the deceased's head He did not actually say that the wound would be found on the right side It is impossible for me to say whether the deceased dropped on the exact spot where he was shot From the collar of deceased's jacket to the bullet mark is about three and a-half inches

Re-examined I could see no signs of the deceased man having changed his position He appeared to have dropped where he was shot

(Signed) E WILLIAMS
Before me (Signed) ALEX STEWART, RM

Alfred Harmsworth, sworn, deposes I am Clerk to the Civil Commissioner and Resident Magistrate of Albert I was present in my office last Friday when prisoner came in He seemed to be excited I asked him what was wrong He said, "I am in for a row, I have shot a Kafir It occured this way I was riding on my farm when I saw a Kafir going through the veldt I rode up to him and asked him what he wanted there He answered, 'I have come to look for a horse' I then demanded to see his pass but he said he had none I told him to leave my veldt, as I did not allow natives to roam about there without passes I then went away some little distance, and on looking back saw the Kafir still in my veldt I thereupon rode up to him and told him that as he did not chose to leave I would give him into custody of the police, and I then sent for two policemen who had passed me a short time previously I reined my horse in front of the Kafir and he then said 'You'll not stop me' He had a bar of iron in his hand, and with this he struck my horse a blow on the nose My horse thereupon became restive and unmanageable, and the Kafir then struck at my leg with the iron I turned the horse round, and as I did so I saw his arm raised again to strike me, and I thereupon shot him " That was what prisoner told me in my office The Magistrate's Clerk then came into the office, and the Chief Constable was sent for He said he had come to give himself up He said he did not know whether the man was dead or not, as he immediately rode home and then to town to report the matter I did not see the horse

Cross-examined Chief Constable was not present when prisoner made the statement to me I know that prisoner used the words " unmanageable " and ' restive " He did not say the horse shied, but he said the horse ran away with him and he had great difficulty in pulling him up Prisoner did not say that ne was arresting the deceased He said he had sent for the police, but did not say whom he had sent

Re-examined After leaving my office prisoner went to the Magistrate's Clerk's office

(Signed) ALF HARMSWORTH
Before me (Signed) ALEX STEWART R M

Marthinus David, sworn, deposes I reside at Roodebergsvlei I know prisoner I am in his service On Friday morning last I was with him in the tramp-floor There were some others there also A native came to the tramp-floor I do not know his name He was a Kafir He spoke in Kafir and asked if there was a black horse which he was in search of One Abo replied He told prisoner through Abo that he was looking for a horse Prisoner asked if he had a pass The Kafir said " No " Prisoner told him to go back and get a pass He said he could not go back as he was in search of his master's horse The Kafir then went away to the right from where we were Prisoner came out of the tramp-floor and stood on the land wall near the floor He then jumped off the wall and went away to the house I saw him ride away on horseback not quite in the direction the Kafir had taken Prisoner had no revolver at the tramp-floor I did not hear a shot fired I remained at the tramp-floor I did not see prisoner again till late that evening I have not since seen the Kafir

Cross-examined I understand Kafir a little Prisoner told the Kafir to go and get a pass from his master Prisoner told him that if he brought a pass he could search for the horse Abo interpreted He told the Kafir through the interpreter that he allowed no one in his veldt without a pass from his master I heard the Kafir say he would go where he would The Kafir went into the veldt of Roodebergsvlei when he went away When prisoner went away I did not think he was following the Kafir I heard him call out as he rode away, but as he was far off I could not hear what he said My son Marthinus was between us and prisoner when he called out I saw Marthinus run to the land and catch the horse which was grazing there He mounted the horse and rode past us He came in the direction of the town I have been a very long time on the farm Roodebergsvlei Lots of stock have been lost on the farm lately, including sheep and cattle, not alone by night but during the day

Re-examined The horse on which prisoner rode away was a black one
(Signed) MARTHINUS DAVID
his X mark
Witness (Signed) W CLIFTON PRICE
Before me (Signed) ALEX STEWART, R M

Abo, sworn, deposes I reside at Roodebergsvlei, and am in the service of the prisoner On Friday last I was at work with him at the tramp-floor A native came to the floor in search of a horse He was a Tambookie I did not notice what colour his jacket was, but he had on light grey trousers The jacket now produced is the one he had on He asked if I had seen a horse, in the Kafir language I said I had not Prisoner then asked what the man wanted I asked the man and he told me to tell the prisoner that he was in search of a black horse I told the prisoner this, and he then told me to ask the Kafir if he had a pass I did so, and the Kafir replied that he had no pass I told prisoner this, and he desired me to tell the man to go back and fetch a pass I told him to do so, and he replied that he could not go back, as the horse was not his but his master's I told the prisoner this and he did not answer The Kafir then left and went towards the other side of the farm The prisoner then went to the house I afterwards saw him on horseback riding in the same direction the Kafir had taken He was mounted on a black horse He disappeared out of sight I did not go to see where he was going I did not hear a shot fired The tramp-floor is on the other side of the house I have not since seen the Kafir I noticed that the Kafir had something in his hand I thought it was a switch It was the same length as the piece of iron now produced

Cross-examined I am a Tambookie The man went into the veldt of the farm Roodebergsvlei The prisoner called out as he rode away from the house I saw one Marthinus go to the land, catch a horse, mount it, and ride in the direction of the town I had previously seen two policemen go in the direction of the town Marthinus rode in the same direction the police had taken I saw the prisoner return from the veldt and go into the house, and afterwards I saw him mount his horse and go in the direction of Burghersdorp He did not remain long in the house Prisoner was riding at a gallop when he returned from the veldt

Re-examined —There is a small dam in the direction which the Kafir took This dam cannot be seen from the tramp-floor on account of a rise in the ground Prisoner rode in that direction

(Signed) Abo, his X mark
Witness (Signed) W Clifton Price

Before me (Signed) Alex Stewart, R M

Frederick David, sworn, deposes —I am a son of Marthinus David, and reside at Roodebergsvlei On Friday last I was herding sheep, and took them to the water at the fountain on the forenoon of that day I did not see a man walking across the veldt nor did I see prisoner I saw a man lying near the fountain I had heard a shot before I saw the man I was then at the spruit, from which I could not see the spot where the man was lying He was lying with his legs crossed and waving his hand I did not go to him because I was afraid I went the following morning, and found the man lying dead I did not know who it was It was before midday when I first saw the man lying there

Prisoner had no questions

(Signed) Frederick David, his X mark
Witness (Signed) W Clifton Price

Before me (Signed) Alex. Stewart, R.M

Alfred Peters, sworn, deposes —I am a carpenter and also a schoolmaster I am employed at present on the telegraph construction near town On Friday last I was near the Dutchman's house, digging a hole for a telegraph pole I was about one hundred yards from the house A native came to me from the direction of the house and said good morning to me, and passed on He sat for half an hour talking to one Swartboy He remained about half an hour It was about twelve o'clock when he left When he had gone I saw the prisoner on a black horse follow the native, who was then about three hundred yards away I saw the native the whole time as the ground was level He overtook the native and they stood talking for some time, and they returned back towards the house I was talking to another man when I saw the smoke and heard a shot, and at the same time I saw the native fall Veldschoen was with me and some others Prisoner stood still for about three minutes and then galloped back to the house, and passed close to where I was He had a leather bag at his side I did not go to the spot where the man was shot as I was afraid I went and reported to my master what I had seen I am quite sure that the man who passed me was the same who was shot He had nothing in his hand when he passed me

Cross-examined —I saw no tramp floor at the house, nor did I see anybody working about the house except the telegraph men From the time the native left me to the time the shot was fired was about half an hour It could not have been more I did not have a watch, I guessed the time After the native left me I worked for about five minutes at the hole I was making I watched the native the whole time, as I had finished the hole I was making My master's name is Mair I went to him after the shot was fired I told him at once what I had seen I also told him all the particulars Veldschoen was working about twenty-two feet away from me The native spoke to me first and then went to Veldschoen He did not go to the house when he left Veldschoen He came from the house when he came to me I could see the house from where I was working

Re-examined —Swartboy was making a hole further on After he left Swartboy he was half an hour walking across the veld The horse on which prisoner was mounted was a black one I did not see prisoner leave the house and come to town

(Signed) ALFRED PETERS
Before me   (Signed) ALEX STEWART, R M

Veldschoen Gcwacwaka, sworn, deposes —I reside at the tents on the other side of the Wool-wash I know the farm Roodebergsvlei I am employed to dig holes for telegraph poles On Friday last I was working with last witness digging holes I was working near the Dutchman's house A native man came to me He greeted me I asked him where he come from, and he replied that he was in search of his master's horse He did not tell me his name There were a number of horses on the other side of the dam, and the man went towards them When he had passed the dam a Dutchman appeared and rode after him He was on a black horse When he got to the man he rode between the man and the horses He was riding after the man towards the house coming back When they were close to the dam I heard a shot and saw the man fall I saw the white man shoot him and then gallop towards the house, I was as far from them as from here to the railway cottage near the waggon road The man was walking in front of the horse on which the Dutchman was riding The horse's head could touch the man as he walked I could not see whether the man fell on his face or on his back

Cross-examined —I know the last witness I was working near him After speaking to me the man did not go to Alfred and speak to him He did not speak to him at the time he came to me The man went from me to the dam, and from the dam to the horses Alfred and I were working near each other I know a man named Swartboy He came to me whilst the native was talking to me Swartboy was working on the other side of Alfred I can't say how far he was from me I was digging a hole at the time I heard the shot and I turned at once and looked I saw them coming I was looking when the shot was fired, and I could see the smoke I heard the shot first, and I saw the man fall Alfred Peters and I are under one master It was not very long after the shot was fired that we went to dinner The shot was fired a little before dinner I went to dinner at the dinner time I thought that I ought to go and report at once what I had seen but I could not leave my master's work

Re-examined —The man did not stay long speaking to me He spoke to Swartboy It was a long time after breakfast It was between eleven and twelve o'clock when the man came there It was about one o'clock when the shot was fired The dinner-time is about the same time that the Court adjourned to-day (The Court adjourned at one o'clock)

(Signed) VELDSCHOEN, his X mark
Witness (Signed) W CLIFTON PRICE
Before me (Sd) ALEX STEWART, R M

Swartboy Mdlunga, sworn, deposes —I am a labourer on the telegraph construction on the other side of the Woolwash I know the prisoner On Friday last I was working on the other side of his farm In the forenoon I was working on this side of the farm When I was working above prisoner's house a man came to me Last witness was with him I found the Kafir with last witness He had on a black jacket The one produced might be the same I asked him what he was looking for, and he replied for a horse He then went on, and I came towards town I did not see him again I heard a shot I saw a man go that way, but not quite in the same direction that Zachariah had taken It was the prisoner, and he was mounted on a dark horse I did not see where he went to I did not see the shot fired I have not seen Zachariah since After I heard the shot, I saw prisoner coming to town

Prisoner had no questions

(Signed) SWARTBOY MDLUNGA, his X mark
Witness (Signed) W CLIFTON PRICE
Before me (Signed) ALEX STEWART, R M

Mtloyiya, sworn, deposes —I am a labourer on the telegraph construction I reside at present on the other side of the Woolwash I do not know the prisoner On Friday last I was working near the house of prisoner's father I saw the prisoner riding on a horse on Friday last before dinner It was a very dark horse I saw a native man walking in the veldt I asked him what he was about, and he replied that he was looking for a horse He then went on to the Flats, and I saw the man on the black horse turning him back The native had nothing in his hand I was about as far away as from here to the Railway Station The man on the black horse shot the native When the native passed me he did not have the iron now produced in his hand I saw the white man shoot him He was about two yards from the native The native's back was turned towards the white man's horse The native fell when he was shot The white man then galloped home I did not go to see because I was afraid of the white man

Cross examined —The man fell in front of the horse I could see that he fell on his side It was not long before the dinner hour I was digging a hole at the time I left off digging the hole and looked on the scene I went on with my work when I saw that the man had fallen My dinner is always brought to me where I am digging holes The cook Jack brought it to me on that day I told Jack of what I had seen I did not go with Jack to the spot I also told my master when I returned from work at sundown I know Alfred and Veldschoen We are under the same master

(Signed) MILOIIYA his X mark
Witness (Signed) W CLIFTON PRICE

Before me (Signed) ALEX STEWART, R M

Breakfast sworn, deposes —I am employed to work on the telegraph construction My master's name is Mair On Friday last I was working on the farm the other side of the Wool wash I was working just on the other side of Alfred and Veldschoen I saw a man on horseback driving another man They were coming down the valley above the dam I heard a shot fired, but did not see anything, as I had then gone into a hollow place I did not see anything further

Prisoner had no questions

(Signed) BREAKFAST, his X mark
Witness (Signed) W CLIFTON PRICE

Before me (Signed) ALEX STEWART, R M

Canteen Nqantweni, sworn, deposes —I am employed on the telegraph construction My master's name is Mair On Friday morning last I was digging a hole at the dam I saw a man being driven on by a white man on horseback, whom I do not know They went round the wall of the dam, and I could not see them I afterwards heard a shot The horse was a dark one I was about as far away from them as from here to the spruit

Prisoner had no questions

(Signed) CANTEEN NQANTWENI his X mark
Witness (Signed) W CLIFTON PRICE

Before me (Signed) ALEX STEWART, R M

Jacob Seelemane, police constable, sworn, deposes —On Saturday morning last I was sent with some prisoners to bury a corpse It was the body of a Tambookie named Zachariah, who had lived at the Location

Prisoner had no questions

(Signed) JACOB SEELEMANE, his X mark
Witness (Signed) W CLIFTON PRICE

Before me (Signed) ALEX STEWART, R M

Edward Williams re-called —It was between 12 and half-past 12 when prisoner came to the office It is about three-and-a-half miles from town to where the body was The revolver produced was handed to me by the prisoner It is loaded The bullet found in the body resembles the cartridges with which this revolver is loaded

(Signed) E WILLIAMS

Before me (Signed) ALEX STEWART, R M

Ferdinand Paul, sworn, deposes —I am the District Surgeon of Albert On the 16th of this month I proceeded to the farm Roodebergsvlei, to hold a *post mortem* on the body of a native I arrived at the spot about two p m Prisoner accompanied me, and pointed out the body to me I found the man dead, and held a *post mortem* I produce my certificate (A) showing the result of the *post mortem* I found the body in the veldt about half-a mile from the homestead It was lying on its back with its head towards the north-east The homestead was due east from the body The man had apparently been dead some hours I found on the left side of the back above the left shoulder-blade, and about one-and a-half or two inches from the middle of the spine, an oval gun-shot wound On examining the wound I found that the bullet had penetrated in the direction of the spine It had fractured the second vertebra of the chest, and was lodged in the middle of the vertebra compressing the spinal marrow I also made a *post mortem* examination of the internal organs, and I found all of them in a comparatively healthy state Except the above-mentioned wound there was no other marks of violence on the body I am therefore of opinion that the deceased died from the effects of the gun-shot wound causing the fracture of the spine and a compression of the spinal marrow The bullet now produced is the one I found in the spine The wound did not bleed freely The jacket and shirt now produced are what I had taken from the body There was a handkerchief tied round the body

Cross-examined —I was in Court when evidence was given that a white man on horseback was driving a black man on foot I heard the witnesses say that the black man was close to the horse's head with his back towards the horse Had a pistol shot been fired then it would have gone straight into the back, and would not have caused the wound from which the deceased died It was a flesh wound until it struck the spine, and the bullet travelled in an oblique direction If the black man had faced the white man on horseback with an iron or a stick in his left hand, and the horse had swerved on one side, and the blow had missed it is possible for the white man on horseback to have fired a shot which would have inflicted the wound which caused the death of the deceased The bullet could in such a case have taken the direction I have already described

Re-examined —The piece of iron was lying close to the man's body There is another explanation as to the wound If the deceased had aimed low at the prisoner with his right hand and missed his blow, and the prisoner had been slightly behind the deceased, then the gunshot wound might have been made It is impossible that the wound could have been made by a man riding behind in the way indicated by the witnesses

(Signed) F PAUL

Before me (Signed) ALEX STEWART, R M

Remanded for further examination to Tuesday, the 27th instant

On Tuesday, January 27, in presence and hearing of the prisoner, appeared also

Edward Williams, who being duly sworn, states —On the 20th instant I gave my evidence regarding this examination Yesterday I proceeded to the spot again, accompanied by Sergeants Strong and Hall and a private in the Divisional Police I took the witness Alfred to point out the place where he stood at the time I placed Sergeant Strong and another where the body was found Sergeant Hall stood where the witness Mtloyiya was at the time From where I was I could see Sergeant Strong on horseback almost facing me Private Venter had his back towards me That was the position in which I understood from the prisoner he and the Kafir were when he shot the Kafir I saw the smoke from the revolver fired by Strong but could not hear the shot I saw smoke from the revolver three times, but heard no shots whatever I could not see from where I was whether one was a black man, the other a white man Had Sergeant Strong been driving the man on I should have seen The distance from the place where Alfred was to where the body was found is about 500 yards and from where Mtloyiya was to the body is about 500 yards The tramp floor is on the left side of the house inside the lands Had the deceased gone to the tramp floor first and then to the place where he was shot he must have passed near to where Alfred was working digging telegraph holes

Cross-examined —I think it was possible to distinguish the colour of a horse from where Alfred was to where the body was I knew that the shots were to be fired but did not hear them

Re-examined —It was windy and dull when Sergeant Srong fired the shots, I think it was much calmer the Friday before last

(Signed) E WILLIAMS

Before me (Signed) ALEX STEWART, R M

William Strong, sworn, deposes —I am Sergeant of the Albert Divisional Police Yesterday morning I accompanied last witness to the farm Roodebergsvlei One of my men, Venter, also went with us We went to the spot where the body had been buried The Chief Constable went to one of the telegraph poles about two hundred yards from the house I remained at the grave and mounted the horse I was facing Williams and Venter was on my right, about a yard and a half from me He made two blows at me with the left arm, he had a riding whip in his hand I fired a blank cartridge with a revolver The cartridge was the same as those in prisoner's revolver I fired after he had made two blows at me He fell on his right side Venter also struck at me with his right arm, and I again fired a blank cartridge I fired a bullet cartridge also first at the grave

Cross-examined —I cannot tell which direction the wind was blowing at the time

(Signed) W STRONG

Before me (Signed) ALEX STEWART, R M

Arthur Lambert Hall, sworn, deposes I am a Sergeant of the Cape Police stationed at Burghersdorp Yesterday morning I accompanied the Chief Constable to the farm Roodebergsvlei, and I stood at a telegraph pole about three hundred yards on the other side of the homestead I saw Sergeant Strong and the policeman in the veldt I saw the man raise his arm, and the other on horseback close to him I could not see if he had anything in his hand I saw the smoke twice, and saw the man fall I afterwards distinctly heard a shot fired I was looking the opposite way at the time, and I turned round and saw the smoke The view was quite open, with the exception of a few small bushes I was nearer to the man than the Chief Constable

Prisoner had no questions   (Signed) ARTHUR L HAIL
       Before me (Signed) ALEX STEWART, R M

David Mair, sworn, deposes —I am Sub Inspector of Telegraphs I am engaged at present in superintending the construction of the line between Queen's Town and Aliwal North I know the witnesses Alfred Peters, Veldtschoen, Swartboy, Mtloyiya, Breakfast and Canteen They were in my service last Friday week and some of them were working about two miles on the other side, and others about two miles this side of Pelser's homestead On that day, between 11 and 12 o'clock, the witness Alfred told me about a man having been shot He had finished his work, and was coming to work further on I can't say where he had been working He told me that a Kafir had been shot by a farmer He told me nothing further None of the others told me anything about it I heard Alfred talking to other natives about shooting, and I asked him about it The whole gang was distributed over a space of four miles The men might have been working near Pelser's homestead I do not know where they were working

Cross-examined —From what Alfred told me he did not lead me to suppose that he had seen a Kafir shot I concluded that he was simply repeating a rumour Had he told me that he had seen a black man shot by a white man I would have made enquiries Alfred Peters is a Kafir man The usual dinner time for my employes is one o'clock I thought it was an idle rumour

Re-examined —It would have taken him from ten to fifteen minutes to walk from opposite Pelser's homestead to where I met him
                         (Signed) DAVID MAIR
       Before me (Signed) ALEX SIFWART, R M

FOR THE DEFENCE

William Clifton Price, sworn, deposed —I am Clerk to the Resident Magistrate of this District I recollect the prisoner coming here on Friday, the 16th instant to report that he had shot a Kafir I took it to be about half-past 11 o'clock in the forenoon I did not look at the time When he came the Magistrate was still on the Bench
                         (Signed) W CLIFTON PRICE
       Before me (Signed) ALEX SILWART, R M

Alfred Harmsworth, sworn, deposes —I am Clerk to the Civil Commissioner I remember prisoner coming to the office to report that he had shot a Kafir It was between 11 and 12 o'clock It was a calm day
                         (Signed) ALFRED HARMSWORTH
       Before me (Signed) ALEX STEWART, R M

Abram de Klerk, sworn, deposes —I reside at Roodebergsvlei. I was on the farm on the 16th instant   I remember a Kafir coming to the tramp floor   I was there   The Kafir said he was looking for his master's horse   Prisoner was there   Prisoner asked the Kafir if he had a pass from his master   The Kafir said he had no pass   Prisoner ordered him back to get a pass and then he could look for the horse in his veldt   The Kafir then went away into the veldt   He had the iron rod now produced in his hand   He spoke as he went away, but we could not understand   Prisoner then went to the house, and I saw him riding his horse   As he passed the floor he shouted to Martinus to get a horse and get the Police   I saw two Policemen pass the house a little before   Martinus caught a horse near the tramp floor   I afterwards saw prisoner returning   He went to the house and I then saw him coming to town   It was about half-past ten o'clock when he left the house for town   When he came to the house he was riding at a canter   I afterwards saw prisoner's father, who told me that prisoner had shot a Kafir, and I was to go and look   There have been many thefts on the farm lately, by day time, as well as by night time   About 14 head of cattle have been slaughtered by Railway Kafirs and about 150 sheep have been lost during the last two months   The reason why Mr Pelser will not allow any native to go in the veldt without a pass is on account of these thefts

By the Court   Martinus was at the tramp floor   I did not see the Police   Martinus said he could not get the Police when he returned   The Kafir who came to the floor was a tall man   He spoke in Kafir which I do not understand   Abo interpreted

(Signed) A J DE KLERK

Before me   ALEX STEWART, R M

Martinus, sworn, deposes —I reside at Roodebergsvlei   On a Friday, some time ago, I was at the tramp floor   The Kafir who was shot on the farm came to the floor that day   He asked about a horse   Abo interpreted   Prisoner asked him where his pass was   He said he had no pass   Prisoner asked him to go back and get one   He said he could not go back as he was in search of his master's horse   Prisoner told him that if he brought a pass he could look for the horse in his veldt   He had the iron now produced in his hand   He then went into the veldt and prisoner went into the house   I had seen two Policemen at the house on foot   They went towards Burghersdorp   I saw prisoner mount a horse and ride away   When he passed the tramp floor he shouted to me to go and get the Police   I went to get a horse and came towards town after the Police   I came as far as the cottage and then turned back as I did not see the Police   Many thefts have been committed on the farm, lately, by day as well as by night

By the Court   I was at the floor when prisoner told me to go and get the Police   I saw some men working at the telegraph holes, on the rise on the other side of the house and this side of the dam   I could not see how many there were   They were working near the homestead

(Signed) MARTHINUS, his X mark
Witness   (Signed) W CLIFTON PRICE

Before me   Sd ALEX STEWART, R M

I

Willem Jacobus Pelser, sworn, deposes —I was on the farm Roodebergsvlei on the 16th instant, when a Kafir came there   Prisoner asked him, through an interpreter, where he was going, and he replied that he was in search of his master's horse   Prisoner asked him if he had a pass   He said he had no pass   Prisoner told him to get a pass from his master as he allowed no one in his veldt without a pass   The Kafir then went away   He had an iron bar like the one produced in his hand   I saw prisoner ride into the veldt and afterwards return home and then ride towards town

(Signed) W J PELSER

Before me   (Signed) ALEX STEWART, R M

Remanded to Wednesday, the 11th Feb , 1885

(Signed) ALEX STEWART, R M

(A) I herewith certify that on the 16th instant I proceeded to the farm Roodebergsvlei to hold a *post-mortem* examination on the body of a native who had been shot by Mr W Pelser of that farm

On arriving at the spot I found the dead body of a native lying on his back and apparently dead for several hours   On external examination I found no injuries except an oval or valvular gunshot wound above the left shoulder-blade and about $1\frac{1}{2}$ to 2 inches from the middle of the spine   On examining the wound I found that the bullet had gone in the direction of the spine, fracturing the second vertebra of the chest, and I noticed the bullet lodged in the middle of the vertebra compressing the spinal marrow   On examining the internal organs of the body I found them all in a healthy state

I have no doubt that the deceased died from the above-mentioned gunshot wound, the bullet having fractured the vertebra and compressed the spinal marrow

(Signed) F PAUL, M D , District Surgeon

Burghersdorp, January 20th, 1885

PRELIMINARY EXAMINATION

In the case of the Queen *vs* Willem Jacobus Pelser, charged with culpable homicide, district of Albert, at Burghersdorp, in the district of Albert, on the 11th day of February 1885, in the presence of Alexander Stewart, Resident Magistrate for the said district, appeared William Jacobus Pelser, an European, twenty-six years of age, born at Koppiesfontein, by trade or occupation a farmer, residing at Roodebergsvlei, in the district of Albert, who having heard the evidence adduced in support of the charge made against him of having on the 16th day of January, 1885, and at Roodebergsvlei, in the district of Albert, wrongfully and unlawfully killed one Zachariah, in his lifetime a labourer, and then residing at Burghersdorp, in the district of Albert, and being asked what he will say in answer thereto, and being at the same time cautioned that he is not obliged to make any statement that may criminate him, and that what he shall say may be used in evidence against him, declares —I am not guilty Latterly we have lost sheep day and night in great numbers   When the deceased came to me I asked him for a pass, as we did not allow anyone to go into our veldt without a pass   Deceased was determined to go into our veldt   Upon this I went to fetch him back   When I got to him he would not come back   At last he did go a few yards in the direction of the house, but he suddenly turned back and struck at me three times in such a way as to show me that my life was in danger I had already my revolver out for the purpose of frightening him The horse got restless, and when the horse gave way for the deceased the revolver went off and hit the deceased I thereupon went to the house and told my father, and requested him at once to see about the man that I had shot I am very sorry that such an occurrence should have taken place, as I had not the slightest intention to exercise malice

(Signed) W J PELSER

The above declaration was freely and voluntarily made by the said Willem Jacobus Pelser, who was then in his sound and sober senses, and having been read over and interpreted to him, he adhered to the same, and affixed his signature thereto in the presence of the subscribing witnesses and

Before me (Signed) ALEX STEWART, R M

Witnesses { (Signed) W Clifton Price
           ,, Alf Harmsworth

Alfred Harmsworth was the first witness called

Mr Solomon You are Clerk to the Civil Commissioner and Resident Magistrate of Albert? Yes And you were in January last? Yes You know Willem Jacobus Pelser, the younger one? I do And you remember him coming into your office on the 16th January last? I do What time was it about? Between eleven and twelve o'clock Tell us what took place as well as you can remember First of all when he came into your office was any one present? No one I saw that he appeared to be excited, and I asked him what was the matter He said 'I am in for a row"

Judge He spoke in English? Yes He said "I have shot a Kafir" I asked him how it occurred He said "I was riding in my place and saw a Kafir in my veldt I rode up to him and asked him what he was doing there He said I am looking for a horse I asked if he had a pass and he said he had not I told him then to leave my farm as I did not allow Kafirs to to be on my farm without a pass I then turned away and went some little distance off and on looking back I saw the Kafir still in my veldt I again rode up to him and told him if he he did not leave my veldt I would give him to the custody of the Police and I then sent for two Policemen that I had seen pass a short time previously I pulled my horse up in front of him and he said 'You will not stop me' He then struck my horse a blow across the nose with a bar of iron he had in his hand The horse became restive and unmanageable He then struck a blow at my legs and I succeeded in pulling the horse up, and I saw his arm raised again to strike me and I shot him" He told me he did not know whether the man was dead Is that as far as you can recollect? Yes Are you quite sure that he said he shot the Kafir as he saw his arm raised to strike

him ? Quite sure   You are quite sure that Williams did not
hear the statement he made to you ? I am quite sure   I was
alone in the office   Can you rember distinctly whether he said
he struck the horse a blow on the nose or struck at the horse ?
He distinctly said he had struck the horse on the nose

Judge   He distinctly said that ? Yes

Mr Solomon   Did you see him in company with Williams
after ? Yes   He was taken into custody by Williams   I want
to ask you certain distances for this reason   The witness
Veldschoen says " I was as far from them as from here to the
railway cottage on the wagon road " How far is that ? There
are a lot of cottages on the wagon road   How far is it from the
Court House to the Station ? About seven hundred yards

Solicitor-General   You say he was much excited when he
gave you the statement ? Yes   And it is quite possible that
here and there you may have misunderstood him ? I cannot
have misunderstood him as the statement made too deep an
impression on me   For instance, here you say he said he saw
the Kafir going over his veldt and he rode up to him and asked
what he wanted—are you certain that he said he rode up and
only asked him what he wanted ? He said he rode up to him
How many times did he strike him do you think from his
statement ? Twice   This man Abo, he gave evidence the same
day you did ? I don't know   I was not in Court   You didn't
go out to the spot where the body was ? No

Edward Williams was next called

Mr Solomon   You are Chief Constable at Burghersdorp ?
Yes   And you were so in January last ? I was   You know
Pelser ? Yes   Do you remember him coming into Burghers-
dorp into the Court House in the forenoon of the 16th January ?
Yes   Did he say anything to you ? Yes, he made a statement
Where did he do so ? It was in the office of the Assistant
Magistrate—Mr Price   And when he made the statement to
you was anyone present ? No, I don't think there was anyone
present, except at the finish, when I think some one came in
At all events Mr Harmsworth was not present ? No   Can you
tell us whether he came from the Magistrate's Clerk's office to
your office—had he been to the Magistrate's Clerk's office before
he came to you ? I cannot say   As far as you can remember
will you give us the statement he made to you on that occasion ?
He told me he had shot a Kafir, and I asked him under what
circumstances, and he said he saw the Kafir come on to his farm to
look for a horse   He asked if he had a pass from his master
He said he had not, and he was told to go back and get one
The Kafir did not do so, so he rode up to him to compel him to
go back, and the Kafir turned round and struck at his horse
With what ? An iron rod about two feet long   The Kafir
struck a second blow at Pelser's knee, and he said, " I out with

the revolver and shot him, and I came immediately to town to report what I have done" Did he say if the Kafir was dead or not? He said, "I do not know" Well, under instructions from the Magistrate you went out to the spot where the Kafir had been shot? Yes At what time was it? About one o'clock, as we had to wait while the Doctor got his horse right And you were accompanied by the District Surgeon and Pelser? Yes What took place at the body? Mr Pelser took us to the spot, and pointed the body out to us It was dead at that time The Doctor examined it to search for the wound Mr Pelser pointed to the right side of the head I was standing on one side and the Doctor on the other, and Pelser said you will find it there somewhere

Judge Show

Witness put his finger on the right side of the forehead over the temple He could not find it there We turned the body over as it was lying on its back and we found the wound in the back Did you see any foot prints of the horse? Not close to the body, Did you see any at all? About five yards— I just paced it off from the body Now you remember the native witnesses giving their evidence—Veldschoen and Alfred Peters, and the rest? Yes Did these witnesses come and volunteer their evidence? No

Judge None of them? No

Mr Solomon I think you went along the line to see if any-one had seen what had taken place? I first sent my boy along, and afterwards I went myself Did you go the same day? I think so, I am not quite sure When you sent the boy was it on the day Pelser went in? I think I sent him at the same time and I must have gone the next morning And after they had given their evidence you went out to the body again did you not? Yes And you were accompanied by Sergeant Strong and Hall, and Private Venter of the District Police You were sent out to test the credibility of the native witnesses? Yes

Judge To see if they could see what took place? Yes, from where they stood, my Lord They showed you the places where they were standing? Yes Alfred Peters took me to the different holes where the men were at work Now just you tell us how did you test the evidence? I stood at the pole where Peters——

Solicitor-General It is not English to lead evidence of the witnesses that you are going to call in the future

Mr Solomon (sarcastically) That was done by the Crown, but the Crown takes up a different position now

Judge I see nothing wrong in it If the witnesses do not come forward and say they stood in the positions he says they were it does not matter

Solicitor-General He is going to ask him how he tested their evidence

Judge It is perfectly in order

Solicitor-General That is a matter for argument

Mr Solomon I am now following the practice of the Crown

Judge (to witness) You had better speak for yourself as to what you saw

Witness From the positions described to us we tried to see whether we could see the spot where Pelser had taken us where the body was

Judge Don't speak for 'us,' speak for yourself Tell us what you saw

Witness I was taken to the pole where Alfred Peters was supposed to have been standing, Sergeant Hall was taken to another pole where Mtloyiya was Private Venter was on foot and stayed with Sergeant Strong on horseback on the spot where the body was found Strong had a revolver and Venter had a riding whip

Mr Solomon What could you see? From where I was I saw Strong—it was about five hundred and sixty yards, the other pole was a little nearer

Judge Between you and the spot could you see Strong and Venter? Yes What were they doing? Strong was on his horse with a revolver in his hand Could you see him? Yes, but not the revolver I could see his arm extended Venter struck at him,

Mr Solomon Could you see that? Oh yes, plainly I could see the arm up and the riding whip He then fell Before he fell did you see anything? I saw the smoke

Judge Which you took to be what? A shot fired from the revolver Venter fell

Mr Solomon Could you see him fall? Yes They went through the performance twice and on each occasion I saw smoke Could you hear the shot? No He fired three shots altogether I believe he told me so Did you hear any of the shots at all? No, not one What sort of a day was it? It was a windy day the wind was blowing pretty strong at the time And the day on which Pelser came and reported the matter to you? It was a beautiful calm day

Solicitor-General The wind blew on that day Was it blowing from the North, South, East, or West? I think it must have been pretty near East There was a kloof coming right down to the spot near the body and it was blowing from the East That is to say that it was blowing from the East downwards? Yes

Judge Which way was the wind blowing? It was blowing from the homestead towards me and on to where the body lay It was strong

Solicitor-General You say the distance from you to the body was about five hundred and sixty yards? Yes What was the distance from the homestead to you? About two hundred and fifty yards The place where you were standing, was it in a direct line between the house and the body? It was not exactly a direct line, but not very far out of it And you looked towards them when Strong fired the shot? Yes And yet you could not hear? Yes You saw the smoke? Yes I suppose he fired in your direction, as they say the horse was coming towards them? Yes Alfred Peters pointed out to you where each of them had been standing? Yes He placed you at the spot where he himself had been standing? Yes He pointed out the place where Zwaartboy had been working? I don't know their names Mtloyiya was one, Canteen another You say he pointed out Mtloyiya's place? I put Hall on that hole Where did Alfred Peters say the other natives were standing? Well I am not quite sure about that point Let us change the subject a little—you cannot tell us? Not exactly When you went out on the 16th with Pelser you passed close by where you said the men were working? If the men had been working there— we went direct out—they must have seen us They must have seen us coming across the line If Peters was working at the spot, could he have seen you go up to the body on that day? Yes, we had to cross the line There was nothing to prevent him What time did you go to the body? I suppose the time we went to the body must have been about twenty minutes to two I am not quite sure I think I got back before the Court closed, and that is at 4 o'clock You were there about two hours? About that You had the body buried? Yes None of these witnesses came up to you to give you any information? No, not before I enquired for their names That was the next day? Yes You know Mr Man? Yes These natives were in his employ, at least that day? I believe so Mr Man did not come up to the spot where the body was that day? I did not see him And he gave you no information? No, I don't think I saw him or the natives that day I may have seen them amongst numbers of others, perhaps

Judge There were many natives working there? Yes, on the railway and telegraph line

Solicitor-General The railway line runs close to the poles— it is the telegraph line in connection with the railway? Yes I do not mean to say I saw all of them I saw natives on the 16th working along the telegraph line from the Woolwash They were working all along the line from Burghersdorp

Judge From the Woolwash to where? To the ballast-hole

Solicitor-General Did you after you had gone to the body go to any of the natives along the line to see if any of them could see the spot—did it strike you to look? I didn't go out of my way I saw none from the spot I did not look about Now you say that when Pelser took you out to the body he said

that he thought the bullet would be found in the forehead?
Yes He did not seem to know where the bullet was to be
found? No he pointed to the right side of the head Now
from what you noticed there did it seem to you that man had
fallen where he was shot or if he had moved after he had fallen?
Judging from the appearance of the ground I should imagine
he had dropped where he was shot and had not moved There
were no appearances of a struggle about there

Judge No appearance of a struggle at all? No Did you
look? Yes

Solicitor-General What did you find about the body? I
found an iron bar on the one side Is this the bar? Yes
Where was it lying? At the right hand side How far from
the body? About one yard from it Where was it lying,
farther back from the head or along side? Along side It was
about the middle of the body about a yard away from it As
if it had been thrown away as the man fell? It may have been
thrown away When you found him what position was he
lying in as regards his arms—was he lying on his back with his
head towards the north-east? I think they were by the side of
the body, I didn't quite notice

Judge Were they extended? No I don't think so—they
may have been a little

Mr Solomon I hope the jury will not want half a holiday
to-morrow

A Juryman We prefer to sit all day to-morrow

Court adjourned at 6 p m, to Saturday morning

SATURDAY, NOVEMBER 14, 1885

The Court resumed at 9 30 a m when the Jury having answered to their names, Arthur Lambert Hall was called

Mr Solomon You are a Sergeant in the Cape Police stationed at Burghersdorp? Yes You recollect some time ago in January last going out with Williams the Chief Constable to Pelser's farm? Yes He was standing at one telegraph pole and you at another? Yes Were you standing at the next pole to his? Yes How far are the telegraph poles apart? I think about ninety yards

Judge Are they all new telegraph poles being put up or old ones renovated? No, it is a new line

Mr Solomon You went to the spot where Strong stood— where the body was? Yes Now from where you were standing —could you see what they were doing? I saw Venter in the act of striking He was in front of Strong who was on horse back He was on foot, he made blows at him Strong fired two cartridges How do you know he fired? I saw the smoke twice

Judge Could you see from what it came? Don't say you could if you could not? Yes I could see the arm extended Afterwards I heard a shot in the same direction It was when I saw the smoke a third time I heard it distinctly

Mr Solomon The view there is quite clear? Yes

Solicitor-General You were standing at the first hole to the left where Williams was standing? Yes, on the left

Judge Was that nearer to the spot where the body was found? Was it ninety yards nearer? No not ninety yards How much nearer to Strong? It was some fifty yards nearer to Strong than Williams was Can you tell me if you went to the place where the body was? Yes Did you look about there? Yes Have you been long in the Colony? No not long, about two years Do you know what creep grass is—do you know the difference between that and other grass? Yes At the spot was there any grass? I don't think there was any grass—it was all dried up

William Strong was next called

Mr Solomon You are a Sergeant in the Albert Divisional Police? Yes

Judge That is a different body to the Cape Police—you are employed by the Divisional Council? Yes

Mr Solomon You remember going out in company with Williams, Venter, and Hall to Pelser's farm? Yes

Judge To the spot in the veldt on Pelser's farm? Yes

Mr Solomon You and Pelser went to the place on the farm pointed out by Williams where the native was found? Yes And Williams and Hall went to two telegraph poles—two separate ones? Yes.

k

Judge   And there stood ?   Yes

Mr Solomon   You went through a performance with Venter ?
Yes   What performance did you go through ?   I was on horse
back and Venter was on my right, and he was to make several
blows at me with a whip, first in his left hand   I fired a shot
whilst he had it in his left hand   I fired a blank cartridge and
he fell according to agreement on his right side   He again struck
at me with his right arm and I fired another shot with a blank
cartridge   I suppose he fell again according to agreement ?   Yes
I then fired a bullet cartridge   That is all ?   Yes   Would the
bullet cartridge make a louder report than a blank one ?   Yes, a
much louder report

Judge   When you were standing there did you look about the
ground ?   I looked about at the spoors Williams had brought
me down to,   You saw the spot where you were standing ?   Yes
You saw under foot — was there grass growing there ?   Short
grass in some places in some places not   In that country was it
tall grass which you saw, or grass such as turf ?   It was not turf
Do you know the difference between them ?   Yes   How was it
that it was so short ?   It appeared to be short, but after a rain I
think it would spring up   It had been very dry previously to
this   Was it a grassy country or not ?   It appeared to be a kind
of vlei, it was a hollow place

Solicitor-General   Oh !

Judge   Have you been long in that part of the country ?   Yes   And
it is your duty to go about to detect crime and if possible to follow
the spoor ?   Yes   From where you were at that place could you
see if it was a spot where you could trace spoor ?   Yes   If any one
had been there could you trace any spoor ?   Yes, I think so

Solicitor-General had no questions

James Fischer was next called

Mr Solomon   You are a turnkey at the gaol in Burghersdorp ?
Yes   How long have you been there ?   Two months   Previous
to that what had you been ?   Assistant Railway Ganger on the
line   And previous to that you had been working for the Municipality ?   Yes, as Superintendent of Native Locations and Street-
Keeper   You knew a native called Zachariah ?   Yes   He was
I believe working for you while you were Street-Keeper   Yes.
What sort of a man was he ?   He was a very good boy as regards
work   Was he a quiet man ?   Yes   Was he a raw Kafir ?   No,
he was a school boy   one of the educated boys   How long was
he working for you ?   About two weeks   Do you know where
he went to from there ?   He had been working in another boy's
place for these two weeks

Judge   As a substitute ?   Yes   What wages did he get ?
Half-a-crown a day

Mr Solomon   After that where did he go to ?   He then went
to Mr Stewart, the Bank Manager

Judge He is dead now? Who, Zachariah? No. Mr. Stewart? Yes

Mr Solomon At the time of his death can you tell us in whose employ he was? He was in the employ of another Mr Stewart—a stone mason

Judge In Burghersdorp? Yes

Mr Solomon This Mr Stewart the stone mason has left the Colony, I believe? Yes What height was this man Zachariah? He was about five feet four or five Compare his height with yours? He was about my height

Judge How high? He was not quite as tall as me And what is your height? I am 5 feet 7½ inches And what do you say was his height? Five feet four inches What did you say in the first place? Five feet four or five

Mr Solomon Did you notice when he was working for you whether he was a right or left handed man? He was a right handed man, On Friday, the six——some day in January you were working on the line as a ganger? Yes I had charge of some boys

Judge Near to Burghersdorp? Yes, just opposite to Mr Pelser's farm On his farm? I don't know You remember there was a railway cottage there? I was about half a mile from it

Mr Solomon You were working then at the ballast hole? Yes

Judge You had men under you? Yes Natives? Yes

Mr Solomon From where you were working could you see Pelser's homestead? Yes How far about was the house from where you were working? About 150 yards And could you see Pelser's tramp-floor from where you were working? Yes There were some natives at that time working at the telegraph poles? Yes, about that time

Judge Are the telegraph poles on the same line as the railway? They run all along the line

Mr Solomon How far where these men working at the telegraph poles from you? Some were above me They were working all along the line? Yes

Judge Could you see them? I could see them as far as Pelser's dam (To Mr Solomon) Have you a plan of the place at all?

Mr Solomon Yes my Lord (Plan handed to witness)

Judge Now just look at this plan You see the ballast hole and Pelser's homestead, and say if it gives a fair description of the locality Look it all through Does it seem to be all right? Yes

It was being handed to jury

Solicitor-General There are memoranda on that plan that ought not to be

Judge   Let me see it   What memoranda do you mean?

Solicitor-General   The explanations of the route of Pelser and—

Judge   Oh, yes   (Plan handed to jury)

Is it fairly correct?   Yes

Mr Solomon   On a Friday morning do you remember Zachariah's coming up to you at the ballast hole?   Yes   Who was with you when he came up?   A boy named Grahamstown   Was he the only boy working alongside of you?   Yes   What direction did Zachariah come from?   He came from Burghersdorp   I see there is a Woolwash marked on the plan, did he come from there?   I saw he came along the line as from Burghersdorp   He spoke to you?   Yes   He came up and said "Good morning"   You had conversation?   Yes, he said to me—you cannot tell us what he said to you   Was he friendly?   Yes   He had a smoke whilst he was there   He had a talk and a smoke?   Yes

Judge   Whilst he remained with you?   Yes   Did he sit down?   No, sir

Mr Solomon   Now when he came to you had he anything in his hand?   No

Judge   Nothing?   You are sure of that?   Yes, I am sure of it

Mr Solomon   You saw him go in the direction of Pelser's house?   Yes   How far could you see him?   When he left me in the first place I noticed him pass off and cross a sluit

Judge   Was this through the veldt—when you saw him come up to you?   He came along the side of the line   Was it where people generally go?   Yes   People used to walk promiscuously there?   People coming from Burghersdorp   And after he left what course did he take—where did he go?   He went about twenty yards down the line, and then turned off to his left in the direction of Pelser's house

Mr Solomon   How far could you see him—when did you lose sight him?   I missed sight of him at the kitchen or milk house at the back of the house as he passed between the kitchen and the house

Judge   That is not on the plan?   No

Mr Solomon   How did you lose sight of him?   I left the spot where I was working and went to another end of the quarry   Did you leave Grahamstown there?   Yes, still working   Well, then, as you were at this part of the ballast hole you did not see the native leave Pelser's again?   No   And after some time you got back to where you were originally—joining Grahamstown again?   Yes   And after you had been there some little time did you hear anything?   Yes, I heard a shot fired   And you made a remark to Grahamstown about it?

Judge   In what direction did it come?   From the right of Pelser's house

Mr Solomon   You know where there is a dam ?   Yes, it was coming from about the mouth of it in that direction

Judge   That was the direction where the body was found ?   I did not go to the spot   (To Mr Solomon)   You had better prove this plan

Mr Solomon   Yes, sir, I am going to   (To witness)   You see on that plan a spot marked "body," is that near the dam you speak of ?   Yes

Judge   The dam is also marked   Is it about where you say ?   You would say the dam was a little more directly between the spots where the body was found and the ballast hole   You do not know where the body was though—so that the dam may be correctly described—the dam is somewhere about there ?   Yes

Solicitor-General   You say that when the native left you that morning he had nothing in his hand ?   Yes   One witness says that when he came to the tramp-floor he had a stick, a little longer than this bar, or a switch as he calls it—are you sure he had not at the time he saw you ?   Yes   And he had not this iron ?   I am quite sure he hadn't anything   He was a Kafir ?   Yes   It would be nothing very singular for a Kafir to walk about with a stick in his hand ?   I think I should have seen it, for at the time he came to me he asked me for tobacco, and I gave it to him, and he stood in this position, and rubbed the tobacco in his hands   At any rate if he had anything in his hand when he came to the tramp-floor he must have picked it up   You say he was working for you about two weeks   In what capacity was he ?   I was street-keeper, and he was working along the street   How many natives did you have in your employ at that time ?   I had five   All the two weeks there were five men in your employ ?   Yes   You say that he merely took the place of another man that had gone away ?   He spoke both Dutch and English ?   I don't know if he could talk Dutch well   I know he could English

Judge   What did he speak to you in when he came up ?   He spoke Kafir   Then he always spoke to you in Kafir ?   Yes   And you understood him - you speak a little ?   Yes

Grahamstown, a Kafir, was next called

Mr Solomon   In January last you were one of the labourers on the telegraph construction line ?   Yes   You were under Mr Fischer ?   Yes   You remember when at work there a Kafir came up to you   He was afterwards killed ?   Yes   Did you know him ?   No, I did not know him, Fischer knew him   What direction did he come from ?   He came from Burghersdorp direction   What did he go up to Mr Fischer for—was there a conversation ?   Yes, he came to speak   While he was there did he do anything ?   Yes, he asked for some tobacco   What did he do with the tobacco ?   He took it and placed it in his pipe   He left you afterwards ?   Yes, after he had lit his pipe   And where did he go to—

in what direction? He left, going towards the farm He had told us that he was in search of a horse Now when he came up to you and Mr Fischer had he anything in his hand? No, I didn't see anything If he had anything would you have seen it? Yes You say he walked towards Pelser's house? Yes

Judge He had nothing when he left? No

Mr Solomon Where did you see him go to? He went to the enclosure? He went to the enclosure which is near the homestead, the enclosure where the horses were I saw him come out of the kraal and go round Pelser's house

Judge He went into the kraal? No, he stood in the gateway looking at the horses Then I saw him go to where the people were at work taking corn off, If he had gone inside would you have seen him? I am not sure about that because there was a little time I went away from the spot You saw him leave again? Yes

Mr Solomon You say he went from there to the tramp-floor? Yes, then after that I saw him leave there and go to where some men were at work at the wire fence

Judge When he went to the men to what point did he go? You had better ask that Mr Solomon

Mr Solomon Yes

Judge Did you see the stone wall there? Yes Round where the men were working? Yes

Mr Solomon Did he go over the wall or stand this side? No, he stood outside of the wall Now you saw how he stood? Well, I was at work and it seemed to me he was standing talking to the people there Then you say you saw him leave and go in the direction where the men were working? Yes Tell us all you know? He disappeared and you went to your work? Yes After he had disappeared some little time I saw a person leave the tramp floor where they were at work and this person I saw come mounted

Judge What kind of horse? A dark brown or black horse

Mr Solomon What direction did the man on horse-back take? He followed the course taken by the Kafir and disappeared where he did Then some little time after his disappearance I heard a shot I was speaking to Fisher Yes, but you must not say what—Fischer was with you when you heard it? Yes Had he been there all the time—was he standing alongside of you? Yes, close to me

Judge What direction did the shot come from? The same direction as where the white man had disappeared I heard the shot but I did not see where it came from

Judge The disappearance, you have not asked that Mr Solomon When he first lost sight of the man on which side was it, was it on this side of the line or the opposite side of the line? He must have gone over the railway to have got there

But when you lost sight of Zacharias first he must have gone over the railway? No, when he disappeared he had not gone on to the railway, but it was close to that spot Is there a hollow there? There is a ridge

Mr Solomon Then you saw him again afterwards—Zachariah? No, I did not after he had disappeared

Judge Now the man on horse-back

Mr Solomon Where did you lose sight of him? He disappeared at the same spot where the Kafir disappeared Over the line yes? Yes

Judge Did you see him again? I saw him return

Mr Solomon How long did you work at the ballast hole on that day? I worked till sunset Then between you and where you heard a shot there is a rising ground is there not? There is a ridge and I heard the report of the pistol

Solicitor-General Is it usual for you Kafirs to carry sticks about with you? Yes, but at Burghersdorp it is prohibited People are caught for carrying sticks

Judge By the Police? Yes They are taken away because they say we quarrel with them and fight

Solicitor-General Then it is not usual to see a Kafir when going into the veldt to find horses carrying sticks? Then a man would be outside the town and he would perhaps carry sticks Oh! it is only in the town that it is prohibited? Yes Then it would not surprise you to see a man out in the veldt carrying a stick? No And you would not take particular notice whether he was carrying a stick or not—it would not strike you particularly? Yes, I should know whether he carried a stick or not

Mr Solomon It would convince you when you saw him take the tobacco in his hands and rub it, that he had nothing in his hands? Yes

Judge Are you sure he had no stick at all? I am sure when I saw him he was not carrying a stick At the kraal you say he stood for some little time? Yes From where you were standing could you see from there if he had anything with him? No, that was some little distance and I should not have been able to see that

Juryman (Smith) Did you see any pieces of iron about where you were working? What sort? All sorts, bars or anything at all? The iron which is there are the rails for the railway (laughter) Were there no broken hand-barrows about? No, our work is to take gravel to that place on the railway in the trucks, we do not work with hand-barrows Did you see any piece of iron like that about? No

Solicitor-General Will your Lordship ask him how it was he did not give the Police this information—he seems to know so much about it—at the time of the preliminary examination (question put) ?   Well I was under the white man and I only said what I was asked   The Police never called at all at that time

Veldschoen was next called

Mr Solomon   Your name is Veldschoen ?   No, it is Gewa-geweka—my Colonial name is Veldschoen (laughter)   Oh ! very well we will take your Colonial name   You were on the telegraph line working ?   Yes   You were employed to dig holes for the poles ?   Yes   You were working at this, when a Kafir was shot on Mr Pelser's farm ?   Yes   Can you give us the names of any other Kafirs that were working there at the time ?   Ntloyiya, Alfred Peters, Canteen, and Zwaartbooy were working lower down   From where you were working could you see Pelser's house ?   No, I could not see it

Judge   Where is the spot, where this man was working, on the plan ?

Mr Solomon   Where the native crossed the line

There is a rise between you and Pelser's house   You remember the Kafir being shot ?   Tell us all you saw of the man—what he did and the whole story ?   He came and sat on a stone near me and whilst he was still on the stone Zwaartboy came   How near was he sitting ?   About four yards   After that they had a conversation—Zwaartboy seemed to know him The man went away after a time—he crossed before the water

Judge   To the right or the left of the water ?   To the left Was there much water in it ?   No, there was not

Mr Solomon   While he was talking to Zwaartboy did he have anything in his hand ?   No, he had nothing   He sat upon the stone and his hands were resting on his knees   You saw him over the dam ?   I saw him go across the dam   After that I saw the white man follow him on horseback and overtake him They spoke a little

Judge   Why do you say they spoke ?   Did you hear them ? No, I could not hear, the distance was too great   They seemed to speak ?   Yes   Why do you say so ?   The white man had gone ahead of him and then they faced each other   He was turned by the white man and came towards us, then they walked along—the white man behind the black man about the distance between me and your Lordship (about four yards)   Then when they got to the dam there was a report

Judge   What report ?   A gun's report   Do you know the difference between a gun and a pistol ?   Was it the report of a gun ?   I cannot say whether it was that of a gun or a pistol Where did it come from ?   From the white man   After the report the white man did not dismount but stood a little while and then turned and galloped off home

Mr Solomon   From where you were could you at any time see the black man turn round and strike at the white man ?

No, I did not see anything of the kind   The man walked along as far as the Judge's desk without looking back at all   You did not know this man Zachariah at all ?   No, that was the first time I had seen him   And when you heard the shot they were some distance from you ?   Yes   How far ?   It was about as far as those three large stores in the street   Did you ever point out to anyone where you were when the shot was fired ?   Yes, to the interpreter in the Magistrate's Court at Burghersdorp

Solicitor-General   Alfred Peters gave that information

Judge   He may have done so

Mr Solomon   How far was Alfred Peters from you when you heard the shot ?   He was about the distance of the front of the Court House (forty yards)   And you say the white man was driving the black man on—in which direction—coming towards you ?   Yes

Solicitor-General   You say the Kafir was walking quietly in front about three yards from the horse ?   Yes   And didn't turn back ?   No   Did he turn his head ?   I was too far see that

Judge   He may have turned his head but you could not see ?   No, if he did I did not see it

Solicitor-General   He was directly in front of the horse ?   Yes, the distance of the Judge's desk   You say you were both talking the whole of the time ?   Yes, I was in the hole—the pole was already up and it was for the stay I was making the hole   And whilst you were making this you heard the shot fired ?   Yes, I saw them coming along, one driving the other on   Yes, and at that time—just before you heard the shot—you were working at this hole ?   No, I was looking at the time the report was heard   Now just listen to what you said before the Magistrate   "I was digging at the time I heard the shot and I turned at once and looked"   Did you say that before the Magistrate ?   No, I said to the Magistrate that when I was looking I heard a report

Judge   Is this the part "I was digging a hole at the time   I heard the shot and turned at once and looked   I saw them coming   I was looking when the shot was fired, and I could see the smoke"

Mr Solomon to Solicitor-General   Read it all, you left out the last evidence

Solicitor-General   The latter is a matter for argument   (To witness)   Where was Mr Mair that day ?   He was a long way away   Tell us how you and the other men were standing—where was Zwaartboy that day ?   Zwaartboy had already left me and had disappeared   Yes, but before he disappeared, where had he been working ?   He was working quite a long way from me, on the Burghersdorp side of me   That was before the man came

L

to you⸮ Zwaartboy came to where I was sitting talking to him Where did he come from, the Burghersdorp side or the other⸮ He came from the side of us going towards Burghersdorp Who was working nearest to you⸮ Ntloyiya On which side— Burghersdorp or the other⸮ No I was nearer to Burghersdorp than him And who was working on the Burghersdorp side of you⸮ Alfred I was between Alfred and Ntloyiya There was one pole that intervened between him and me and that was finished

Judge Had Zwaartboy been working nearer to Burghersdorp on the same line with Alfred⸮ Well where Zwaartboy was at work was nearer to Burghersdorp than I was And nearer to Peters⸮ Zwaartboy was not on the Burghersdorp side Tell us where he was⸮ This side You were between Ntloyiya and Peters⸮ Yes Now where was Zwaartboy—nearer to Peters or Ntloyiya⸮ He was nearer to Canteen (laughter) And where was Canteen⸮ Nearer to Ntloyiya

Solicitor-General Who was working nearest to Canteen⸮ Where was Breakfast⸮ He was behind Zwaartboy again (laughter) From where you were working, could you see Breakfast⸮ Yes I could see him—there was a bend And Mr Mair—where was he working— on the Burghersdorp side or not⸮ Burghersdorp Alfred Peters was nearest to him⸮ No (laughter) How far was he from Peters⸮ A long way

Judge Could you see Man⸮ No, he was hidden out of sight

Solicitor-General After this when did you see Mair that day⸮ That evening You did not think it worth your while to tell him what had happened⸮ No I did not go Well, that afternoon you recollect some people coming on horseback from the direction where the man had been shot—some policemen⸮ What I saw after this was the father come to where I was I am coming to that Did you see the police going towards the body⸮ No, I did not see them Where were you working after dinner that day⸮ I went to sleep a little in a sluit and then went to work in the same hole What time do you take your dinner— They go by the sun (Mr Ayliff) —How was the sun⸮ Was it noon⸮ Yes, at noon And how long after noon did you go to work again⸮ We have no watches so we cannot tell (laughter) Mr Man takes good care to see that you stick to your work⸮ Yes Then you say you had a short snooze and then went to work again⸮ Yes It was a warm day, and after we had eaten I rested a little while, and then went to work (laughter) Do you recollect Pelser and some other people coming from Burghersdorp and going to the spot where the man had been shot⸮ I do not You were saying that old Mr Pelser came to you, when was this⸮ It was before dinner Then the man had been shot before dinner⸮ Yes Did you tell him anything about the man being

shot ? No, I did not say anything about it I was with Ntloyiya He came to me for a crowbar

Judge How far was the old man from you ? He came and
stood close to where I was working He said "What are you
working here?" I said "I am digging a hole for a stay" Did
you tell him anything about a man being shot ? No What
did he say ? He made some remarks about the pole saying it
was a strong pole, and then he left

Solicitor-General You saw him come towards you Yes
And he came from the house Yes And after he had spoken
to you where did he go to ? He went back in the same direction
He did not go to where the body was No, he did not Now
the man that you had seen shoot the Kafir, did he return to the
spot again after he had ridden off to the house I did not see
him return I did not report to old Pelser that a Kafir had been
shot because I was afraid

Mr Solomon You knew the man that had shot the Kafir had
come out of the same homestead Yes Was it usual for him
to come and see you at work at the poles? No, that was the
first time I had seen him

Judge Do you know the man Frederick David who gave his
evidence before the Magistrate? No (read evidence) This
was one of Pelser's servants and I should like to know from the
man if he can describe the spot

Solicitor-General I would like to ask him if he saw any boy
herding sheep near the spot where the man was shot? No

Mr Solomon The boy (Fred David) says he was herding
the sheep in the spruit

Judge Have you no idea where it is—is the spruit marked
on the plan ?

Solicitor-General No, my Lord

Judge I should like to know where it is (To witness) Now
from where you were when you heard the shot fired were you
looking in that direction? I saw the smoke and heard the shot
Before you saw the smoke, could you see anything—could you
see the direction of any arm or hand? No I could not Why
not I saw nothing of that kind at all If you were looking
at the white man on the horse at the time you say, did you—
could you see anything? I saw him fire at the Kafir man
Then could you not see how the shot was fired—was it too far?
It is some considerable distance (witness again pointed to the
three large stores) When you say he was that distance from
you can you say it was—mightn't it have been farther, or might
not it have been nearer? I thought it was about that distance
If it was nearer you could have seen his arm? I did not say
that what I saw was smoke and then I heard a report

Zwaartboy was next called

Mr Solomon In the beginning of the year you were a

labourer on the construction line making holes for poles? Yes You were working at the poles on Pelser's farm when a Kafir was shot there? Yes That Kafir was Zachariah? Yes You knew him? Yes What kind of a man was he? How do you mean? His manner—was he a civil or a quarrelsome man? Well to me he was very good indeed and I never saw anything opposite to any one else You saw him that day when he was shot? Yes Just tell us where you saw him and how you came to see him? I saw him at the wire Where were you working? I had finished making one hole where I was at work and coming to another when I saw the man come up to Veldschoen The man had come from Pelser's I saw him approach Veldschoen before I came up to him, and when I came up he was there I greeted him

Judge You went up because you knew him? No, I had finished the work I was occupied upon there and I was going to some other Beyond Peters? Yes I came to Veldschoen before I got to Peters I shook hands with him

Mr Solomon Did you notice if he had anything in his hands? Nothing He asked me then about a horse You must not give his conversation He stood a little while talking? After a little while he left and went in the direction of the dam At the same time he left in that direction you went in the direction of Burghersdorp? Yes When I got over the bridge which is beyond the homestead—a culvert? Yes I saw the white man coming out mounted and ride in the direction of the native man When you saw this had you already passed Alfred Peters? Yes, I had And you went on when you saw the man on horse back? Yes Did you afterwards hear anything? Yes, when he had disappeared I heard a shot

Judge Were you at work then? No, I was walking—going there I heard it come from the direction the man had gone I am not able to say where it came from, I was going along and heard it Then after a little while I again saw the white man still upon his horse and galloping towards the town

Solicitor-General This Kafir Zachariah, he was talking by you for some time? It was not long Were you sitting down? No, he was sitting down, I was standing When you came there was he already sitting down? Yes, he had just sat down

Judge Do you have your meals with Veldschoen? No, I have it alone Do you work by the day or by the job? Well, we receive our wages weekly though we are hired monthly, but we do not always get it all (laughter)

Ntloyiya was next called

Mr Solomon You were also in January last a labourer on the telegraph construction? Yes And you were working on that part of the line on Pelser's farm where the Kafir was shot? Yes. Alfred Peters, Veldschoen, Canteen and Zwaartboy were working there? Yes   Next to whom were you working? I was nearest to Veldschoen   Did you see the Kafir before he was shot? I had seen him

Judge   That day—had you never seen him before that day? I had never seen him before   Tell us how you came to see him and where you saw him? I saw him coming out of Pelser's and coming up to us where we were at work   To whom did he come up to first? Veldschoen   Then I saw him converse with him and went up to listen   He stayed a little while and then went on   Was there anyone else there? No   Was Zwaartboy there? Zwaartboy simply greeted and went on   The Kafir then went on? Yes   In what direction did he go? He went past towards the dam in that way

Judge   Had he anything with him?

Mr Solomon   I forgot that

Witness   No, he had nothing in his hands

Judge   How near were you to him?   I was about the distance of the Judge from him (4 yards)

Mr Solomon   You saw him go in the direction of the dam? Yes After he had passed the dam the man passed down on horseback— passed to our right   How do you mean, between you and Burghersdorp? Yes, he went and turned the Kafir that had passed me

Judge   How do you know that? I saw him turn him

Mr Solomon   Tell us exactly what you saw?   After he had turned him they stood a little while   While I was looking I saw smoke and then I heard a report and when the report was heard the man dropped, the horse stood   I was all the time with Veldschoen   When you saw the white man drive the black man in front of him, did you see the black man turn round to strike at him? No, I did not

Solicitor-General   The black man walked quietly in front of the horse and did not turn back at all? No

Judge   Quietly? Yes

Solicitor-General   And when the white man shot him he was not looking round at all? He did not turn round   I said look round? He did not look round   You say he was walking three yards, do you mean three yards in front of the horse's head? Yes   When you saw the smoke you were looking at them as they were coming along? Yes   And did you see the white man take up his pistol and fire at the man? I saw him in the act of firing   And at that time he was walking straight in front of the horse? Yes   Straight in front of the horse? Yes   And then while they were coming you say you were standing with Veldschoen? Yes   And you had a little conversation? He was talking at the time   And you were standing talking to him? I had come there for a crowbar

Judge   After the man left did you go back? No   You originally came for a crowbar and stopped there? Yes

Solicitor-General And then you told us you saw the man talking to Veldschoen and you came there for the purpose of listening? Yes, I went up And while you were talking to Veldschoen you kept your eye on the man all the time until he went into the veldt? Yes, I could see him well You kept your eyes on him continually? Yes, we could see him walk along You say the man came from the homestead? Yes Did you actually see him come from the house? I did not see him go out of the house, I could see that he came from the homestead You say you continually kept your eye on the man going into the veldt—when had you time to turn round and look at Pelser? We could see the man walking along, and then by looking the other side we could see the white man too Where was the Mi Man working that day? Beyond Nearer to Burghersdorp? Yes How far from you? It is a long way from me When did you first see him that day? Well, I worked for him After the man was shot when did you first see him? Late that evening after I had finished my day's work Did you tell him about seeing a man shoot a native that day? Well, I spoke to Alfred, and told him about it I did not mention it to the white man You were present in the Magistrate's Court when Mr Man gave his evidence? Well, I was there I had been there to give my evidence Did you hear Mr, Man give his? No, I remained outside You gave evidence? Yes Do you recollect telling the Magistrate " I also told my master when I returned from my work at sun down?" I said I had mentioned it to Alfred Did you mean that Alfred had interpreted it to your master? No, I was not there I understand that you told Alfred that that evening? Yes, I told him to tell the white man

Judge Did you tell him that evening the first time? Yes

Solicitor-General You say Velschoen worked next to you that day? Yes And who worked next to him on the other side? Alfred Then between you and Alfred there was only one pole and that was the one at which Veldschoen was working? There was no one at the middle pole

Judge Between Veldschoen and Alfred there was no one working? Alfred stood here, Veldschoen was second, and I was third here, and Canteen below me (Witness intimated position by putting his fingers in consecutive places) You saw the native approaching the line that day? Yes You were the first man he spoke to? Yes And did he not go to speak to Alfred Peters before going to Veldschoen? No And did he speak to Zwaartboy at all? Yes, he did And you say Zwaartboy greeted and passed on? Yes And he only returned the greeting and passed on? Yes What was Zachariah doing when you and Veldschoen were talking to him, was he sitting down or standing up? He was standing You say he had

nothing in his hand when he was speaking to you? No As
he was standing up was it possible for him to have had a stick
hanging down by his side without you noticing it? No, I did
not see him with a stick Might he have had it without your
noticing? Well, my eyes saw nothing

Judge If the stick had been there would those eyes have
seen it? Yes, if he had carried anything Why? Well, if
he had carried a stick my eyes must have seen it

Solicitor-General You say you saw the man on horseback
holding his arm like this (extended arm)? Yes Now look at
me—can you say that he had a pistol in his hand like this? It
is only a pistol

Judge Did you see the pistol? We did not see the pistol
exactly but we saw the smoke

Solicitor-General Did you see anything in his hand or not?
Something was visible And do you not know whether it was a
pistol? No, I am unable to say

Mr Solomon From where Alfred Peters was that day he
could see what took place? Yes And when you saw what you
say did you speak about it afterwards? Yes, we were telling
each other And you suggested to Peters to tell your master?
Yes, I did He spoke English? Yes And you do not? No
Zwaartboy then talked to Zachariah? They greeted How
long did Zwaartboy remain there talking to him? Quite a little
while

Judge Did what? Greeted Did it appear from what took
place that Zachariah and Zwaartboy had ever known each other
before? Yes Why? Because they appeared pleased to meet

Mr Solomon And Zachariah remained some time talking
do you mean? No, he did not How long did he stay? Quite
a little while Did he sit down while he was there? No You
don't remember

Judge When you came first up to Veldschoen was Zachariah
there? Yes, he went up before me

Mr Solomon And then who came up first you or Zwaartboy? I did You kept your eyes on the man on horseback--
why did you do that?

Judge He did not say those words, he said he saw him

Mr Solomon And you are quite sure you saw him riding
behind the native? Yes, he followed him and then turned him
And you are sure he was behind the native when he fired? Yes

Judge You saw him riding after him, what distance did he
come back after speaking to him before he fired—describe about?
The horse was following the man at the distance of your desk, and
going along that way he fired How far did they go? It was
not very far from where he turned him How far? I cannot
explain distances at all You know the distance between the
telegraph poles that you were working at? Yes, I saw them

And when they were travelling back in that way from the spot where he was stopped did they travel back a distance of one telegraph pole to another or less or more? They were not near the poles at all (laughter) Supposing there had been poles there—how may do you think they would have passed, or if they would have passed any? I am unable to say Give us some idea? I am unable to say Could you have thrown with a stone from the spot to the firing or was it too far or too near? I could not have thrown a stone as far as the spot where the man was shot to the spot where he was turned And could you see them going along? Yes And you did see them? Yes And while they were going along was there anything to show a disturbance, was the man hurrying him along and did the man go near the horse and the horse swerve? No, I did not see any of that Before the shot was fired, did you see the horse swerve? No After that did it swerve, if it had done so must you have seen it? I did not see anything but the two following each other If he was behind the man how could you see that he was armed? The man was armed Could he not have been to the left or the right of the coloured man? No, he was behind him If he was behind could he have been a little to the left or right? No, the man was in front and the horseman behind Yes, I know that, but could he not have moved? A horse does not always go the same going through the veldt Now as he went along did he go on one side or the other? The horse did nothing at all, but simply followed the man

Solicitor-General If your lordship will look at the plan your lordship will see that the line taken by Pelser and this man would not be perfectly straight towards these people but at an angle

Judge That plan may not be correct All of them describe the dam differently to what it is on the plan It is only a rough idea

Solicitor-General The line between the house and where the body was found is at an angle with where the natives were working

Judge If we could know the pole where the man stood we could know it at once, and I should be glad if you could find out

Court adjourned at 1 15 p m for tiffin

On resuming at 2 26 p m ,

Alfred Peters was called, and on being sworn was asked by the interpreter, Mr R Ayliff, if he spoke English, he replied he did a little

Solicitor-General Oh yes, he is a schoolmaster, and speaks English well enough to be understood

Mr Solomon You are a carpenter and schoolmaster? Yes In January last you were employed on the telegraph construction, and you were working on it when the native was killed? Yes Did you see the native before he was killed? Yes Tell us what you saw of him? I saw the native come towards where I was working He came and said "Good morning" I was alone I said ' Good morning," and then he passed on towards where Veldschoen was working And about half-an-hour afterwards I saw the Dutchman come out of his house

Judge You went on with your work? Yes

Mr Solomon Before that, was there anyone else there? Yes Ntloyiya I saw him go up to Zwaartboy Did you see him talk there? Yes

Judge Veldschoen came up? Yes

Solicitor-General Let him give his own statement

Mr Solomon Yes I will not lead

Witness The native had gone on in the direction of the dam, behind which there were some horses Then I saw the Dutchman come on horseback, and he passed about ten yards between me and Veldschoen, and followed the native What sort of horse did he ride? A black horse He went up to the native and he stood talking for a few minutes They both returned in my direction Who was in front, who behind? The native was in front I was standing looking at them all the time Then I saw smoke and heard a report, and I saw the man fall down in front of the horse, and then I heard him shout three times "Hi! Hi! come this way" He was speaking Kafir

Judge Did you think he was calling you? Yes I thought he was calling to the men on the line I did not go because I was frightened of the Dutchman shooting me I was at Veldschoen's pole when the Dutchman shot the native and I stayed there for a few minutes, and then went for some water to drink I came back, and when I got there I saw the Dutchman return

Mr Solomon In what direction? Going back to the house

Judge Between whose poles? Between mine and Veldschoen's

Mr Solomon Then you went back to your pole? Yes Now when this man Zachariah passed you and stood, did he have anything in his hand? No, sir And when you saw him shot, did you see him turn round attacking the farmer? No You afterwards pointed out to Williams the constable where you were standing when you saw this? Yes

Solicitor-General Now you say that the native passed close to you within about ten yards? Yes Between you and Veldschoen? Yes There was no man working between you and Veldschoen that day? No And as he passed you, you say he greeted you and passed on? Yes And where did he go to

M

from you, who was the next man he came to ? Veldschoen
Well, now tell us exactly   Well he first met Veldschoen   Now
what happened after ?   Let's know everything   When he
came to Veldschoen I was working at my place   And the next
thing that happened ?   The next thing was that the Dutchman
came from his place after the Kafir and I then came up from
my pole and went to Veldschoen as I was finished   When you
went to Veldschoen, Zachariah had already left Veldschoen ?
Yes   Then where was Zwaartboy ?   He had already passed
Did you see Zwaartboy at Veldschoen's pole when Zachariah
was there ?   Yes   Who besides ?   Ntloyiya   You recollect
what you said before the Magistrate ?   Yes   You are a Schoolmaster, and of course you recollect ?   Yes   Did you say before
the Magistrate that this Zachariah was sitting talking about
half-an-hour to Zwaartboy ?   Yes, I did   And that was true ?
And that is true   Perhaps you can tell us who was the first to
go, Veldschoen, Zachariah, Ntloyiya or Zwaartboy ?   Ntloyiya
and then Zachariah   And then Zwaartboy I suppose ?   Yes
And did they stop together talking until Zachariah went
away ?   Yes   They were all there for half-an-hour standing
talking ?   Yes

Judge   Was Zwaartboy there when Zachariah left ?   Zwaartboy left about five minutes before

Solicitor-General   I thought you said they were all there—at
any rate Zwaartboy had been talking there and so was Zachariah
before he left ?   Yes   Well then I understand you to say that
when the shot was fired you and Ntloyiya and Veldschoen were
all together there ?   I am sure

Judge   Was this at Veldschoen's hole ?   Yes

Solicitor-General   When did you leave Veldschoen's hole—
well never mind, it was after Zwaartboy and Zachariah had left
that you left ?   Yes

Judge   Who left first ?   Zwaartboy, and came in the direction
where my pole was, and he went on and did not stop

Solicitor-General   Then Zwaartboy left ?   And then I left
my pole to go to Veldschoen's pole after Zachariah had left
You are not quite so stupid as that   You know what you are
saying—I do not want any confusion   You have said that
Zachariah—tell it over again ?   Zachariah went to Veldschoen's
pole first   Ntloyiya was there before Zachariah then Zwaartboy

Judge   Where were you then ?   I was by the pole

Mr Solomon   That is what he said before

Solicitor-General   That is what he did not say

Mr Solomon   You tried to confuse him

Witness   Then Zwaartboy left Veldschoen's pole and came to
where I was and passed me, and then Zachariah left Veldschoen's
and I went there

Solicitor-General.   Will your lordship refer to your notes

(Judge did so and what he read corresponded with the witness'
last statement only it was abbreviated)

Solicitor-General I don't think he said that

Judge I want justice to be done Mr Solicitor, and I do not
want confused statements   There is no interest to serve but
that of justice, and as long as I sit here I shall endeavour to do
it

Solicitor-General I should think so, my lord, and I should
not suggest anything to the contrary

Witness I did not go to Veldschoen's pole until Zachariah
had left

Solicitor-General When you got to Veldschoen's pole who
was there ? Ntloyiya And Veldschoen   Yes What was he
doing ? He was working And you three stopped there till
the Kafir was shot ? Yes And I suppose as soon as the Kafir
was shot you had some conversation about it, such as "Look
there, there is a man shot ?" Yes You did   Yes Can you
explain how it is that Ntloyiya did not speak to you about it
until the evening

Mr Solomon Ntloyiya did not say that He said he told
him in the evening to tell his master

Witness I talked to him at once

Solicitor-General He is wrong if he says so ? Yes Did he
speak to you in the evening about it ? Yes I told Mr Mair
before dinner time, about 12 o'clock Mair did not know this
before At any rate you did not request Ntloyiya to tell you
the man had been shot because you had seen it ? Yes There
was no necessity for him to come and tell you ? No, he told me
that a man had been shot and I must tell my master

Judge Did he tell you so in the evening also ? Yes You
understand what I say ? Yes Did you tell your master that
evening   No, I had already told him

Solicitor-General Did you tell Ntloyiya when he told you
that you had already told your master ? No, when he spoke to
me in the evening I told him I had already told my master
Veldschoen says that Zachariah never went to you at all, he
came to them direct   If he says this he must be wrong One
thing you are certain of he spoke for half-an-hour to Zwaartboy
before he came past and spoke to you ? Yes Do you mean to
say he was sitting down   Yes And Zwaartboy also ? Yes
Who were all at the pole when the shot was fired ? Ntloyiya,
Veldschoen and myself How do you account for it that
Ntloyiya and Veldschoen say that you were not at the pole at
all, and that Ntloyiya did not speak to you till the evening ? I
was there and Ntloyiya did speak to me in the evening When
the shot was fired you must have seen the same thing as Ntloyiya
and Veldschoen, you were all looking the same direction   Yes
Let us hear the exact position the white man on horse back and

the black man were when the shot was fired? You saw him as if he were driving him towards the homestead? Yes And the next thing you say? I saw smoke come out from the pistol I heard a report and saw the native fall down in front of the horse How far in front? I think about six yards How was he going? At a slow walking pace Did you see the white man about six yards behind him? Yes When you say six yards do you mean from the man or the horse's head? The horse's head And you saw the white man raise his arm to shoot? Yes He was just behind him? Yes And the native did not turn round and assault him? No He did not turn his head round? No And the horse was straight behind him? Yes After that the man dropped What did Ntloyiya do? I didn't see him do anything What did you do, did you go back to your hole? Before I went back to my hole I told them that if I was not afraid the Dutchman would shoot me I would go and see what he had shot at I then went back to my hole As a matter of fact neither you nor Ntloyiya nor any of the natives on the line went to the spot? No, not at the time I was there Well, then you went back to your hole? Yes And Ntloyiya? I do not know I was finished and I had only to get my jacket and go where my master was

Judge · And you went where? Towards Burghersdorp to another hole? Yes

Solicitor-General Then you saw nothing of old Mr Pelser? No Will you tell us exactly what you told Mr Mair—what time was it? About 12 o'clock Well what did you tell him? I told him a Dutchman had been shooting a native In English? Yes He could not understand you—did you speak as well as you are speaking now? Yes, he asked me what Dutchman I said Willem Pelser He said, "Was he shot dead?" I said "I think so, as the native was shouting three times" He said "When did he shoot him?" I said "I do not know, I did not go there" The time-keeper who was present with Mr Mair asked me

Judge Was anyone else present? Some natives were working there Is the Time-keeper a white man? Yes

Solicitor-General This is the first time I have heard of him

Mr Solomon Oh yes, it is the first time we have heard of him at all

Solicitor-General He asked you where the Dutchman had hit the native and you said you did not know as you did not go and see? Yes Then I went further on What did Mr Mair do? I don't know—I went on You say the Time-keeper was there and some natives? Yes

Judge Where did you speak to him? At the cutting Do not be in a hurry—do you know where the ballast hole is? Yes It was by the ballast hole I spoke to the Time-keeper and Mair This was before dinner? Yes

Solicitor-General· Let us not make any mistake You say when the shot was fired the native was about six yards in front of the horse's head? Yes Point out how far it was (witness pointed to the leg of the Barristers' table—about the same distance from him as the Judge's desk)

Judge There are two things natives cannot determine, that is time and distance

Solicitor-General Yes, my Lord I ask because something will be made out of it

Judge Were you right in front? No, I was slightly to the left side

Solicitor-General Would your Lordship put the question When he says on the left does he mean that they were on his left or he on their left? By this I mean I was slightly on their left and they were slightly on my right

Judge How was it before the Magistrate you did not say anything about hearing the native cry out three times? I told the Magistrate so Did you speak in English? Yes

Judge This preliminary examination is much like a great many other preliminary examinations It does not give a grain of information whether a witness has been examined through an interpreter or not [Solicitor-General He spoke English] All the evidence I take down, and it is fifty times more than a Magistrate does, I always make a note and say whether it is taken through an interpreter or not, and it is easy to refer to In the whole of this preliminary examination there is no mention of an interpreter It is very important in the event of a witness being dead or out of the way or sick

Dr John Baldwin Greathead was called

Mr Solomon You are a medical man practising in Grahamstown? I am You were in Court when Dr Paul gave his evidence? During his cross-examination And during the evidence of the native witnesses ʳ During most of it, not the whole You heard the Doctor describe the course the bullet took after entering Zachariah and where he found it lodged? Yes Now in your opinion if the bullet had travelled right in whereabouts would it have come out? Let me have a native (native placed in front of witness with deceased's coat on) It would have come out about the right breast above the nipple If the bullet instead of remaining where it did after it had entered had gone on it would have come out there   .

Judge It would have taken an almost horizontal course? Almost I believe Doctor Paul said almost

Mr Solomon What distance is the hole in the coat from the middle of the spine? (Witness measured it with a small pocket measure) Two inches In your opinion what stopped the bullet going on? The body of the second vertebra as described by Doctor Paul In your opinion as a medical man what are the probable ways in which the bullet must have been fired? There are several. It must have come from a point at an angle of forty-five degrees to a line drawn from one shoulder to the other

Judge. Why do you say that? Because I take the depth of the wound and the position where it has been found from the surface and it penetrated the skin two inches from the centre of the spine

Mr Solomon. The bullet would have taken that course if Pelser had been behind the native and had the native slightly on his right? Yes. If the native had been immediately in front of Pelser and just slightly turned round could the bullet have taken that course? Yes

Judge. Do you mean if the native had his back turned to him? If the native had been walking with his back turned towards him

Mr Solomon. If the native had walked in front of Pelser and merely shrugged his shoulders? That is the same question you asked Doctor Paul. I think it would have been possible—not shrugging his shoulders—but if he had been moving his shoulders backwards and forwards. In your opinion could the bullet have possibly taken the course if Pelser had fired at the man as he was in the act of striking? Whilst he was in the act of striking it could not have taken that course. Can you say how the bullet could possibly have taken that course if Pelser had shot at the man whilst he was facing him? No. You heard Pelser give his explanation of how the bullet might have taken that direction? I did. You heard him say that as the native struck at him with his right hand he leant forward like that? (leant his body forwards) I did. It could not have made such a wound, the bullet would have gone down

Judge. And not horizontally? No

Mr Solomon. You agree with Dr Paul that the most probable way in which the pistol was fired was behind the man?

Judge. Is your description correct?

Mr Solomon. If the horse had swerved round can you say how the bullet would have taken that direction? If the man had stood still and the horse had backed and swerved a good deal round he might have possibly shot him in the back. The man must be then in an upright position. Right round?

Solicitor-General. He said a good deal round, not right round

Mr Solomon. How much? A semi-circle backwards so as to get round to his back

Judge. Then he would have been in very much the same position as a man shooting from the back? Yes. He must have got to the back

Mr Solomon. I suppose you will say that is a very improbable theory? I should say it was

Solicitor-General   I do not quite understand that last theory of yours   Take this to be the horse (places iron bar in front of him)   When the horse swerves he comes round on his hind legs?   He swerves away from danger, if you will give me the iron I will show you [bar handed to witness]

Solicitor-General   Say the horse had backed

Mr Solomon   Let us all see it [witness placed iron bar in front of him, and took one end in his hand and turned it from him]

Witness   If the horse had swerved on his hind legs he must have swerved in a complete circle to get there   I see now that if the horse had swerved in a semi-circle and backed at the same time it could have been inflicted

Judge   Dr Paul said if he had swerved and backed he could have done so

Solicitor-General   No, my Lord, he did not say so, as I had the iron bar describing it   [To witness]   You have heard what the natives said that the man was walking three yards off and the Dutchman took up his pistol and shot him in the back   Could it have made this wound?   Not unless the man turned   They say he did not   Supposing the man had been walking with his back towards the horse?   Well you cannot say that   I suppose you agree with Dr Paul, you heard him describe the wound, that the bullet was compressing the spinal marrow   Do you think in this case that he would have dropped at once?   Most probably   If he did so would he drop on his knees or face?   If he was walking slowly the probabilities are that his knees would have given way first and the centre of gravity being towards the back he would have fallen on his back   If the man was walking due east his head would be towards the west?   If he had one foot in front of the other it may influence the direction a little and the head would not be exactly west   In this particular case we find the man lying towards the north-east and you would take it that he was facing more or less towards the south-west?   Roughly speaking

Mr Solomon   You will admit that at a distance of five or six hundred yards that it would be very difficult to say if a man was immediately behind another or a little at his side—Yes, I should think so

Dr Ross was next called

Mr Solomon   You are a medical man practising in King William's Town?   Yes   You heard the evidence of Dr Paul in this case?   Yes   You know whereabouts the bullet entered Zachariah and where it lodged?   Yes   You have heard the evidence of Dr Greathead?   Yes   Do you agree with the whole of his evidence?   Yes, every word   Do you agree that it was impossible for a bullet to take the course if the pistol had gone off whilst Zachariah was attacking Pelser?   Yes, if he was facing him and striking

Solicitor-General had no questions

Canteen was next called

Mr Solomon You were employed on the telegraphic construction last January? Yes You remember one Friday morning you were digging a hole and you saw something? Yes What did you see? I saw a horse driving a man (laughter) Who was on the horse? A white man Did the white man drive the black man any distance? It did not appear to me to be very far What became of you then? I was working in a hollow, a dip, in the dam

Judge What dam, not this one?

Witness Below the dam

Judge Did you hear anything? I was out of sight and I heard a shot And you did not see what took place? No From where you were could you tell the distance between the black man and the horse? He was the distance of the Judge's desk

Solicitor-General had no questions

Mr Solomon That will conclude my case

David Mair was called by the Solicitor-General

Solicitor-General Your name is David Mair and you are sub-inspector of telegraphs? Yes In January last you were putting up a line of telegraphs in connection with the railway of Ahwal North crossing the farm of Mr Pelser? Yes On the 16th January you recollect hearing something about a man being shot? Yes And that day you had in your employ Alfred Peters, Veldschoen, Ntloyiya, Zwaartboy, Breakfast and Canteen? Yes Now you say you heard something about a man being shot, what was the first you heard? Alfred Peters told me What time? About eleven or twelve o'clock How did he come to tell you? I heard him talking with the other Kafirs about shooting You understood a little? Yes And then you asked them about it? Yes Will you tell us what you asked him and what he answered? I asked him who had been shot and he said a Kafir had been shot by a farmer Was that all? With that I asked him to tell me Did he tell you that he had seen the white man shoot a Kafir? No From the way in which he told you did you think the Kafir had been shot by the white man?

Mr Solomon That is for the Jury to say

Solicitor-General Well he has already said it Did he say the Kafirs saw it? No Did he tell you that he did not know because he had not gone up to the Kafir and that he cried out three times "Hi! Hi! come this way?" No Did you ask him whereabouts the Kafir had been hit? No Did Ntloyiya tell you anything about the shooting at all? No

Mr Solomon At all events he told you a Kafir had been shot? Yes And this was between eleven and twelve o'clock?

Yes   Did you not have the curiosity to ask further? No   You were very busy at the time? Yes   And I suppose he may have said something more that you have forgotten? He was speaking to the Kafirs about it, but not to me

Judge Where did you understand that the Kafir had been shot from what he said? He said up on the railway You say he did say more—try and recollect what he said

Mr Solomon Did he not mention Pelser's name? No   I hope you will not wish us to believe that you took so little interest in human life that you did not ask where? No

Judge   When he said on the railway did you not ask where? No

Mr Solomon Were there any Kafirs present? Yes Did you ever find out where the spot was? No You do not know now where it was? Yes, I know somewhere near Alfred Peters and Veldschoen were working at the telegraph construction that day? Yes   And they were working on Pelser's farm? I cannot say, they were about there

Solicitor-General That is the case We cannot finish the arguments this evening, but we shall finish in good time for my learned friend to get away on Monday, so there is no need to go on now

Judge Is there much civil business?

Solicitor-General I believe there is not much, I am sorry to say (laughter) Is there Mr Registrar?

Registrar The provisional cases will take about half-an-hour

Judge Very well, I will adjourn till Monday, when we can then call on the civil business and adjourn it till this case is finished (To the Jury) I hope gentlemen you will not discuss this case with anyone at all

The Court stands adjourned till Monday morning

MONDAY, NOVEMBER 16, 1885

The Court resumed at 9 30 when the attendance was very large, and many ladies occupied seats in the gallery

Judge Barry introduced the new Judge Christian Maasdorp, Esq, who after the civil business had been formally adjourned retired

At 9 38 a m the Solicitor-General commenced his Address to the Jury as follows —May it please your Lordship Gentlemen of the Jury By referring to the indictment of which you have a copy you will find that the accused stands charged with the crime of publishing a defamatory libel The actual libel is the portion of a letter which appeared in the *Cape Mercury*, a paper published in King William's Town, on the 14th of April last To that indictment several pleas have been filed by the defence, first, the general issue, and then some under the head of special The special pleas of the defence are first, that these words are a fair comment on the circumstances as appearing in the preliminary examinations, and further they state in their plea, that the words are absolutely true, and what is meant by that is that William Jacobus Pelser did wrongfully, unlawfully and maliciously kill and murder one Zachariah in his lifetime a labourer residing at Burghersdorp I shall first deal with the last plea, because if you find Pelser guilty of murder the whole case is disposed of When I have finished that part of the case, I shall proceed to that part of the case to which the defence has set up the plea of fair comment, which means that it was one of public interest and that the words used were justified by the circumstances which were before the public On the charge of murder a number of witnesses have been called in support of that charge In all, four witnesses have been called who have sworn to seeing the crime actually committed At the outset I think you can only come to one conclusion as regards their credibility, and it is only on the question of credibility that you can come to a conclusion whether the comment is justifiable or not I will first refer to the witness Veldschoen who appears to have been working on the line of telegraph poles with Zwaartboy, Ntloyiya and Alfred Peters Veldschoen swears that on the morning the deceased man Zachariah came to where he was working—he first went to a man named Alfred Peters—and whilst he was talking Zwaartboy came and he had a short conversation, and then went on Veldschoen only swears to himself and Zwaartboy being together at this time What they saw I do not think will weigh very much with you after the medical evidence which you have heard, and I think they go to corroborate to a certain extent the evidence of Pelser Then Ntloyiya is called who tells you that he saw the man talking to Veldschoen and he then went up, and that Zwaartboy had been up and greeted the man, and then went on and had no conversation with him. Alfred Peters says that when he went up to the hole all of them were there. It seems evident that this is a conspiracy amongst the natives or it must actually be true. He says they were all there and that Zwaartboy was sitting talking to him for half-an-hour. Another says that he merely greeted him and passed on. These are small discrepancies, but still they are discrepances that will have importance later on. It would seem that the natives on the telegraph line on this particular day seemed to have being doing everything besides their work, for we find what an object of attention Zachariah was. He goes to Grahamstown and smokes his pipe, and this native paid him particular attention, and then he says he was standing with Fischer. Here I must remark that neither of these last witnesses gave their evidence at the preliminary examination. They did not volunteer their evidence or give their evidence to the Police. Grahamstown tells you that the man stood at the kraal on Pelser's homestead and then corroborates what one of the witnesses for the prosecution has said about the kraal. He then follows him to the tramp floor where he goes out of sight. It is remarkable the amount of attention this unfortunate native received until he got out of sight. It is said that he then went away from the house about five hundred and sixty yards when he was overtaken by Pelser. And according to the witnesses Pelser turned him back and he walked for a short distance on before him, the natives appear to be most positive on this point—he turned back quietly and walked slightly in front of the horse's head, and whilst he was in front —three yards it is told you—then Pelser took out his pistol and shot the man in the back. Now in the first place what earthly reason could he have had to do it? You have heard that he first ordered the man off his farm, and then he said to his men " I will go to him and turn him back and fine him 2s." He thought better of it and sent Marthinus to call two Policemen that had been on the farm that morning, and Pelser then pursued the man in order to give him over to the Police. Whilst I am on this subject I may say that he had every right to go after the man to apprehend him, for under the Police Offences Act of 1882 a crime was created that had not been in existence before. I refer to Section 7 sub-Section 12 of Act 27 of 1882 which reads " Wilfully trespassing in any place and neglecting or refusing to leave such place after being warned to do so by the owner or occupier, or any person authorized by or on behalf of the owner or occupier." That gave the owner a right of arrest if he declined to leave the place. The 18th Section of that Act reads " Any person found committing any offence punishable under the provisions of this Act may be taken into custody without a warrant by any Constable or any member of any Police Force, or may be apprehended by the owner of the property on, or with respect to which the offence shall be committed, or by the servant of such owner or by any person authorised by such owner, and such person may be detained until he can be delivered into custody of a constable or a policeman to be be dealt with according to law" There is also another Act he may have done it under. Any man committing an offence under this Act may be taken into custody by Police Officers, owners or occupiers of property or by their servants or persons authorised by them Pelser was acting within his right in attempting to arrest the man His only object was to get him and give him to the police who he thought would be at his homestead when he returned If he did turn him back it was in order to go to the homestead, and what object could he have had to shoot him? None whatever He was going at a slow pace according to these people and he took up his pistol and shot him Does that seem common sense? Does it appear to your reason as likely? I should say that it was most unlikely Then the medical evidence has entirely exploded this evidence They say he was directly in front of the horse's head about three yards off, and they would not allow him to turn his head. Dr Greathead says such a wound could not have been made in that way My learned friend did not examine him on that point—he only confined himself to prove that Pelser's theory was not right It is the duty of the prosecution in a charge of murder to prove their case and show that a murder has been committed Then we have the Doctor's evidence to show that it was utterly impossible for the shot to have been fired as the man was directly in front Then the man's head was lying due east to where Pelser and the boy were The Doctors agree that when a shot is fired into the spinal column there must be an immediate collapse and the man must fall on his back I am now supposed to be looking due east and if as I am walking I am shot in the back as described and I fall on my back, how would my head be found? It would be found due west, but the man's head you hear was found north-east therefore he must have been looking south-west We want to know how he would fall and the medical evidence tells us on his back, and you have the medical evidence to show it is impossible and opposed to common sense to say that a man who falls with his head to the north-east could have looked east Let us follow up the theory Pelser says that the native turned round and struck him, and there must have been a moment or so between every stroke He made three blows at him, and each blow he struck the horse swerved round What position would he then be in? he would be backing towards the north-east and looking to the south-west—the native would be somewhat in advance of Pelser, and then the pistol went off—the native having veered round to the north-east And this is how he was actually found To meet this evidence of Pelser's an attempt has been made (and you will have to consider that, when the question of malice is considered, for the defence allege it is a malicious act on the part of Pelser) and my learned friend wants to make out that Pelser took the bar of iron and put it by the man's side to make out his case The evidence I have led you on this bar of iron discredits that of the native witnesses for the defence It is possible that he did not have it when he saw Fischer and Grahamstown, but they did not give evidence at the preliminary examination, and it is possible that they might not remember if he had anything in his hand I say it is possible that he may not have had it in his hand when he was with them, but there is no doubt that he had it in his hand when he went to the tramp floor, and where he got it from nobody knows Abo, a witness called for the prosecution, is the most favourable to the defence, and after consulting with the Attorney for the defence in King William's Town he comes here and says that when the man came to the tramp-floor he had something in his hand, and shows us in what attitude he was standing He corroborates Pelser as to the attitude At the preliminary examination he says he *thought* it was a switch, but after he has paid two visits to King William's Town he says " No, I did not think, I know it was a switch," and he says it was a longer switch than this iron Even if Fischer and Grahamstown did not see this switch, Abo, who is favourable to the defence, says he knows he had a switch You will take his evidence as conclusive against the other witnesses Then you have to consider how the iron could have been placed by the deceased From the time he was shot to the time Williams went out no one had been to the body Old Mr Pelser went and had a conversation with the natives on the—

Judge You stopped Mr Solomon when he was asking about that conversation and you had better not refer to it

Solicitor-General This is no evidence that he went near the place, and he did not go there, and until Williams comes upon the scene no one had been there The shot was fired about 10 o'clock, and between 11 and 12 when he went there——

Mr Solomon No, no, about a quarter to two

Solicitor-General Well about a quarter to two When you have the question of a man committing a crime you must prove it. Where could he have got the iron from ? Pelser himself was in town and could not have put it there, and Abo says his master had no irons like that on his farm The iron was found near the body, and there were no spoors nearer to it than five yards After this you can come to no other conclusion than that they have laid their heads together to tell a lie, but why they did so you cannot say Kafir evidence must always be borne out and corroborated, and you would expect the first thing for these men to have done would have been to tell their master Did they do so? No, they did nothing of the sort Alfred Peters says he went and told him, but Mr Mair says that he did nothing of the sort, but he heard them talking about shooting and asked them about it, when Alfred Peters said a native had been shot on the line Mr Mair said that from the way he told him he thought it was a rumour What Mr Mair said was this "He did not tell me he had seen it He told me a man had been shot on this railway line, and he spoke as if it was matter of rumour" If he had said "I have seen a man shot," he would have made enquiries, but he thought it was only a rumour that had come down the line Taking all these things together I think you will consider that this charge of murder is absolutely false and that the account given by Pelser is the correct one If you do not believe the witnesses for the defence in this then you must disbelieve them altogether And you must conclude that they have absolutely put their heads together to make a serious charge against a man in that he shot a native and that in the worst form If they did not see what actually took place they are not to be believed at all in any particular of their evidence in their attempt to make out this most serious charge If you object to this evidence then you come to the evidence of Pelser himself In taking this evidence of Pelser you have no reason to disbelieve him I will take his evidence after that of the medical man—but there is one fact you must remember—the man's head was lying to the north-east In addition to this you have Dr Paul's evidence He has several theories, and he does not mince the matter He says that if the horse had swerved as Pelser described and got behind the native the wound might have been given, and the wound would have been horizontal He also says if he had been stooping, and had his shoulder like this (raised shoulder slightly and bent it forward) it might have been caused You have frequently seen them in their fights with their kernes—they have a blanket over one arm, then they put up their arm after giving a blow—it is a sort of second nature to put up the arm in defence Pelser does not say it happened like this He says that as he was pulling the horse up—and he does not deny that if the native did not discontinue attacking him he intended to shoot him—he says as he pulled up his horse he accidentally pulled the trigger and it went off As I said before take away the natives and you only have the statement of Pelser who says he was acting in self-defence, but it went off too soon Therefore, as far as justification is concerned, I hope you will accept Pelser's evidence, and not that of the defence, as it is borne out by the facts of the case and by the position of the body, and the evidence for the defence is contradicted by the Doctor's evidence and the position of the body, and the evidence of the natives was disproved   Now to pass on to the plea of fair comment   You have all already seen the letter of Don's attacking Pelser   This letter arose out of an article which was published in the *Cape Mercury* on the 24th March last   That article purports to be a fair and impartial discussion on the preliminary examination   The article is most untrustworthy, and amongst other things it says the Government is corrupt and dishonest, and for party reasons they had ordered the Solicitor-General not to prosecute, and in addition to this they imply that the Solicitor-General is corrupt and dishonest, and further that the Government had not done its duty   I would ask you if this is fair comment on judicial proceedings, which should be impartial ?   I shall call your attention to the evidence given at the preliminary examination which is in favour of Pelser, and which is really the same evidence which has been more fully developed in Court to-day, and to which I have already more fully referred   Several of those portions of evidence that are favourable to Pelser have been systematically left out of the article   The Doctor in his evidence said it was impossible for the wound to have been inflicted in the way the natives described   This most important piece of evidence has been entirely omitted from this *impartial* and *fair* article !

Mr Solomon   Mr Don is not indicted on the article

Solicitor-General   No, but I am coming to what he is indicted on   He adopts this article

Judge   No, Mr Solicitor, he merely says, These statements have been published and they have not been contradicted and therefore I must take it as true

Solicitor-General   Well, all that is left out   Then the evidence which states that Pelser had sent for the Police in order to arrest the man—this has been left out and they unhesitatingly stated that there was no evidence in support of this !   Then again there is the evidence of Mair who says that he thought what the natives told him was nothing but idle rumour—all this is left out of this article   Mr Don very innocently swallows it and adopts it   He says " I am reluctantly compelled to come to the conclusion that your statements are true, in short, that our rulers have been influenced by political instead of such legal considerations as are alone applicable to the case   It may be safely assumed that if a white man had been the victim, the murderers would not have been left untried and unpunished   Indeed it may be confidently affirmed that had the same thing happened in this district, the offender would have been brought to justice   But it would seem that in the district of Burghersdorp if a Dutchman shoots a Kafir, the crime must be overlooked   Government refuses to do its duty, and the conscience of the whole community is offended   I fully expected that when your article went forth through the country, especially after its statements remained unchallenged, the press would have taken up the question and compelled the Government to break silence, if not to alter its decision   But the press with few exceptions has paid no attention to the case   I confess I have met with nothing more disheartening for a long time than this immoral apathy in connection with such a grave business   Is the matter to rest here *   Is the Government to be permitted ignominiously to abdicate its functions in this fashion ? and to offend the conscience of all not blinded by race prejudice or party feeling   Even were the evidence against Pelser less damning than it seems to be, he himself admits a criminal act, whether murder or manslaughter, which ought to be dealt with in the prescribed and proper manner, tried by a Judge and Jury in open Court, instead of settled off-hand by Solicitor-General or Attorney-General in a hole and corner fashion   Nothing less can satisfy justice, not to speak of decency, and, I trust, nothing less will satisfy the country "   This is the inference he draws from the article—the Government are corrupt and dishonest and had hushed up a foul crime for party purposes   You will keep this in view when you come to consider your verdict on the plea of fair comment Is this the way in which fair comment is to be made ?   Then it is suggested that it is the duty of the Government to have contradicted the statements made by the *Cape Mercury*   This is really most absurd   The Government is supposed to be composed of gentlemen who are alive to every interest it is their duty to serve, and when they are attacked by the press they must go hat in hand to the Editor of any country newspaper and say " You may think that we are dishonest and corrupt but we are not quite so bad as you think "   It is not an action that any gentleman—any man would take up   The government have taken no notice of it, and before Mr Don wrote that letter it was his duty to go and seek in a cool, deliberate and impartial manner for evidence to justify his words, but he became so reckless that he did not consider the effect on Pelser or anyone else , and deliberately said a murder had been committed   He charges Pelser with having committed murder in the following words ' That poor man's blood cries to heaven, not merely against the wretched murderer, but against the Government which refuses to prosecute "   That is, that it cries to heaven not merely against Pelser for having committed a deliberate murder, but against this dishonest and corrupt Government   The circumstances connected with the case and the position of the body bear out that the evidence of the native witnesses is improbable   The circumstances are in favour of the innocence of Pelser, and the evidence of Mair also who says that he thought it was a rumour—a mere idle rumour   All these circumstances point to the conclusion that there was no murder, yet the

defendant in his letter charges him with the crime   If you wipe
out the evidence of those natives you have but the statement of
Pelsei, and that statement is the statement that he has given
you to-day only not so full (read statement of February 11th
already published by us)

Judge   I see the Jury have had copies of the correspondence
in which appears the preliminary examination   It should have
been sworn to—it is irregular

Mr Harmsworth was put into the box and swore to the preliminary examination as being correct

Solicitor-General   If you wipe it out you have only the statement of Pelsei   Now besides this statement which my friend
will no doubt comment upon, there are those made to Harmsworth and Williams   You will know that Pelser was excited
when he came to them and that will account for the differences
in the statements, and when he had calmed down he gave a more
correct account to Williams than he had done to Harmsworth
Harmsworth says he understood Pelser to say that he was riding
in the veldt when he saw the native   That could not be, as all
the witnesses have sworn that the man came from the veldt to
the tramp-floor, and that this conversation took place at the
tramp-floor, so he could not go to Harmsworth and tell him that
Harmsworth seems to be under the misapprehension that Pelser
said "I was riding on my farm when I saw a Kafir going through
my veldt"   I say this wrong impression was made on Harmsworth's mind by excitement, and I contend that there has been
a satisfactory explanation of Pelser's conduct   Williams says
" I asked him under what circumstances, and he replied that the
Kafir had come on the farm to look for a horse"   He does not
say where it took place and he does not say that Pelser was
riding when he met the Kafir   When he spoke to him he was
more calm than when he spoke to Harmsworth and explained to
him what actually took place   You have in your hands the
preliminary examination, which should have been calmly and
impartially criticised by defendant, and to show you how far he
could justly criticise I will quote you a few authorities   It must
be remembered that a citizen in a free country like this has a
right, and you may almost say a duty to fairly criticize and comment on the acts of public men, not only politicians, but Judges,
Public Prosecutors, Barristers and all who are concerned in
any way with judicial proceedings and the administration of
justice   The press has no further liberty than this, and I have
no objection nor has his lordship, the learned Judge, to be
criticized in any of our actions   This is the right of every
citizen, and a clergyman has no more right than another of the
public   The question for you to consider is whether this is a
fair comment on the proceedings instituted against Pelser, in the
first place on the Government and then indirectly on the

o

Solicitor-General You are not trying Mr Don for a libel on the Government, but you must understand what was the state of his mind when he wrote the letter—was it written in the interest of justice, or was it written in a fit of spleen for party purposes? I have pointed out to you the improbability of the crime being committed by Pelser—the position of the body, and if the native witnesses saw the murder why did they not tell Mair? All these circumstances went to the Public Prosecutor, and you have no evidence as to whether there was anything further, and with these facts before him the Law Officer of the Crown determined to go no further It was competent for Mr Don to discuss the act of the Public Prosecutor, and he may have inferred that he had been guilty of a gross error, and he could have said that it was his duty to have gone on with the trial, this he might have said, but it does not lie with him to say that it was not due to error but to corruption Now I come to the authorities on fair comment The first I quote is Odger, page 44, which lays it down that the administration of the law and the verdicts of Juries are all matters for lawful comment as soon as the trial is over, but I had better read it for the information of the Press

Judge I should not read it for the information of anybody but the Jury

The Solicitor-General then read extracts from the cases of Regina vs Sullivan, Odger page 44 Regina vs Fitzgerald, page 49 The latter is from the address to the Grand Jury and shows that the defendant could have discussed the conduct of the Public Prosecutor or the Government in a spirit of *bona fides*, but instead of that he launches against Pelser and the Government this libel I read again at page 53, which is a charge to the petty jury (read extract), and the same principles are laid down at page 57 Then again there is the case of Foster vs Finlayson, Cockburn page 216 in which the same doctrine appears

Judge I hope those who take books from the Law Library will not scratch through portions of the passages I can say this now, but cannot do so in addressing the Jury

Solicitor-General Then there is the case of Hedley vs Barlow You will see, gentlemen, that Mr Don could have approached the matter in fair discussion You will also see from these authorities it is not necessary for Don to have known Pelser to infer malice, but merely to write in a careless manner is evidence of malice, and using words on the occasion which are excessively severe You will find—

Judge The *Cape Mercury* published the article and has been indicted, and the *Cape Mercury* is responsible for the attack You have withdrawn the charge and if anyone is guilty of imputing motives it is the *Cape Mercury* The Government had power to interfere and prosecute that paper for imputing corrupt motives It is a great difficulty in the case, but I should like to hear from you in argument to throw all reference to the Government out of it

Solicitor-General The Government would have its hands pretty full if it prosecuted everyone who libelled it throughout the country and it has systematically avoided it But, gentlemen, I say Mr Don wishes to be a judge of these matters and not the jury I say this excessive language is sufficient to establish *malice though there was not personal knowledge between the two parties* It is for you to decide whether the language used calling Pelser a murderer was intended to elucidate the subject or was written in an excited state of mind in order to injure the Government and the accused, and I think you will find that it was to injure the Government and not to elucidate the matter in the case of justice I now come to another authority on fair comment The particulars of the case are simple An officer shot another in a duel and he was tried It came out that the night before the duel he was engaged in target practice, which was held to be an intent to kill, and a newspaper said this fact was sufficient to prove premeditation and that though he was acquitted he was actually guilty of murder, an action was brought and it was held that the paper had no right to say that That is clear enough I think *you will come to the conclusion, on the authorities I have laid before you,* that to call Pelser a murderer on the evidence which appeared at the preliminary examination was libel I have already trespassed too long on your time and I must conclude by again urging you to consider what I have put before you, and I do not doubt that you will come to a decision which will unmistakably prove that it was a libel and nothing else

The learned gentleman resumed his seat at 10 50 During his argument on fair comment, besides the authorities already noticed, he quoted from Cockburn, pages 223, 203 and 111, and Fisher volume 5 page 9,437

Mr Solomon rose at 10 52 a m , and said May it please your Lordship Gentlemen of the Jury When my learned friend *opened this case I heard from him a statement that I was* surprised to hear from a gentleman occupying the high position of Solicitor-General in this Colony He said that, after a statement made by Pelser which closed the preliminary examination had been received and he had declined to prosecute on the evidence before him, there the matter would have rested if we had no party politics in this country , but if the influence of such is to raise the voice of public opinion to clamour for justice and to compel even the highest of the Crown officials to deal out justice with an even hand, then I pray heaven it may continue, and if it should be the means of bringing criminals to justice I trust it will continue to examine into the judgments of the Crown Prosecutor The circumstances of this case will not allow them to be hushed up as these have been hushed up by the Public Prosecutor, but that they should be tried in open Court by Judge and Jury Another thing is this I hope your verdict will be such as to deal a death blow to that measure of oppression which tends to stifle that free discussion of public events which is dear to every Englishman I allude to the Criminal Libel Act When this measure was introduced into the Legislature Mr Leonard said it was his intention to reach a certain class of publications on behalf of the parties who were assailed, and which publications were not worth powder and shot, but it has completely missed that object, and its tendency is to stifle the free discussion of public men and public acts It is impossible to think that this action is brought by Mr Pelser for the purpose of clearing his character, for if that had been his only object he could have brought a civil action before a board of Judges, but no, he thought Mr Don would go to prison and become acquainted with the abominations which have been pointed out by the Bedford Editor during his incarceration But he reckoned without his host, and he did not think it would come before an intelligent Jury Before going further I must say that I trust you will consider the case before you and the important issues that are at stake, and in doing this you can only give one verdict, which will not only be a credit to you and a credit to the Colony, but which will be a credit to the country from which you came Let me proceed to the circumstances which have led to this case On the one hand we have Mr Don, a gentleman of the highest respectability and social position, not only in this country but in the country from which he comes, and he is placed in the position in which he is to-day What for? Because he has done his duty as an honest man and because he has the courage of his own convictions On the other hand we have Mr Pelser—he laughs—Why? Gentlemen I will leave you to form your own opinion, and I trust you will exercise your opinion on such conduct It is not so much a question of whether Mr Don is simply guilty of the charge but there are other issues which have made it an important question to the country and one which is being looked upon with the deepest interest by all classes of colonists It is because of its import- ance that I will, whilst using every endeavour on behalf of my client, be perfectly fair to Mr Pelser, and I shall steadfastly endeavour to uphold the cause of law and order During the examination of Mr Pelser my friend made a remark which I tried to stop but unfortunately it reached your ears, it was to the effect that Pelser had lost a number of stock by theft My friend had no right to make such a remark, because it can only prejudice your minds against the poor man Zachariah I am

unfortunately aware of the evil of stock-stealing and I heartily
sympathise with those who lose their hard-earned property by
theft Another thing which surprises me is that the Solicitor-
General should have made such a statement with regard to
Zachariah, as it seems to imply that he went on to the farm for
for the purpose of stealing But Zachariah was not a wild or
barbarous native prowling about the country but had adopted
English customs and he had gone to the farm rightly and
straightforwardly on his master's business in open daylight,
and I should like to know if this will justify anyone in having
the slightest suspicion that he went for any other purpose He
first went to Fischer and Grahamstown and stood talking and
then went away from them and proceeded to the tramp floor and
asked for his master's horse, and according to the evidence of
Abo there was no sign of incivility in his manner When he
heard Pelser tell him to go back and get a pass he did not answer
him uncivilly but merely turned away and left the place You
know what followed Do not think, gentlemen, that I want to enlist
your sympathies on behalf of my client or the dead man
Zachariah, but I want you to consider the case on legal considerations and those alone It has been insinuated that Mr
Don has been influenced by party politics and that he wrote the
letter because he was a "political parson," but if you want to
know who he is I will tell you

Judge The evidence of Hay states that he is not

Mr Solomon No, he is not interested in party politics, and
the letter was not written for political purposes You can read
it yourselves and you will find that he was actuated by motives
which were a credit to him and the country, and I rejoice that
there is a man who has the common pluck of a man and an
Englishman to come forward and challenge the conduct of the
Crown Prosecutor You will never make the people a law-
abiding and contented people until you deal out even handed
justice to them This was what was done in the case of the
natives in India, and the same example must be followed here
I hope you will consider this case apart from the question
whether Mr Pelser was a loser by stock thefts or whether
Mr Don is a "political parson", consider it upon the broad
principles of justice In this case there are two defences—the
first of which is fair comment, and the second defence is that
the words contained in the indictment are true in substance and
in fact His Lordship will tell you that it is not every statement
which is defamatory that is punishable by law—

Judge You are not stating the law rightly Truth in our
law is not considered an offence

Mr Solomon If I prove a statement to be true in substance
and in fact the law holds me blameless, and if I published a
defamatory statement of a man, without malice and believing it

to be for the benefit of the public, I should not be guilty of libel even if it were proved to be untrue, and on these principles the liberty of the Press depends   If you find this case proved and that the words used are a fair comment you are bound to acquit Mr Don, and if you do not you will give the liberty of the Press a blow that it will take years to recover from   The first thing I have to do is to prove to you that the words used are a fair comment   It is not for me to tell you whether Mr Don had a right to take up the position he has done, because my learned friend has told you that he had a right to do so   I shall probably be rather long in my address but I trust the importance of the case will convince you of the necessity to give it your whole attention   The second question is—was it an honest comment or not and was the writer actuated by honest motives?   Did he do it with the object of damaging Pelser or for the benefit of mankind?   And I think you can have no doubt whatever that the latter course was that which influenced Mr Don   What political motives could he have?   He belongs to no political party   It was done to awaken the conscience of the country and to have a public investigation into the facts of the case   Anything I can say to you cannot be more eloquent, or more fully explain his action than the language used by him in his letter   This is what he says   "Is the matter to rest here?   Is the Government to be permitted ignominiously to abdicate its functions in this fashion and offend the conscience of all not blinded by race prejudices or party feelings?   Even were the evidence against Pelser less damning than it seems to be, he himself admits a criminal act, whether murder or manslaughter, which ought to be dealt with in the prescribed and proper manner, tried by a Judge and jury in open court instead of settled off by Solicitor-General or Attorney-General in a hole and corner fashion   Nothing less can satisfy justice, not to speak of decency and I trust nothing less will satisfy the country   I belong to no party   I am not a politician, I never was in Burghersdorp, I know nothing of its people, and never heard of Pelser before, but am a member of the community which has to bear the responsibility in the last resort of the Government's unchallenged acts, and a Minister of a Religion which knows no distinction of race, caste, class or colour, and my conscience refuses to put up silently with this offence   'What hast thou done?   The voice of thy brother's blood crieth unto me from the ground'   That poor man's blood cries to heaven, not merely against the wretched murderer, but against the Government which refuses to prosecute, and the country which condones such conduct   I for my part will have no share in this responsibility   Therefore to clear my own conscience I solemnly protest, in the name God, of Law, Justice and order against the manner in which this foul crime has been dealt with "

Gentlemen, these are the words of an honest man! His object in thus writing is to see justice vindicated. Gentlemen, it is needless for me to dwell upon this part of the question for it must be unmistakeably clear to you, and there is not a single man upon this Jury who will say he was actuated by any other than honest and conscientious motives. Whether you agree with his opinions or not I am perfectly certain you will give him credit for the honesty of his motives. My learned friend has told you that Mr Don has said that the circumstances of this case were hushed up for political motives. Gentlemen, I am sorry to say this, and no one can regret the necessity to say so more than I do, but Mr Don had before him the records of the case and the whole of the circumstances connected with it and there was enough in them to lead a reasonable man to infer that this prosecution had been dropped for political considerations. He saw the evidence, and found the Government did not contradict the statements made and he came to the conclusion that the man should have been tried by Judge and Jury, and when he was not tried and considering the peculiar circumstances of the case he came to the conclusion that the prosecution was dropped not on account of legal but political considerations.

Judge   Why don't you prove it?

Mr Solomon   Because my friend has said that we must not go into politics

Judge   As it is not in evidence you should not have said it. You say that he was led to believe this because the Crown had not challenged these statements. Mr Don may have had reasons but you have no right to say that Mr Don had these reasons

Mr Solomon   Quite so. Well, gentlemen the only thing you can have any doubt upon is that of fair comment. To come to a decision you must take the preliminary examination and read it through, and when you have considered it you must ask yourselves whether a man—a reasonable and impartial man—would come to the conclusion that the crime was one of murder. If you come to this conclusion you must find it a fair comment. You may read it through and you may think it only one of culpable homicide, but it does not follow that Mr Don is wrong in his conclusion, for different men have different opinions, and it does not prove that he was unreasonable. Then you must ask yourselves if it is such a harsh conclusion that no reasonable man could come to it, and if you find it was you will find the pleas not proved. To illustrate the differences of opinion I may tell you that the Solicitor-General after reading the preliminary examination in a case might indict for murder, and the prosecuting barrister on the same documents thinks it only culpable homicide; it does not follow that the Solicitor-General is wrong, and in the same way the Solicitor-General may indict for culpable homicide and the prosecuting barrister may deem it murder. If you come to the conclusion that anyone after reading the preliminary examination could come to the conclusion that it was murder you will find it a fair comment My friend has given you some authorities and I will supplement them The authority I quote from is Stephens' Criminal Law Volume 2 page 374, a libel displayed on a placard, and page 367 which case arose out of the publication of a certain pamphlet and Lord Kenyon asked the Jury to take the pamphlet and read it in a lenient spirit, and this is what I ask you to do, take the preliminary examination and Mr Don's letter and read them carefully over in a lenient spirit I shall not trouble you with any more authorities I must again impress upon your mind that the preliminary examination justifies Mr Don in coming to the conclusion he did, therefore the words are fair comment I was much surprised to hear my friend comment upon the article in the *Cape Mercury* because it has nothing to do with this case If he had taken the article alone and written the letter it would have been all right to do so, but we are quite ready to compare the letter with the preliminary examination The preliminary examination shows clearly that Pelser killed Zachariah and the presumption is that he murdered him and the onus of proving otherwise lies with him, and if it was found that he committed the act under great provocation he would still be guilty of culpable homicide At the first stage of the preliminary examination it was found that there was a great difficulty in finding out the facts, and it was found that Pelser had made two statements, then at the close of the examination he made another which entirely contradicts either of the previous statements made to Harmsworth or Williams He told Harmsworth that when the native raised his arm he deliberately fired, and then to Williams (these statements were made before he had seen the postmortem examination, and seen the direction of the bullet and he did not know it would not tally with it) he makes another statement which differs from that made to Harmsworth, and then another at the close of the examination in which he says the revolver went off before he was ready These, gentlemen, are all contradictory statements and when a man makes contradictory statements after an act has been committed you are justified in not believing him Pelser has taken up the position that his statement is true and Mr Don had to look through the evidence for corroboration, but if you look through it you will not find a single statement to corroborate it I shall come to it directly It is quite clear on Pelser's own admission, without the statements made to Harmsworth and Williams, that he is guilty of culpable homicide There is nothing in the proceedings to lead one to the conclusion that Pelser shot Zachariah in self defence Pelser was on horseback armed with a loaded revolver, and Zachariah was on foot armed, I will admit for the sake of argument, with the bar of iron I ask you,

as men of common sense, if the native attacked Pelser could he
not have gone away and summoned his servants instead of shooting the man   His Lordship will tell you that if a man cannot
get away from danger he can take life (Judge   In no other case)
If a policeman has a warrant to arrest a man he is bound to do so,
and if he resists and continues to resist or tries to get away he
is at liberty to shoot him   The Solicitor-General has drawn your
attention to the fact that Pelser had a right to arrest, but he is
not a policeman and had no warrant   If you take his own statement he is as guilty of culpable homicide as any man has been
in this country   I will now go on to the plea of justification
All the probabilities are in favour of murder   Will you believe
for a moment that the Kafir, a quiet and inoffensive man, armed
with that ridiculous bar of iron, would turn round and attack an
armed man on horseback   He knew that Pelser had a loaded
revolver ready to fire, because he tells you that he took it
out in order to frighten him   I ask you whether he
would attack knowing this, and you must agree that it
is altogether improbable that he would do so   But, gentlemen,
I do not rest my case upon mere probabilities   When Mr Don
read this evidence, and that of the Doctor, who says distinctly
that he found the bullet had gone in about two inches from the
spine in an oblique direction, and that therefore the shot must
have been fired by Pelser at an angle of forty-five degrees, the
only conclusion he could, with any other reasonable man, arrive at
is that he must have been behind when he fired the shot   Taking these two facts by themselves what conclusion do you come to?
First that he was shot by Pelser in the back, and that Pelser deliberately shot the man whilst he was behind him, and not when
he was making an attack   My friend says that what Pelser has
said is quite consistent with what he said at the preliminary
examination   Take his statement to Williams   In it he says
he fired when the man had his arm raised to strike him   Now
if he had been striking he would be facing him and how could
the wound have been inflicted in the back?   The statements
made to Harmsworth and Williams are entirely inconsistent
with the Doctor's evidence   Then there is the statement he
made at the close of the examination   He says " The horse
became unmanageable and when the horse gave way for the
deceased the pistol went off and hit the deceased "   I ask you
if it is possible that the bullet could have taken the course it
did?   There is not a single statement made at the preliminary
examination by Pelser that is consistent with the Doctor's
evidence   You must not think that Pelser was not acquainted
with the seriousness of his position and you must remember
that he had an Attorney to watch his case and cross-examine
witnesses   The Doctor tried hard to make the bullet take this
course but it was impossible, but he says " If the black man had

P

faced the white man on horseback with an iron rod or a stick in his left hand and the horse had swerved on one side and the blow had missed it is possible for the white man on horseback to have fired a shot which would have inflicted the wound that caused the death of the deceased The bullet in that case could have taken the direction I have described" Pelser has never made a statement that the man was striking with his left hand, and why was this theory put to the Doctor? It should not have been put Then the Doctor again says, " If the deceased had aimed low at the prisoner with his right hand and missed his blow and the prisoner had been slightly behind the deceased then the gunshot wound may have been made" This is inconsistent with Pelser's statement, and I am surprised to hear my learned friend say it is not I think I have shown you that the different statements made by Pelser from time to time are entirely inconsistent with the evidence taken at the preliminary examination Now, gentlemen, I say that when Mr Don had read the *post mortem* examination, and when he had read the whole of the evidence, he was perfectly justified in coming to the conclusion that Pelser had committed murder You must remember that when a man reads a preliminary examination and when he is anxious to find out whether a man is guilty he must take into consideration the probabilities of the case But this was not the only evidence that Mr Don had before him There was the evidence of Williams, who says that he went out to the spot about two o'clock in the afternoon, and he tells you that there were horse spoors about five yards from the body There is no evidence from the prosecution to contradict that it was as he described How could he have been attacking when he was five yards away He must have got up nearer to attack him with a rod two feet long With these facts before him Mr Don was justified in saying that a murder had been committed, and considering this he was right in saying what he did Then it was brought out at the preliminary examination that when this man went to the tramp-floor to look for his master's horse, and was civil in his enquiries, Pelser did not do as a man who had any respect for human life would do, that is take two or three servants and go and bring the man back, but he went to the house and got a loaded revolver Would not a sjambok have been enough to bring him back? Anyone who read the preliminary examination and took into consideration these facts would be justified in coming to the conclusion that he was guilty of murder, and you are justified in coming to the same conclusion If that had been the only evidence, the Solicitor-General would have been justified and should have indicted him for murder But that is not all, for you have the native evidence—that of eye-witnesses to the crime When you consider the plea of fair comment you must not take into consideration any of the evidence that has been given here, but only that given at the preliminary examination. The natives at the preliminary examination swear distinctly that they saw the crime committed, and that the native did not make an attack upon him. That was the evidence before Mr Don when he wrote. If you come to the conclusion that there is any evidence to show that the men were swearing falsely Mr Don had no right to believe it, but I challenge anyone to point out a tittle of evidence to lead one to believe that they swore falsely. A doubt has been thrown on their evidence, first because the wound is inconsistent with their evidence, but I never heard a worse argument or a more lamentable contention. The men were in the line of vision with Pelser and the man coming towards them, and you know natives have no idea of a straight line. The unfortunate man may have been a little on the one side or the other, and then supposing Pelser to be slightly behind and Zachariah gave the slightest twist of his shoulders the bullet may have taken the course it did. On the plea of justification alone there is nothing to lead a reasonable man to suppose that there was anything inconsistent in the native evidence with that of the Doctor. As to the Doctor's evidence, gentlemen, I say it is a disgraceful way in which Dr Paul was examined at the preliminary examination but he is an honest man, and now to-day he tells you that the bullet may have taken the direction it did if he was a slight distance behind the native and the latter had slightly turned his body. I say that Mr Don in calmly reading the evidence concluded the evidence of the natives was perfectly consistent with the Doctor's, and he was justified. What evidence is there to show that they did not positively see what they say they did see? None whatever. Their evidence was tested by the Police Constables who were sent there, and two men were placed at the spot where the body was found, and others where the natives said they were working and the evidence of these men corroborates the evidence of the native witnesses. The only point that is not quite clear is the hearing of the shot, and the Police on the line say they could not hear it. The first two cartridges were blank and then a third ball cartridge was fired, and one of the policemen says he heard it. And it must be remembered that when Pelser shot the native it was a calm day but when the Police were there the wind was blowing pretty strong. Otherwise they corroborate their evidence in every particular. Therefore, gentlemen, I say that you must conclude that Pelser was driving the native in front of him and that he deliberately shot him in the back. Now I come to the iron bar, and I tell you plainly, gentlemen, that it is a mystery. The witnesses I have alluded to say Zachariah did not have it in his hands, and some of the witnesses for the prosecution just as emphatically swear that he had it when he came to the tramp-floor and there is nothing to say where he got it from if he had it at all. Again I must impress upon you the necessity for taking the evidence given at the preliminary examination and not that given in Court now   The natives say most distinctly that Zachariah had nothing in his hands when he passed by them, but they are contradicted by the witnesses at the tramp-floor—Abo, the accused, and a cousin of his   These are the only three   Now I ask you how was Mr Don to come to any other conclusion than that the three men on the line were swearing truthfully—was there anything to point otherwise?   Nothing at all, but rather the opposite   Those at the tramp-floor were interested and the men who swear they saw the crime committed are entirely independent witnesses and never saw the native before, and this being the case Mr Don was justified in coming to the conclusion that it was these three men who swore truthfully and not those at the tramp-floor because—

Judge   Didn't Marthinus David say anything about it?

Solicitor-General   Marthinus, my Lord

Mr Solomon   He did not say at the preliminary examination that he had seen the bar at all   There is another reason why he was justified in the belief that the witnesses at the tramp-floor were not speaking the truth   They all say they were some distance from Zachariah and it is so peculiar that they should notice so particularly and be able to swear so positively, and after the bar was found to come to the Court at the preliminary examination and identify it   And then one of them has to-day told you that he knew it was the same iron although he had only seen a small portion of it   I say it is absurd and I prefer to believe the evidence of the three natives on the line because it is disinterested   You have only to read the evidence   Take that of Zwaartboy   He says Zachariah was his friend and he went to meet him just before this bloody crime was committed   He said at the preliminary examination, and he says here, that he had nothing in his hand   He did not swear he saw the crime committed, and if he had been at all anxious to favour Zachariah he would probably have perjured himself on his friend's behalf   Does this look like a conspiracy?   I say it completely upsets the theory that the natives had conspired   The evidence is of such a nature that I challenge any honest man to believe it   I say it is extraordinary that these natives should not have been believed on a question of the kind which is entirely open for a Jury, and it should have gone to one   I say Mr Don was perfectly justified in coming to the conclusion that Zachariah had nothing in his hand   If you agree with him on this point, no matter whether you disagree with him on others, you must come to the conclusion that Pelser is guilty of murder   There is one more point about that iron bar   There was a witness examined at the preliminary examination named Marthinus David who is a servant to Pelser, yet he was not asked one word about the iron bar   He was in Court, and why was he not asked?   Gentlemen, this is suspicious and from this Mr Don had a right to come to the conclusion that these three natives were speaking the truth Now let us look at the magnanimous conduct of Mr Pelser, and the material service he rendered the Crown As soon as he had shot the man he rushed off to town to protect himself, and left the poor unfortunate native weltering in his blood That was the conduct of this man which the Crown looked at with such complacency Was it not enough to bring a blush of shame to an honest man's face? If he had shot him even in self-defence the common instinct of man would prompt him to get down and help him, but I say that shooting the man and rushing into Burghersdorp to gain protection is a proof of his guilt, and that this prosecution is a lie from beginning to end I will put it to you as nine honest conscientious and impartial men—Pelser went from the tramp-floor to the house, and got a loaded revolver to arrest a quiet man He got his horse and went after him and then occurred the foul act that has come out in evidence Then there is the fact that the body was found five yards from the spoor of the horse, and then the evidence of the eye witnesses who saw him come and go into the veldt, then Pelser's statements to Harmsworth and Williams, and in the face of these facts I challenge any nine honest men to say that Mr Don was not justified in saying that it was a foul murder That is the only result you can arrive at Where was the reason to commit the crime if the man was doing all he wished? Pelser tells you that the poor wretch would not walk fast enough for him, so he pushed his horse on him to drive him on, saying "Cannot you walk faster, I cannot stay here all day"— that is the explanation, gentleman—what do you think of it? Now, gentleman, after hearing these facts you may come to the conclusion that the language was strong, but in this case you must remember that the circumstances are in direct violation to what he professes Mr Don is a teacher of morals and religion which knows no distinction between black and white and when a case of this description occurs it gives the lie to his teaching —can you wonder now why his words were strong Considering how he must have felt they are not a bit too strong There is only one more point My learned friend argues that the mere fact of pleading justification is evidence of express malice and that therefore the defence must all break down If Mr Don had pleaded justification in this case, and persisted in it without any evidence to support it, you would then conclude that he was guilty of express malice, but, gentlemen, the mere fact of raising this plea of justification, and leading evidence in support of it does not lead you to the conclusion that he was actuated by express malice In the case of Stigant vs Hofmevi, the defendant pleaded as we have (quoted case) I want you to compare my conduct in this case with the conduct of my learned friend, and

I am satisfied that there is nothing from which you could infer malice   I have endeavoured to be perfectly just to my client and fair to Mr Pelser from beginning to end, and I say that my learned friend is not fair in saying that the way in which I have conducted this case shows malice.   Gentlemen, I am as certain as I am of to-morrow's rising sun that the first plea has been established as clear as ever a plea has been in any case   It may be that if you find the first plea proved you will not care to give a verdict upon the second plea

Judge   Before you go on you may say, if you have anything to say, why Mr Don pleads justification and Hay does not

Mr Solomon   I do not appear for Mr Hay

Judge   Under the plea of the general issue there is more evidence against Hay than Don

Solicitor-General   My letter will explain that a difficulty arose with regard to the pleas

Mr Solomon   I do not appear for Mr Hay, he appeared for himself and he can explain   I have an idea why he did not plead justification, but it would not be advisable to say as it is trenching on the article   (To the jury)   I said that you might not like to give a verdict on the second plea but still it must be considered   Let us come to it   I must admit in fairness to Mr Pelser that I must prove to your satisfaction that he murdered Zachariah to go on to the second plea   If in the facts I have laid before you I have not supported the plea of justification and from them you can only come to the conclusion that the crime committed is only that of culpable homicide, then in Heaven's name do not give me a verdict on the second plea   We do not seek for a verdict on the second plea but simply wish to lay the facts before you that ought to have been elicited at the preliminary examination and made the subject of a trial   With regard to the plea of fair comment you must form your own idea—You saw Pelser in the witness box, and noticed his demeanour and other circumstances connected with these proceedings   Here I cannot help calling attention to what has been said in one of the local Newspapers (*Star*) during the hearing of the case   It is to the effect that the Judge had congratulated Pelser on the way in which he gave his evidence

Judge   I have not seen the paper, and I did not congratulate Pelser, and if there has been any comment by any paper it is a contempt of Court

Solicitor-General   I have seen comments in the *Journal* and the *Star*

Judge   Then they must not have understood their business to have done so   I have exercised the privilege of allowing the Jury to go out of Court during adjournments, and if the papers have commented on the case it is contempt   I get the local papers, but have purposely abstained from reading any papers that I take in

Solicitor-General   My attention was drawn to it

Judge   I think it is an error that ought at once to be cor-
rected especially at a town where the Eastern Districts Court
sits, and if such conduct is persisted in it may be concluded that
this is not the place to have such trials tried

Mr Solomon   It is a baseless fabrication and an insult to this
Court   Well, gentlemen you saw Pelser in the witness box
carefully guarding his defence   You heard his explanation and
I may say that I never heard such a miserable attempt to throw
off a crime   He told you that Zachariah struck at him with his
left shoulder forward and that he fired the pistol and that the
bullet went into the back, but the Doctor says in that case the
bullet would have taken a downward course and not a horizontal
one   I put the witness through a course of cross-examination
to endeavour to prove to you how it was inflicted and he could
not show you   His statement before the Magistrate was different
to that he made to Harmsworth or Williams because in some he
says he shot and in others that the pistol went off presumably
accidentally, but in the witness box he made another statement
and tells you that he fired at the native's arm for the purpose of
disabling him   If this is so why did he tell Williams when he
went out at two o'clock that he would find the bullet in the
head ?   There is not an intelligent man in this Court that would
come to any other conclusion than that it is murder and nothing
else   All the Doctors that gave evidence in this case—Paul,
Greathead, and Ross—go to show that the statement of Pelser
is inconsistent with the direction of the bullet   We have on the
plea of justification circumstantial evidence which was strong
against Pelser—the evidence of the eye-witnesses   I ask you if
you believe the native witnesses on the line ?   What is to justify
you in thinking they came here to swear what is false ?   My
friend says there is a doubt that they actually saw what did take
place, but how was it that they could go to the Magistrate at
the preliminary examination and each of them tell exactly what
had taken place ?   That Zachariah came to the dam and Pelser
followed him on a black horse—turned him and drove him back,
and then shot him   If they did not see this where could they
hear it from— Did Pelser tell them ?   I think not   I think their
evidence will lead you to one conclusion only, that they are
speaking the truth and did see what took place   And if they
saw it, what motive had they to say that Zachariah did not
attack Pelser ?   They would rather please the white man if they
could   My friend says that their evidence is inconsistent with
the Doctor's evidence because they say Pelser was behind
Zachariah, but is it so ?   The men were five hundred yards off
and it was impossible to see whether he was immediately in front
of the horse or a little on one side, and when they say that he
was behind Zachariah it is quite probable that he was a little

on one side. I have carefully looked over their evidence, and I cannot find a point that is inconsistent with regard to the important facts of the case. My friend cross-examined them, and they are not educated men and could not see to what each question would lead, but did he shake their evidence on any material point? No, not one. There is the point about Zwaartboy not speaking but merely greeting and passing on, but this is not a contradiction and when they are right on the important facts of the case and only err in small details that it is possible to forget after a lapse of nine months, I say you should take their evidence. What on earth was the reason Pelser shot the native who had a right to breath God's free air peacefully pursuing his way? This is it. He drove his horse upon the poor wretch and because he could not go on as fast as the horse he fired, that is the simple story, and there is nothing in the evidence, I ask you to believe, that is inconsistent with this. Then my friend says you must not believe them because of the evidence of the iron rod, because the witnesses at the tramp-floor say he had it and they do not. Let us examine their evidence for a moment. Abo says he was standing in the middle between the deceased and Pelser, and if there is one man more than another who should have seen what Zachariah had in his hand it was Abo. He was the interpreter and saw all that passed at the floor and he tells you that he had no iron rod but a switch. Then there is the others, amongst whom is de Klerk. Gentlemen, I am sure you all pitied him from the bottom of your hearts. He was bound to stick by Pelser with whom he lives and with whom he has been brought up. He says he was at a distance of forty yards and he could see only an inch or so of what he tells you was an iron bar and he is able to go into the box next day and swear that this was the same bar the native carried. I shall say no more, but I ask you if you can believe a man who can swear so positively on such knowledge.

Judge. De Klerk did not go into the witness box until the 27th January.

Mr Solomon. Thank you, my Lord. Then again de Klerk tells you that he had never seen a bar like this in a Kafir's hands before, and that it was most uncommon, and then Pelser says he had seen iron bars like this about the homestead. Then Marthinus tells you he had a good look at him, and he went into the kraal. This is the first time we have heard of this kraal and why does he say it now? Because he has been told what to say to make out Pelser's case, because they knew when we got up the case that a man could not identify the bar at a distance of forty yards. If Pelser knew anything about his going into the kraal would he not have said something in his statements or at the preliminary examination? I tell you that what Marthinus tells you is a deliberate falsehood. These are the men who tell you that he had the bar in his hand, and who are those who do not? First there is Fischer, a most respectable and trustworthy man He tells you that Zachariah came up to him and Grahamstown and took the tobacco he gave him, and rubbed it in his hands, and if he had got the iron bar when he got to the tramp-floor he must have picked it up on his way there, but then de Klerk tells you there are more about the farm Then there is Grahamstown If he wished to make the evidence against Pelser stronger he could have said that when Zachariah went to the tramp-floor he had nothing in his hand, but he says clearly and honestly "No, my Lord, I could not see so far" Then there is Zwaartboy, who recognised his old friend, and went up to Zachariah and shook hands Why is he not in the conspiracy? I rely upon his evidence very much If he wanted to make it stronger against Pelser he could have told you what Ntloyiya and the others told you, but he says that he went away and merely heard the shot Ntloyiya and the others tell you he had nothing in his hand, and I think you should believe them If you come to the conclusion that he had nothing in his hand then the whole of Pelser's defence is taken from under his feet, as it rests on this iron rod, and the plea of justification is proved up to the hilt If it is proved that he had the bar, he must prove that he shot the man in self-defence, and that he has not done He is able to make different statements at different times yet he cannot reconcile them with the direction of the bullet From these facts, gentlemen, you must come to the conclusion that the wound was inflicted from behind when the native was not making the slightest attack There is one more thing and I have done My learned friend tells you that Mair contradicts Alfred Peters, but Mair gets into the witness box and tells you that he did come to him, but he did not say that he had seen the occurrence Now, gentlemen, this is hardly credible, for from what Peters told him any reasonable man would have concluded that he had seen it, and if he had been an intelligent man he would have asked for the particulars, and I believe he did, that is a supposition I say, gentlemen, that it is very seldom indeed that native witnesses give their evidence in such a straightforward manner as these three witnesses in this case, and there is nothing in the evidence to justify you to come to the conclusion that they swear falsely If you believe them you must conclude that the plea of justification has been proved, but even should you take it away I say it is proved Any one going into the circumstances of this case is justified in coming to the conclusion that Pelser wilfully murdered Zachariah I do not think there is any more for me to say I am not going into details, but I lay before you the broad principles of justice If you find every plea proved you are bound to acquit Mr Don I don't think it is necessary for me to tell you the importance of this case—it is watched with interest by the whole colony, and a healthy public opinion will be brought on by your verdict in this case   I am quite sure if you give a verdict in favour of Mr Don, I feel perfectly certain, that the verdict will be approved of by the intelligent portion of the inhabitants of this country, and as years roll by, you will look back to this day and be proud of it and of your verdict, as one which has fortified the discussion on public matters in this country and vindicated the principles of justice I do not make an appeal on behalf of Mr Don but in the interest of two great principles—even-handed justice between black and white, and the liberty of fair discussion on matters of public interest, and in conclusion I cannot do better than quote the words of Erskine, which so eloquently apply to this present case "They, however, who may be disposed to censure me for the zeal which has animated me in this cause will at least, I hope, have the candour to give me credit for the sincerity of my intentions It was the first command and counsel to my youth always to do what my conscience told me to be my duty, and to leave the consequences to God   I shall carry with me the memory, and, I hope, the practice of this parental lesson to the grave   I have hitherto followed it and have no reason to complain that the adherence to it has been even a temporary sacrifice, It is impossible in this country to hurt an honest man, but even if it were possible, I should little deserve that title if I could upon any principle have consented to tamper or temporise with a question which involves in its determination and its consequences the liberty of the Press, and in that liberty the very existence of every part of the public freedom "   (Hear, hear)

The learned gentleman spoke with warmth and earnestness, and resumed his seat at 12 25 p m , having spoken one hour and thirty-five minutes   The Solicitor-General's speech was not quite so long, occupying one hour and ten minutes

The jury expressed their desire to remain for the Judge's summing up, instead of adjourning for lunch

THE JUDGE PRESIDENT'S ADDRESS.

At 12 28 p m , the Judge President commenced his address, as follows —Gentlemen of the Jury   The defendant stands charged with the crime of Criminal Libel, and the libel complained of is set forth in the indictment as follows —"That John Davidson Don, a Minister of the Gospel, residing at King William's Town, is charged with the crime of publishing a Defamatory Libel, in that, whereas one Willem Jacobus Pelser, a farmer, residing at Roodeberg's Vlei, in the district of Albert, did upon or about the sixteenth day of January, in the year of our Lord one thousand eight hundred and eighty-five, and at Roodeberg's Vlei aforesaid, in self-defence, and as he lawfully might, shoot and kill one Zachariah, in his lifetime a labourer residing at Burghersdorp, in the said district, the said John Davidson Don contriving and wrongfully, unlawfully and maliciously intending to injure, vilify and prejudice the said Willem Jacobus Pelser and deprive him of his good name, fame, credit and reputation, and to bring him into public contempt, scandal, infamy and disgrace did on or about the fourteenth day of April, in the year of our Lord one thousand eight hundred and eighty-five, and at King William's Town aforesaid, wrongfully, unlawfully and maliciously write, print and publish, and cause and procure to be written printed and published in the *Cape Mercury*, in the form of a letter purporting to be written and addressed by the said John Davidson Don to George Alexander Hay the following false, scandalous, malicious and defamatory words, that is to say 'That poor man's blood' (meaning the blood of the said Zachariah) 'cries to heaven, not merely against the wretched murderer' (meaning the said Willem Jacobus Pelser) 'but against the Government which refuses to prosecute and the country which condones such conduct,' the said John Davidson Don meaning thereby that the said Willem Jacobus Pelser had wrongfully, unlawfully and maliciously killed and murdered the said Zachariah and that the said Willem Jacobus Pelser was a murderer, to the great damage, scandal and disgrace of the said Willem Jacobus Pelser, the said John Davidson Don well knowing the said defamatory libel to be false, and thus the said John Davidson Don did commit the crime of publishing a defamatory libel" The charge proceeds to say that Mr Don meant thereby that Pelser had murdered Zachariah and knowingly published that which is false with the intention of defaming the character of Pelser To this charge there are three pleas The general issue, under which defendant can prove that he did not publish the alleged libel, that the document does not convey the meaning attached to it, and that there was no malice on his part in publishing it In addition to this there is a special plea which perhaps can be dealt with under the general issue and that is " fair comment," which is that there was no malice in the publication of his letter, and that it is a fair comment on the proceedings it relates to Then there has been a plea of justification, and that is, that the words are true in substance and in fact, and that Pelser did commit a murder I do not think I need explain now the various pleas more fully because I shall deal with them as I proceed In the pleas referred to, appears the letter which is relied upon by the Crown as the libel and which the defendant relies upon as evidence, or some evidence, of the absence of intent to traduce I shall not now read that letter which is attached to the copy of the pleas, because I mean first to deal with the plea of justification, and because, as the Solicitor-General has told you, if this plea is proved, not only is defendant entitled to the verdict of not guilty, but to public encomium for publishing a letter which was the means of proving that a serious crime had been committed, and which perhaps would not have

come before you but for the publication of that letter Now
with regard to that letter it appears from what has been said in
the course of argument, that there has been some comment in the
local newspapers on this case during the course of this trial If
so, I very much regret it I don't care from which side it comes,
for no side has a right to comment upon a case during the time
it is before the Court I trust you will not be influenced by it
If you are, you will be neglecting your duty It is possible that
you may have read it without knowing that you have trans-
gressed your duty in reading the article, if this should be so, I
hope you will not be influenced by such comment In dealing
with this case I ask you to dismiss from your minds every
possible prejudice that may have been created This is a case
that involves most serious issues, and must be impartially
considered It is Pelser appealing to the Crown to clear his
character by a criminal prosecution It involves his character,
and it also involves most important questions concerning the
administration of justice It also involves very important questions relating to the liberty of the Press, and last, but not least,
it may involve the liberty of the subject With regard to the law
on the subject of libel, criminal libel is now regulated by a recent
Act, under which criminal proceedings can be instituted by the
Solicitor-General issuing a hat, and by this law the publication
of a libel is punishable with imprisonment and fine You see,
gentlemen, that this case involves most serious issues from
every point of view, therefore I do entreat of you not
to burden yourselves with any prejudice or sympathies one way
or the other It is a case which requires all your reasoning
faculties, honesty, impartiality, and sense of justice to enable
you to deal with the facts that have been put before you I
hope you will not import into this case any class or race feeling,
or any political feeling The law has appointed you as sworn
judges to do justice upon the evidence, and I ask you to honestly
fulfil your high office If you have any feeling against the Kafir
because you know him and find him not on a social equality with
yourselves, or that he is inferior to you in intellect or under-
standing, do not import it into this case Then again, gentlemen,
do not import any sort of personal prejudice towards the
man Pelser because something has been said about Dutch and
English Set aside all race feeling and political feeling, and
approach it as judges, which you really are As regards the law
you will require to know from the Judge what the law is upon
the subject, and I shall endeavour to tell you plainly what that
law is Libel has been defined to be a publication without
justification or legal cause, tending to bring a person into contempt and ridicule, and injuring the fair fame of any person
That is a definition, and for the purpose of this case a very
proper one Intentional insult to character is a libel, and in

any community character becomes important The law presumes
every man to have a good character until it be taken away from
him by evidence showing he is not entitled to it And the law
also presumes that it is his property, and shall not be taken from
him unless the law decides he has forfeited it But the law goes
further, and says that any one who injures that character intentionally is liable to be punished Intention to injure is the
most important feature in libel On the other hand, if one
man uses language about another man which detracts from
his character, he would scarcely be able to say that he
did not mean to convey what the language plainly con-
veys In this letter the language is, that Pelser is a murderer,
and the Crown asks you to infer that if the publication
was by the defendant, that he did intend to impute murder, and
therefore injury to Pelser's character The defendant, however,
by his pleas, says there is no injury because he is a murderer, and
there was no intention to injure because even if he is not a
murderer, the circumstances are such as to lead Don honestly to
believe that he was And not only this, but that he had a duty
to do in expressing what he did, and that it was a fair and honest
expression of opinion With regard to the character of the words,
they are *primâ facie* libellous The words are "That poor man's
blood cries to heaven not merely against the wretched murderer,
but against the Government which refuses to prosecute " *Primâ
facie* I think you will have no difficulty in coming to the conclusion that the words mean that Pelser is a wretched murderer,
and what you have now to determine is—First, is he a murderer ?
Next, did Don mean to injure him by saying so, or had
he a better and higher motive, and if he had, did he express
it in a proper and not an unfair way ? As to the plea of
justification, to substantiate it the defendant must prove the
truth of his statement that Pelser is a murderer, and that it was
in the interest of the public that it should be stated About the
question whether it was in the interests of the public there
cannot be much difficulty, for if a man commits an offence against
the law it is for the benefit of the public that it should be stated
You will also have no difficulty in coming to the conclusion that
unless the defendant succeeds in proving his special defences, the
words are a libel The first issue is, truth The law says, and I think
fairly, that truth is not always justification For instance, if
you rake up things against a man that have occurred thirty or
forty years ago, is it for the good of a community to know these
things unless there is something special which calls for it ? When
a thing occurs quite recently, and anyone thinks that the administration of justice has been impeded, he may have a right and
even a duty to come forward and state it, if it is fairly done   I
have urged you, gentlemen, to dismiss prejudice from your minds,
and judge the case on the evidence before you It sometimes

happens that the fear of consigning a man to death induces juries where men are tried for murder to acquit where there is no reasonable doubt of guilt In this case there is no such fear Pelser cannot by your verdict suffer death But the plea of justification cannot be found without proof of murder Approach the evidence without any prejudice—look first to the law, and then to the facts Look to the law It is said that "killing is murder," and so it is, to a certain extent Every man who kills another is presumed to have intended to kill, and so must clear himself I hope you will all follow me in what I say There are several kinds of homicide The first is, killing intentionally—without legal justification or legal excuse that, is murder The law holds that every man who kills intended to kill , and every man who intended to kill, is held to be guilty of murder until the contrary be proved, or until, in other words, justification or legal excuse is proved Just as I said before, in the same way as a man who publishes a document which imputes murder is presumed to be a libeller, until he proves justification or absence of malice, so he who kills is presumed to be a murderer, until he proves justification or legal excuse There is another sort of homicide, and that is, killing without intent, but still without legal justification or legal excuse—that, is culpable homicide Again there is another sort of homicide—justifiable homicide—which is that of killing another in discharge of a duty, such as that of a public executioner For instance, there is the duty imposed on a policeman who has a warrant to apprehend a man on a serious charge He has to apprehend the accused, and if he resists, or if he runs away and he cannot apprehend him in any other way than by killing him, he may do so There is another kind of justifiable homicide, and that is where a man kills another who is in the act of committing an atrocious crime These are justifiable homicides, and the particulars I have mentioned must be proved But this is not the case with Pelser, who does not say "I had a duty imposed on me by law to apprehend the man" He cannot say "I had a duty, and in the discharge of that duty I shot him" He cannot say that, because the law which has been referred to did not impose upon him that duty The recent Act which has been referred to by the Solicitor-General only imposed upon Pelser the *privilege* of arresting, but it does not say he is *bound* to arrest When he attempted to arrest and found he could not do so without shooting, he was bound to desist Justification does not apply to such a case, and the learned Solicitor-General has not relied upon it I draw your attention to this as it is possible that it may be floating in the minds of some of you Pelser can, however, excuse himself by proving that he shot the man in self-defence, and this comes under a different class of homicide, which is excusable homicide A man is excused by law if he kills another by pure accident If a man kills another while doing a legal act without carelessness, it is a pure accident   This implies that he must be acting legally, and that he must be doing it without negligence, if not, he would be guilty of homicide   There is another excusable homicide, and that is, shooting in self-defence   With regard to this sort of homicide, I think I had better quote to you the language of our Criminal Law, which is founded on Roman Dutch Law, and which in every way states the law both here and in England or to what is homicide in self-defence—that is when one kills another in defence of his life and person   To establish this it requires, first, an unexpected and unjust assault—it requires Pelser to prove that there had been made on him by Zachariah an unexpected and unjust assault, next it requires him to prove a great and actual danger, and, thirdly, he must prove that it was impossible to defend his own life in any other way than by taking the life of Zachariah   To prove that it is a killing in self-defence, he must prove that there was an unjust and unlooked for assault, and that there was a great and actual danger, and that he could not avoid it without killing   If he does not do this the law decides the killing to be a murder of culpable homicide, and Pelser cannot be free from guilt   In this case the Crown, by its indictment, raises on behalf of Pelser the plea of self-defence, and it says " We are prepared to prove it "   Mr Solomon, in telling you that when he tendered the plea of justification all that he had to prove was, that Pelser did shoot in such a way as to allow of the reasonable inference being drawn that Pelser had murdered, is strictly correct   To quote again from the same law, it says that a man may be justified if he can prove that at the time of assault he was under the apprehension of a great and impending danger, and he must show that he was placed in the position as provided by the law, and that he could not avoid it without killing   All this Pelser must prove   The law is very clear, and says a man who has killed another shall be presumed to be guilty of murder until it is proved that he is not   Now has Pelser proved that he is not guilty?   And that is what you have to determine   He has had the opportunity of saying in the witness-box why he is not   You have heard his statement during the course of this case, and it is for you to say if it has satisfied you that he did not shoot the man intentionally, and without there being any necessity to do so   Unless there was absolute necessity, or unless it was a pure accident, he is guilty of a crime, and should have been indicted   If there was sufficient provocation to unhinge his mind from the effect of his being placed in a difficult and dangerous position, and that he lost his temper on the spur of the moment, he would still be guilty of a crime—that of culpable homicide, for which he is not, but ought to have been, indicted   Now, bearing all this in mind, are you satisfied that he shot the man in self-defence?   In dealing with this question the law has told you that the defendant must prove an unlawful and unjust assault, and the first question you will ask is—Was there an assault at all? You have heard all the circumstances, and you have it in evidence that Zachariah was known before, was a workman, had a master, and was then looking for a horse, He came to the place openly—these points are not in conflict between defence and prosecution He came to the tramp-floor Before going there he saw a man in whose employ he had been—Fischer —after that he went to the kraal—looked in and passed to the tramp-floor There he had a conversation—he spoke to those inside and said he was looking for a horse Some discussion then took place about a pass—and he said he had none From that he passed on into the veldt After he had left, Pelser (who up to that time had no pistol), went into the house, got the pistol and followed him Before he left he said he was going to bring him back for the purpose of making him pay two shillings That is in evidence for the Crown Then Pelser got up to the man, and something happened It is for you to determine what that was Zachariah was found, at that spot afterwards, with a bullet in his back, and the medical evidence says the shot which inflicted the wound must have been fired from behind at an angle of forty-five degrees Pelser from there went to his house and communicated the circumstances to his father, and told him to go to the place and see about the man, and then he went to Harmsworth, the Magistrate's clerk, and made a statement, then he made another to Wilhams This was on the 16th of January The preliminary examination took place on the 20th, but before this the police had made enquiries on the evening of the 16th, and the result was, that on the 20th several natives were brought forward—Veld-schoen, Zwaartboy, Peters and Ntloyiya, and in addition to these Abo and the two Marthinus Now, gentlemen, these are undisputed facts There are some facts in dispute, and with regard to these your most earnest attention is requested The first is, whether Zachariah was armed in any sort of way This point becomes very important in determining the question of assault, for if Zachariah had no weapon, the probabilities are that he could not have assaulted Had he a weapon? Had he an iron rod? You have heard the evidence elicited by the Solicitor-General and Mr Solomon The Solicitor-General says you ought to be satisfied there was such a rod in Zachariah's hand, because his witnesses swear that he had it when he came to the kraal and tramp-floor, or one similar to this produced in Court Are those witnesses swearing truthfully, and are they correct? It is for you to say Mr Solomon says they are not, and in his defence he has said they were interested in telling a lie to aid Pelser Is there sufficient evidence before you to come to that conclusion? In the first place there is Pelser, who is a relative of the prosecutor, then there is de Klerk, who is also in a similar position, he is living on the farm with Pelser You have it in evidence that he on a previous occasion was concerned with Pelser in a criminal charge, and the connection between them is very close—they are very intimate Then there is Marthinus, with regard to whom it is proved that he is a servant of Pelser, and has been some time in his employ, and there is also this other circumstance with regard to him—before the Magistrate he said he was at the tramp-floor and saw Zachariah with the rod, but he did not say he had seen him at the kraal This statement about the kraal is a very important feature in this case He says he saw Zachariah there, and he went into the kraal to look, and that he had the rod in his hand, and he was about three yards from him Is this true or not? If it is not a lie, it is important In enquiring into the truth of the statement you may ask why he did not say it before the Magistrate He was examined not on the 20th of January, when the first examination took place, but on the 27th The time is most important Would you not expect that if he knew he had seen the man in the kraal with the rod in his hand he would have said so? From the preliminary examination it is difficult to know which witnesses were called for the defence and which for the prosecution, and I trust this will never occur again Then you must remember that Pelser had an attorney, and would *he* not have asked the question? Marthinus before the Magistrate does not say he went to the kraal, that he was three yards off and that he saw the iron bar in Zachariah's hand then, but he does say he was at the tramp-floor Marthinus' credibility is impeached from two causes The first is, that he is a dependent, and the second is, that they found it necessary to put some one in the kraal so as to bring him close to Zachariah From the nature of the examination one would infer that such an important question would have been asked And why was it not asked? If you think he has been tampered with in any way, you will attach less importance to his evidence in his attempt to prove the man was armed with the iron rod It is an important feature, and you must determine why he was not examined on this point Then we come to the witnesses Pelser, de Klerk, and Abo Abo, before the Magistrate, said he thought the man had a switch across his shoulders He says, "I noticed that the Kafir had something in his hand I thought it was a switch It was the same length as the piece of iron now produced" That is what he said He says to you, ' I did not *think* it was a switch, I say it *was* a switch" He was called by the Crown to support Pelser, but because he is called to support him you must not necessarily suppose that Pelser is prejudiced because Abo says something that is not in accord with what the other witnesses for the prosecution have said You must test Abo's evidence by what you think to be facts Before the

R

Magistrate he said, " I thought it was a switch " Do you think this was produced by an impression—such an impression as the Solicitor-General has attached to Harmsworth and Williams ? If so, you will not attach much importance to the change Then, there is the fact that he has been twice to King William's Town, and consulted with the defendant's attorney Mr Solomon asks you to dismiss the idea that his attorney would suggest anything of an improper nature If this is so, you will not consider the departure unfavourable to Pelser, but to the defence If you conclude that he has been tampered with, you must conclude that he is capable of telling a lie—and therefore his evidence about the switch will go for nothing— and that Pelser had people in his employ who were untruthful The defence says that the men could not have seen the iron rod at the distance they stood from Zachariah Abo was nearest He was at the tramp-floor and acted as interpreter He had the best opportunity of judging as he was the nearest and he says it was a switch, and was examined in his master's interest on the 20th January If he thought it was a switch, could the others know it was not ? There was no cross-examination whether he thought it to be a switch or a rod Abo now swears positively that it was a switch, and that he said so before the Magistrate, and as he was nearest the defence asks you to come to the conclusion that the other witnesses at the tramp-floor could not see whether it was a rod You are asked to disbelieve them as much as the Crown asks you to disbelieve the other witnesses who say they saw the shooting If the witnesses at the tramp-floor are not to be believed, you have them swearing it was a rod when they had no opportunity of seeing it Then you must remember that they say he held it on the ground with one hand resting on it Pelser says there were such things about, and he might have picked it up Again, is it not likely that seeing a stranger with such a thing he would have wondered what he was doing with it, and asked him for it ? The evidence of the rod rests with Pelser, de Klerk, Marthinus and Abo The last man was nearest to the deceased, the other is a servant, and one of the other two a dependent and the other a relative Passing on, we come to witness Grahamstown—he says he saw Zachariah, and so does Fischer, and he saw him at a short distance before he came to the tramp-floor They give strong evidence that he had no rod He came up to Fischer without a rod, and had none when he left, and he fortifies his evidence by saying that he gave him some tobacco and he rubbed it in his hands It is an important feature of the defence that he was seen some little distance, just before going to the tramp-floor, without anything in his hand I am glad the Crown does not ask you to disbelieve this evidence, as there is no reason to do so Grahamstown did not know the man before, and he says the same as Fischer Then you must look at the character of Fischer He was in the employ of the Municipality, he is respectable, and he does not seem to have any object to serve in saving what he has He says this is what he saw, and the only question is why did he not come forward before? The authorities at Burghersdorp have shown a great laxity in the matter, and if they had gone into every detail this evidence could have been discovered Fischer did not know it was going to become so important a matter, and it is possible that he did not read the preliminary examination Then again, some months afterwards the Crown was challenged by the *Mercury* newspaper, to publish this evidence, but did not do so Why should Fischer come forward and volunteer a statement about a man if he did not know anything about him? Inasmuch as Fischer did not come forward before, it can scarcely be said that he has a motive to come forward now and tell a lie His antecedents do not lead you to that conclusion Then, to lead you to the conclusion that what they say is true, you have Grahamstown, who was working with Fischer, and when I asked him if he saw Zachariah go into the kraal after he had watched him approach it, he said ' No" If he had wished to tell a lie would he not have said " Yes "? Who was to contradict him ? This has an air of truthfulness What would prevent him from saying he had seen him go into the kraal? But he says, " I cannot say if he went into the kraal or if when he went up to the tramp-floor he had a stick in his hand, I saw him there It was too far" Now did Zachariah perhaps pick up anything, and if so what? And if he picked anything up he must have done so by the kraal—was it the rod or what was it ? You have had some evidence that similar rods belong to ploughs used for agriculture, and that it may have been on the farm, Pelser says so It is also in evidence that they do not use such bars Then it has been said that such rods were not on the line, but that it was in all probability on the farm The question for you to consider is, whether it is likely that he picked it up on the farm, and is it likely that he picked it up before he went to the kraal, or, was it a switch that he found ? If it was a switch, how was it converted into a rod ? Is it likely that Pelser got some one on his farm to put the rod by the dead man's side, or did anyone put it there without his knowing it ? The assault was committed at about half-past ten, and from that time to a quarter past two Pelser was still in town, and then came out Is it possible that between eleven o'clock and two o'clock some one might have gone there ? I do think it most unfortunate that the evidence of old Pelser was not taken at the preliminary examination so as to get at the truth of the matter The Crown should have got the man and if he could have given a statement aiding Pelser, let him do so We cannot want to injure Pelser, but to get at the truth

Why was he not brought forward? Pelser says he went and first saw his mother, then his father was sent for, and he told him to go and see about a man that he had shot. Is that true? If so, you would have expected the father to go to the man and see him, and you have had it in evidence. If he was told to go, why did he not go? It comes out in evidence that he came up to the line and turned round there, and when he came there he was seen with a stick. Why did old Pelser ask questions about the telegraph pole in the way he did? Why did he not ask the natives whether they had seen the native his son had shot? Man has been called to contradict the natives, why was Pelser not called to contradict them also? As he was interested in the matter, if conscientious you would have expected him to say to the natives on the line, "Have you seen this unfortunate Kafir? tell me, I want to see him." But instead of this he goes up to the men and asks questions entirely unconnected with the affair. Why did he do so? There was no difficulty in getting to the dead man, and there were other people on the farm. Now why was this man not called? His evidence would be legal. This is a gap, and why was it not filled? —that is for you to determine. The defence says Pelser may have put the rod, or caused some one after he left for Burghersdorp, to put this rod near the body. This was possible. It was necessary in the interests of justice to show that it had not been done, or that it had been. The Crown at the preliminary attempted neither. Thus we are left in a state of uncertainty, and now the position is this. Fischer says he saw nothing in Zachariah's hand, Grahamstown says that also. Abo, a witness for the prosecution says it was a switch, and then several other witnesses called by the Crown say they saw no stick but an iron bar. It is said that the witnesses for the defence tell a lie to injure Pelser. You have heard what Mr Solomon has said about race feeling, and I wish to say this—do not because a man becomes a champion of natives have contempt for him because you may not also wish to become their champion. The law puts black and white on the same level. But in testing their credibility, you, who are acquainted with the Kafir, may perhaps think that he would invent lies in order to condemn the white man. If these have done so, it is fatal to their credibility. But while I advise you to act cautiously before you accept any evidence as correct in this conflict of testimony—ask yourselves, why should these natives at once concur in inventing the absence of the rod, and speak of Pelser riding behind Zachariah and firing at him from behind? They must have seen Zachariah first alone, and afterwards followed. Did they mean that they saw more than the firing in a position which appeared to them from behind? They were proved to be five hundred yards away. You have heard the evidence, and you will ask yourselves whether men who were at that distance could see the man pass, see him driven back, and see the white man apparently without any motive fire at the black man If they could, then their evidence becomes important, because it is not inconsistent with the medical evidence The Doctor told you that if the native shrugged or swayed his shoulders whilst walking in front, the wound could have been inflicted, and also if he had been walking slightly to the side, and one of the natives has told you that he was slightly at the side as he could not be direct in the line of sight according to his description which you saw If that is so, then their evidence is not inconsistent with the truth Then again, are they speaking the truth when they say they saw him following the black man? You must now look at the preliminary examination Pelser made a statement on the 16th January to Harmsworth—this was before anybody had said anything as he had come straight into town from the farm In that statement he says, 'As the native raised his arm to strike me, I thereupon shot him' Soon after this the natives all come forward as witnesses, and they said at once, "Between us and the man we could see distinctly, and we saw the white man follow the black man" Pelser did not state that he had followed the man Pelser in his statement said that he went to stop him, and because he would not be stopped and struck at him he shot him There was nothing said about the native being followed by Pelser—that was introduced by the native witnesses on the line, and they all concurred in the assertion Afterwards Pelser in his statement to the Magistrate said, 'I did follow him," and then he says "I did not raise my arm to shoot, it went off by accident" Look at these statements, gentlemen In the first instance he says he shot when he stopped the native, and a few days afterwards the natives give their evidence and say that he followed the native, and then Pelser makes another statement which shows their statements to be correct I think it is important that I should read to you Pelser's statements on this point, because his statements become very important I will read each statement he has made His first statement to Harmsworth, second to Williams, the third at the preliminary examination, and the fourth here That made to Harmsworth is as follows "I am in for a row I have shot a Kafir It occurred this way I was riding on my farm when I saw a Kafir going through the veldt I rode up to him and asked him what he wanted there, he answered, 'I have come to look for a horse' I then demanded to see his pass, but he said he had none I told him to leave my veldt, as I did not allow natives to roam about there without passes I then went away some little distance, and on looking back saw the Kafir still in my veldt I thereupon rode up to him and told him that as he did not choose to leave I would give him into custody of the police, and I then sent for two policemen who had passed me previously I reined my horse in front of the Kafir, and he then said, 'You'll not stop me' He had a bar of iron in his hand, and with this he struck my horse a blow on the nose My horse thereupon became restive and unmanageable, and the Kafir then struck at my leg with the iron I turned the horse round, and as I did so I saw his arm raised again to strike me, and I thereupon shot him" Now it is said that this statement must be correct, as Mr Harmsworth has twice sworn to it But the Crown says it is incorrect, because Pelser was so excited that he did not know what he was about It was Harmsworth's duty to put down what was said, and he has sworn to this statement twice, but never examined on the point about raising the arm and shooting Of course one would expect Pelser to be more or less excited, but then there is this other circumstance When Pelser had come in to give this information it appears that he had been to the house to change his clothes, and the excitement had not prevented him from doing this This would point to the conclusion that the excitement was not such as to prevent his knowing what he was about He spoke to his mother and father and then went away to town The first words he said to Harmsworth were, 'I am in for a row" What does that mean Does it mean that he had become contrite and was sorry for what had occurred, or that he came and said the words to put himself right with the authorities in order to allay rumours There is the statement that he said this, and four days after Harmsworth repeated it, and he was not questioned Immediately after this Pelser goes to Wilhams, and he makes another statement, which is as follows —" On the forenoon of the 16th I heard him make a statement in the office of the Resident Magistrate's Clerk He said he had come in to report that he had shot a Kafir on his farm I asked him under what circumstances, and he replied, that the Kafir had said he had come on to his farm to look for a horse He asked the Kafir if he had a pass, and the Kafir replied he had no pass He then ordered him back to town to get a pass He insisted on his going back, but the Kafir would not do so He then rode up to the Kafir to compel him to go back The Kafir turned round and struck at his horse with an iron rod about two feet in length He then struck a second blow at him (Pelser), and he then drew his revolver and shot the Kafir, and then came to town to report having done so He said he did not know whether the Kafir was dead or not" Here, gentlemen, you see he says, "He then drew his revolver and shot the Kafir" Now in this statement there is nothing inconsistent with the evidence with the exception of the last part about the shooting You will find that in the last part of Pelser's evidence he says he had the revolver out all the time, and therefore Wilhams' statement is questioned There is not a word in either of these statements about following the native, nor that he turned round and pretended to go quietly and all at once darted upon Pelser and assaulted him There is no mention of following him at all and it must be remembered that when Pelser made those statements, he had just come from where the scene had taken place This was on the 16th January, before the natives appeared and before they said he followed the man on horseback After their evidence was given he made this statement He was not obliged to make it, and was duly warned that anything he might say might be used as evidence against him This is his statement made on the 11th February, at the preliminary examination "I am not guilty Latterly we have lost sheep day and night in great numbers When the deceased came to me I asked him for a pass, as we did not allow any one to go into our veldt without a pass Deceased was determined to go into our veldt Upon this I went to fetch him back When I got to him he would not come back At last he did go a few yards in the direction of the house, but suddenly turned back and struck at me three times, in such a way as to show me my life was in danger I had already my revolver out for the purpose of frightening him The horse got restless, and when the horse gave way for the deceased the revolver went off and hit the deceased I thereupon went to the house and told my father, and requested him at once to see about the man I had shot I am very sorry that such an occurrence should have taken place, as I had not the slightest intention to exercise malice" Now this statement was voluntarily given, and you must consider whether it is a truthful statement To-day he makes the following statement "I said I would go and bring him back and fine him two shillings and give the men the money I went to get my revolver and rode after him to bring him back When I got up to him I said, You are my prisoner now'" This is the first time he has said that He goes on to say "He stood still I then pushed my horse up towards him" Did he say this before? 'I took out the pistol in order to frighten him and he moved a short distance towards the house He was walking very slowly in front of my horse, and I told him to go on a little quicker, and I pushed my horse up a little nearer Then he turned round suddenly and attacked me" You see, gentlemen, he says he was riding behind the native— you will remember what the natives say about riding behind him Then he says, "As he struck at me the last time the pistol went off and hit deceased" Now is this statement true— is it probable? You have heard what has been said about the evidence of the natives—that they are to be considered untruthful and liars, because they say that this man was in front of Pelser Here is Pelser to-day saying the same and using almost their very words He says "He was walking slowly in front I was on my horse riding behind him" One would think that if the imputation is to apply to the natives, it must apply to Pelser   Then he says "I told him to go quicker, as he was going slowly, as I had no time"   It this is what the natives describe, ask yourselves if they are truthful or not   Here is Pelser admitting that he rode behind him, and was not, as he had previously stated, right in front of him in order to stop him   It would seem that Zachariah was obeying the law in going slowly in front of Pelser   Then he says "I then pushed my horse towards him, I cannot say against him"   Did he do that—can you say the natives are wrong when they describe what they saw?   It is said that the native testimony is untruthful   Pelser has made four statements — one to Harmsworth, one to Williams, then one to the Magistrate, and again another to-day   And if he is allowed to veer about in this way are you in a position to say that his defence is truthful—that he shot because he could not escape with dear life?   If you believe Mair, who does not come here favourable to the defence—he puts the native where they say they were at work   They were all there, although Pelser says he did not see them   It is a strange circumstance that he rode across the line and did not see them   That is what he says, but they were proved to be there by Mair   Do you think they saw what they say they saw?   They say on the 20th January, before the Magistrate, that Pelser followed the man, and he is obliged to admit this afterwards, and in reality corroborates them in this, and the only point now is, did they see the actual shooting?   The law says, that if a man kills another he is a murderer unless he proves the contrary, and it is his duty to reduce it from murder to manslaughter, or self-defence   It was his duty at the preliminary examination to do so   If he did not, there would be evidence, either of culpable homicide or murder, and to this extent Mr Don is to be commended for bringing about these proceedings   The Crown must prove that Zachariah assaulted Pelser   The Crown says he did, and puts the rod in his hand   The defence says, No, if he had anything in his hand it must have been a switch, because Fischer and Grahamstown say he had nothing in his hand when he left them   Then the witnesses on the railway had an opportunity of seeing the man and they say he had no rod   These witnesses are not to be dismissed   They have aided justice in showing that the prisoner passed over the line, and they remember the circumstance that Pelser followed the man, and this Pelser admits   Zwaartboy says he did not see the actual firing, but he heard the report of the discharge of firearms   Witnesses, who saw Zachariah before he went to he tramp-floor, say he had no rod, and those at the tramp-floor say he had, but one says he had a switch   Was there any motive to put a rod or switch in his hand?   Did Pelser say to anyone, "Go and take something and put it down by the man so that I may say I have been assaulted?"   Why was not old Pelser called to say why he stopped at the line, or whether he went to the place? Was it to see whether the coast was clear, or anything of that kind? All these things must enter your minds, and it is for you to answer them. I put it to you, as intelligent and reasonable men, do they prove to your satisfaction that the rod was in the hand of Zachariah? If Pelser has proved that he was unaided by anyone, and that the rod was in Zachariah's hand, he must prove that he was assaulted. It is not Zachariah who speaks, for he is dead, but it is only his wounds that speak to us. That is the only voice we have. He cannot speak, but Pelser can, and you must not only accept statements made by witnesses but look at the circumstances, and say, even if the rod was there, would Zachariah have assaulted him? Pelser says he would and did. If he had his pistol out in order to frighten him, then what Pelser told Harmsworth is not correct. Williams also is sure he said he fired after the second blow. There was no evidence to show that Zachariah was not honestly and *boná fide* looking for a horse, and is it likely that he would turn round on the man's own farm and assault him? Look at the rod of iron—is it likely that a man would have struck at him with it without provocation? and does not Pelser provide that provocation? He pushed his horse up to him, nearly upon him, and if so, had he not a right to strike at the horse, and had Pelser a right to use the pistol? It is likely that after striking the horse on the nose he would have followed it up by other blows, and if so who was to blame? The law says, to clear himself of the inference of murder Pelser must prove that he was assaulted and in great danger. Pelser in the first place tells us an extraordinary tale. He says "I was going to make him pay two shillings." Was this merely sport? He had no right to say "I will go and fine the man." If he had done so, then the man's resistance would have been perfectly justifiable He says it was a joke, and it is for you to say if it was so or not The men he said it to did not think so. If he had gone after him for the purpose of handing him over to the police the act would have been legal. The Act allows farmers the privilege to arrest natives and take them before the Magistrate, but it does not allow them to fine a man and make sport of him. Although it allows you to take a man into custody, it does not allow you to persist in arresting him if he resists, or when there is danger to yourself or the man. Suppose the man resisted—the moment he resisted Pelser should have desisted unless he could prove danger to himself. Pelser ought to have stopped, and ought not to have invited a fight between him and the native. A policeman is different, as he has a duty to apprehend. But there is no duty on the farmer to apprehend—the farmer has only the privilege. Pelser should have stopped the moment he saw there was danger to himself. Where a man has the privilege and has not a duty to arrest, he should not persist. If he had

8

an opportunity to go off, he should have done so   Does this
show that he was in danger of his life, or that he wanted to
apprehend the man at all hazards ?   You can raise a defence of
taking life in self-defence when the man you killed committed
an illegal assault upon you and a great and actual danger was
impending, and there was no other possibility of saving your life
except by taking that of another   But the law clearly says that
you shall have a stigma attached to you of killing a man if you
cannot prove you did so in self-defence   Ask yourselves if he
could not have saved his life in any other way than by shooting
Why did Pelser prod him on when he was walking slowly ?
When the natives say they saw the man going on, it is an
important fact, because Pelser has admitted it   If you do not
believe they saw what they say they saw, give him the benefit of
the doubt   Pelser started the prodding, and if in consequence
of this the Kafir turned round and faced him, he would be
justified in doing so , but Pelser would not be then guilty of
murder if the Kafir was in a position to kill and was going to do
so   But he must prove that he was in this position   If Pelser
went there to fine him and the Kafir resisted, it was a legal
resistance   Gentlemen, I have now told you what is the law, and
I have pointed out to you the various facts with regard to the
charge of murder, and you must form your own conclusions
If you believe Zachariah committed an illegal assault on Pelser,
and Pelser could not escape except by killing, you will find
him not guilty of murder   If you come to the other conclusion, and that is, that although Pelser had provoked this
man, that then Zachariah turned and assaulted him with
intent to kill, he was guilty of taking life but not of
murder   If you think it was only a crime of culpable homicide,
you will find that the plea of justification has not been proved
If it is not proved, you will then consider whether the defendant
commented fairly on the preliminary examination in using the
words   The words are contained in a long letter which has
been put before you in the plea of fair comment, and it is
important for you to bear every part of this letter in mind
The particulars on which this letter is written are these   After
the preliminary examination of the 20th and 27th of January,
there is the statement made by Pelser on the 11th February,
when the papers were forwarded to the Solicitor-General, and
on the 16th February he declined to prosecute   Then there
appeared in the *Mercury* on the 24th March an article which has
been read to you, and which purports to be a summary of the
preliminary examination taken by Mr Hay when he was in
Burghersdorp on a visit   In this summary it is stated   " Police
were sent for, but there is no evidence in support of this "   It is
said by the Crown that there is evidence of this   Another passage
which is objected to is where it says   " The production of the

revolver with one chamber empty and the Doctor's evidence fully completed the chain of proof " It is said that this summary is unfair, and that it contains statements which are liable to mislead the public If you think that he did try to mislead, and that he misled Mr Don into unwarily accepting the statements it will not excuse the defendant altogether But it is remarkable that no other portion of that summary is objected to Mr Solomon says this summary has nothing to do with the case, but I think it has, as it refers to this subject, and says "At Cathcart last Circuit, Mr Filmer was charged with shooting to frighten a native and wounding him in the hip, for which he was fined £30, but then he had the misfortune to be an English European farmer, and therefore had to stand his trial Our duty is done We might add to this bare statement the gossip of railway men and others, but we are content to leave the indisputable facts to the public The Premier has had much to say lately in defence of lawlessness, perhaps he knows something of this case We challenge the Government to publish the full text of the official record to disprove these extracts, which have been copied from those documents " Between the 24th March and the 14th April, the date on which Mr Don's letter appeared, notwithstanding this challenge nothing was done The Government, if doing its duty, would be foolish if it attended to everything that was said of it All Governments are attacked violently, and in this country we have party government and party politics, and those out of office try and find fault with those in office Therefore for the Government to take up every challenge would be absurd, and you would not expect them to do so Something has been said about the Government interfering, and the Solicitor-General has told you that they could not do so I may say for your information that the Attorney-General can take any prosecution at any time out of the hands of the Solicitor-General He could have interfered at any time, but there is no evidence that he has interfered in this case Some time ago, before the liberty of the press was defined and properly understood, it was supposed that preliminary examinations could not be published, but it is not so now After the Solicitor-General had declined to prosecute, every paper could publish the preliminary examination and comment upon it if the comment was fair It is said that if the comment it contains was unfair the Government could have taken action I do not say what the Government could or should have done, but Government did not publish the preliminary examination Nothing was done Mr Don then came forward and said, "I am a citizen I have made my home here, here I have to live, and what is done in this country affects more or less every man in it " We are not under a despotic government, and every man has a right to speak his opinion, provided it is honest and fair   He says, " There has been a prosecution abandoned, and there is abundant evidence to my mind for a prosecution on a charge of murder , and as the *Mercury* has asked the Government to publish the records of the preliminary examination and it has not done so, I assume that their summary is correct, and I have written this letter   'I read with painful interest an article in the *Cape Mercury* some weeks ago on the Pelser case, consisting mainly of evidence culled from the official records   It was plain from that evidence, indeed it was practically confessed by Pelser himself, that a foul crime had been perpetrated , and every right thinking person must have recognised it as a necessary consequence that Pelser should have been committed for trial   It seems, however, that the man is still at large and that the Government has declined to prosecute '" Then it goes on   " The statements in your article were such as the Government was bound to rebut and refute, or by silence be held to admit their truth and force   I have been looking anxiously for such explanation or defence of the action of the Government, such as it was its duty to the country as well as its interest to issue, if defence is possible, but none has appeared   I am reluctantly compelled to come to the conclusion that your statements are true, in short that our rulers have been influenced by political instead of such legal considerations as are alone applicable to the case   It may be safely assumed that if a white man had been the victim the murderer would not have been left untried and unpunished   Indeed it may be confidently affirmed that had the same thing happened in this District, the offender would have been brought to justice   But it would seem that in the District of Burghersdorp, if a Dutchman shoots a Kafir, the crime must be overlooked   Government refuses to do its duty, and the conscience of the whole community is offended "   Now is this an attack against Pelser, or against the Government? Does it not infer that he is appealing to the Government and saying   " I am anxious as a citizen that this matter should be looked into   I say he should have been put before a Judge and jury and tried   I do not say convicted   He committed a crime and he should have been tried by a jury "   If this part of the letter is not an attack upon Pelser, it is upon the Government, and all the motives are imputed to the Government, and the Government could have proceeded against him   It is for you to determine if the letter means an attack against Pelser, or upon Government, because it had not brought a criminal to justice Then it goes on   " I fully expected that when your article went forth through the country, especially after its statements remained unchallenged, the press would have taken up the question and compelled the Government to break silence, if not to alter its decision   But the press, with few exceptions, has paid no attention to the case   I confess I have met with nothing more disheartening for a long time than this immoral apathy in connection with such a grave business " Now what does this mean ? First he attacks the Government, and now the press Then he says " Is the matter to rest here ? Is nothing more to be said or done ? Is the Government to be permitted ignominiously to abdicate its functions in this fashion, and to offend the consciences of all not blinded by race prejudice, or party feeling ? " What does that mean ? Then it goes on " Even were the evidence against Pelser less damning than it seems to be, he himself admits a criminal act, whether murder or manslaughter, which ought to be dealt with in the prescribed and proper manner, tried by a Judge and jury in open Court, instead of settled off-hand by Solicitor-General or Attorney-General in a hole and corner fashion Nothing else can satisfy justice, not to speak of decency, and, I trust, nothing less will satisfy the country " Is this comment fair or unfair ? Is it unfair for a man after reading over the evidence that you have heard during the last four days, to say that Pelser should have been put in the dock and tried ? The law says whoever kills another is guilty until proved not to be Is this man to be let off because the natives say the native was a little behind him, and because it is said they could not see what actually occurred ? Was he justified in saying " If the evidence against Pelser was less damning than it seems to be," and so on What does this mean ? Does it mean " Have a trial for murder There ought to have been a prosecution—it never ought to have been abandoned " Then he says " I belong to no party I am not a politician I never was in Burghersdorp, I know nothing of its people, and never heard of Pelser before but am a member of the community, which has to bear the responsibility, in the last resort, of the Government's unchallenged acts, and a Minister of a religion which knows no distinction of race, caste, class, or colour, and my conscience refuses to put up silently with this offence " If he knew a crime had been committed, it was his duty not only his privilege, to point it out Does this mean " My conscience is not satisfied, and I condemn the Solicitor-General and the Government for not going on with the prosecution ? " Then come the words " ' What hast thou done ? The voice of thy brother's blood crieth unto me from the ground ' That poor man's blood cries to heaven, not merely against the wretched murderer, but against the Government which refuses to prosecute, and the country which condones such conduct I for my part will have no share in this responsibility Therefore to clear my own conscience I solemnly protest, in the name of God, of law, justice, and order against the manner in which this foul crime has been dealt with " Now, gentlemen, here are the words complained of I have told you how the letter bears upon one different thing after another First the Government, then the press, then the country's immoral apathy, then that there should be a trial Does this letter simply mean this "I tell you after reading the records what my opinion is If the Crown had prosecuted on a charge of culpable homicide or murder, I should have been satisfied I conclude there is no evidence of self-defence I express my opinion, and this is it" Did he wish to malign the Government because he was a party man, did he wish to malign the press because he had a grudge against it, or did he mean to show that there had been a killing which he thought was murder, and that it should have been tried? The law says, a man has a character which is a valuable possession If the words are true, then there is no injury to Pelser because he has no character Then if he is not a murderer, there is another ingredient which the law says must be satisfied before there can be a conviction,—that is, did defendant intend to injure? Has he brought forward facts showing that he did not intend to injure, or has he brought forward facts proving that he was justified in coming to the conclusion that a murder had been committed after reading the preliminary examination which was public property? There is a further requirement, and that is, that the comment should be honest and fair The administration of justice in a free country is of universal interest, and is aided by publicity and comment, but then, in commenting, honesty and fairness must be preserved It is not expected that comments which are fair and honest shall agree or be infallible Fair and honest men may, even while acting fairly, arrive at different conclusions A righteous judgment may even be biased without the slightest reflection on his good faith, and therefore if his comments were fair, no one has a right to complain This is the substance of what Lord Chief Justice Cockburn has stated to be the law of England, as it may be said to have recently grown to This immunity rests upon a two-fold ground, first, because malice is the gist of the offence of libel, and although presumed to accompany a wrongful act, that presumption may be rebutted by the circumstances or occasion Secondly, because the advantage to the community from publicity being given to the proceedings of Courts of justice and fair comments thereon is so great that the occasional inconvenience to individuals arising from it, must yield to general good As long as you do not impute motives to a Judge or any public official you have a right to comment on their acts After you leave the jury-box, your verdict, gentlemen, can be commented on one way or the other in the way I have said After the Solicitor-General has declined to prosecute in any case, it becomes public property, and it can be commented upon, and if the proceedings seemed to show that a wrong had been done comment may be severe provided it be honest and fair, and a reasonable degree of judgment exercised in that comment If it does not impute motives it must not be taken that strong language is in itself too strong for the occasion, nor must it be taken to show that there is malice or unfairness when the letter taken altogether shows that the object of the letter is not to malign but to aid the Government, or the administration of justice In conclusion, gentlemen, I ask you to consider first—Are the words libellous? Would they be libellous if there was nothing said in defence? I think they would, but they would not be libellous if they were true Is there evidence to show that there was murder? If there is no evidence to prove that Pelser killed in self-defence, is there evidence to prove that he is a murderer? If you think that something happened, and from that cause the native rushed upon Pelser in order to kill him, you may possibly find there was culpable homicide If you come to the conclusion that murder is not proved, but culpable homicide has been, and that if murder has not been proved that there is still sufficient evidence before you to satisfy a reasonable man to come to the conclusion that there was murder, you will find, not that Pelser is guilty of murder, but that Mr Don is perfectly justified in coming to such a conclusion If you think the Crown has proved to your satisfaction that Pelser is not a murderer, and that the Crown has proved that Don acted maliciously in using these words, and that it was not an honest and fair comment, then you will find Don guilty of this charge I don't know that I have anything more to say You have heard from the defendant's Counsel a brilliant address, and I am sure you must be pleased to find that such addresses can come from the Bar I stopped Mr Solomon once or twice when he travelled outside the issue, but with this exception there is nothing that he did say which was unfair, or not to be admired The Solicitor-General has put before you every point that he could possibly urge on the part of the prosecution It is now for you to say whether Pelser has been injured at all or whether he has been maliciously injured by the defendant

The learned Judge closed his address at 3 15 p m when the Jury retired At 4 45 p m the Judge requested the jury to be sent for as they had not agreed, and asked them if he could enlighten them on any point One of the jurymen (Mr Smith) asked his Lordship to explain the law on murder and culpable homicide, and he did so in the same terms as those used in his summing up The jury then retired again At a quarter past six the jury filed into the box, and the Registrar asked them if they had agreed on their verdict The Court was densely packed, and a breathless silence prevailed when the foreman pronounced a verdict of " Not Guilty " Hardly had the words escaped from the foreman's mouth when the building re-echoed with a burst of spontaneous applause After this had subsided his Lordship said " Mr Don, a verdict of not guilty has been returned , you are discharged You have the satisfaction of knowing that the principles for which you have contended have been established (To the Jury) Gentlemen, I thank you for your patience, and am sorry the case occupied so much of your time, but it was important "

Mr Don was congratulated upon his victory by many persons in Court and as he left the building he was cheered The Court house was soon deserted, and thus ended a trial that has caused intense excitement throughout the Colony

WAITING FOR THE VERDICT

(*The Journal*)

The case of Regina *vs* Don had passed by steady stages from one stirring scene to another For three days the trial had dragged its long, slow length, and yet there was no weariness about it One witness after another came forward and passed through the ordeal of examination and cross-examination Some of them seemed to tremble at the prospect of answering the sharp, rapid questions put by that boyish-looking barrister for the defendant, whose brilliant eye seemed to look through the man who stood forward to describe what he had seen of that terrible tragedy enacted in the broad light of God's sun The last witness had given his evidence He was one named Man, *a valuable* witness for the Crown When he had finished, as it was Saturday evening, the Court adjourned, so that mens' hearts might be soothed and stilled by a Sabbath's rest

Monday morning came, and soon the Court was crowded The Judge President looked stronger than ever, and more dignified, there was about him a bearing as if he was conscious that the eyes of men here and afar were watching his demeanour The jury had lost the jaded appearance they wore on Saturday evening Looking down at the benches, the barristers, robed, came trooping in one after another, very bright and cheery, and greeting each other with that hearty friendliness which is such a marked characteristic of the profession to which they belong The Advocate for the defence was sprightly and merry among his group of friends and admirers All this, however, was suddenly brought to a close by the Registrar of the Court reading over the names of the jurymen Then followed the address of the Public Prosecutor He had evidently mastered his case, and had now detected its weak points, and was conscious that he had a formidable task before him His voice was at times tremulous, and now and then the hesitancy with which he spoke, as well as the strange quivering of the piece of paper which he held in his hand, indicated that his heart was beating above its ordinary pulsations He did his best At times there was scorn in the tones of his voice, as when he referred to the native schoolmaster Alfred Peters Then there was supreme contempt when he suggested that the native witnesses had got up this as a conspiracy All through, the bearing of the Crown Prosecutor

T

was that of a man who was only half-hearted in his address He made long quotations from ponderous tomes, endeavouring to instruct the jurymen They listened stolidly, and as he closed, it was remarkable that he made no appeal whatever to the jury It was at this point and by this fact that his true character came out, for as every one knows he is right at heart, whatever may have been this singular episode in his official career

No sooner did the Crown Prosecutor resume his seat than Mr Solomon rose to his feet There was breathless stillness in the Court There was no flurry or restless anxiety about him The long-looked for moment had come, when he would be free to speak the traditional sentiments of his nature The very first sentences he uttered told The Judge's eyes were riveted upon the young Advocate There were no whisperings anywhere now Note-writers ceased scribbling missives one to another All interest was concentrated upon the speaker There was no faltering, no hesitation, about him With logical clearness, and yet with burning eloquence he proceeded from one point to another, making it evident that he had never before to conduct a case which from first to last was in fuller accordance with his sympathies than this With convincing power he showed that this prosecution of his client was not in accordance with the principles of justice which have established the rule of "our Lady the Queen" He spoke as an Englishman, as one who gloried in the freedom of bearing that honoured name He described in graphic language the significance of this trial, that it tampered with the liberties of free-born English citizens, and he pointed out to the jury the results which would follow if they gave a verdict such as would be unfavourable to his client And as he concluded perhaps the very ablest and most eloquent speech which was ever spoken in this colony before a Judge and Jury, his hearers felt that the Cape Colony ought to be proud of having as one of its sons, Mr Advocate Solomon

Then followed the Judge's charge to the jury It was long It was minute It was clear as a sunbeam It showed the marvellous acuteness of that vigorous brain The Judge President has the reputation of being a first-class lawyer, and the foremost man probably among his brethren In fact if there had been a man present who had any suspicion whatever as to his abilities, all such impressions must certainly have been dissipated yesterday, for he rose to the occasion His charge was bold, trenchant and fearless Certainly, the universal verdict must be with reference to that charge, that it was dignified, honest and true, and every lover of justice must thank God that the President of the Eastern Districts' Court at this critical period of the history of our colony is a man who is not afraid to deal out even-handed justice The summing-up was so clear, that it was with some considerable astonishment that the Jury were heard to ask to retire. And as they did so the lash of the Judge President must have been acutely felt by one who had been seated in the Court, and who ought to have been the man tried

And now that they have retired to deliberate, there is time to glance around and note the various personages who have been in the Court He who had been called "the prisoner," at the commencement of the proceedings by the Crown Prosecutor, sat with great dignity immediately behind his counsel, as indeed all through the ordeal he had comported himself as a man of sterling worth Beside him were several clerical friends and sympathisers, conspicuous among whom was the Rev Dr Stewart of Lovedale, the embodiment of strength, noting doubtless some facts which men may yet hear when occasion requires Then here and there were to be seen representative men Here, side by side, sat the true friends of the accused, Messrs Weir and Peacock, of King William's Town, who had come to testify their confidence in the man who had dared to be singular Before them was the Civil Commissioner's Clerk of Burghersdorp, tall and handsome, a man morever, whose conduct in the witness-box showed that we have in the Civil Service men of solid worth, who are not afraid to do their duty The very tones of his voice, rich and sonorous, as he gave his evidence, will not soon be forgotten Immediately to the right of Mr Solomon is a young barrister of ruddy complexion From the commencement he has been using his pen, now, for the first time, he sits erect, and his features are seen to advantage He has a massive head That is the Junior Counsel for the defendant—Mr Advocate Frames, a most promising member of the bar, and withal a distinguished scholar On the opposite side of the barristers' table, seated on a chair facing the audience sideways, is the delinquent editor of the *Cape Mercury*, which was so contemptuously spoken of by the Crown Prosecutor in his address to the jury That is Mr George Hay, a mere stripling to be sure, but nevertheless a man of some power, else he could not have dared to unearth this whole case He is so quiet and modest looking that no one would suppose that he would for one moment venture for the sake of justice to make a martyr of himself There, looking towards the Counsel for the defendant, and to his left, is seated a young man, pale-faced, with jet black hair His eyes resemble black diamonds, so bright, clear, and penetrating are they He is clearly a great favourite He sits there with heavy topcoat on, showing that he is in very delicate health Who is he? That is Richard Rose-Innes, second son of the Under-Secretary for Native Affairs, and the Attorney for the defence It is he who has wrought up this case from the beginning, who when the injustice perpetrated was first heard of, wrote a short letter crying for "more light and air" He has the satisfaction of having got it, and now that it is being given he every now and then casts a furtive glance around, as if to discover whether his fellow-colonists had got what he had wanted for them. He is the soul of honour, and though the Crown Prosecutor when wildly clutching at every straw to save his favourite tried to cast insinuations upon him, the Judge President scattered all these to the winds, and showed other men that Richard Innes' conduct of this case cannot be impeached. But who is this, about whom such a fuss is made by the chief constable, who has a chair placed for him amid the rattling noise of a cumbrous sword? He is evidently some great personage. As one turns and looks in the direction whence the noise comes, the hero of the moment is seen to be none other than the hon. member for Victoria East, the intelligent exponent of farmers' grievances. Whether he has come out of sympathy for the accused, or whether he is a dear friend of the accuser, it were vain to say. The judge's charge, however, must have given him some fresh knowledge for he has a receptive mind, and it will doubtless be wisely used within the House of Assembly.

Looking over the audience, there are local celebrities belonging to the clerical, medical, and legal professions. The editors of the various newspapers are present also, watching the whole case with keenest interest, for the liberty of the press is endangered. The clerical gentlemen no doubt are deeply interested about their brother, still none of them seem to be anxious. They talk and joke with doctors and barristers, and one would like to know what sparks of wit those are which convulse one group of friends after another. There is a general hum within the court.

Looking up to the gallery it is seen to be crowded with ladies who have graced the court with their presence. They all have papers before them, somewhat similar in size to those which were put into the hands of the jurymen. Surely there must be some very momentous interests at stake when ladies are found sitting so patiently, hour after hour, in such a heated atmosphere. It is for them to describe the cause of their presence.

Five o'clock comes. There has been no adjournment of the Court. At last the Judge sends for the jury to enquire if he can give them any further light. One of them, clearly an intelligent gentleman by his appearance, asks in return if it is permissible to state how far they are agreed. The Judge President checks the proffered information at once, but then the secret comes out. A burly-looking juryman, proud of the position he occupies, probably for the first time in his life, and desirous to prolong the post for himself as long as possible, asks a question which from a little distance sounds something like "What is the law with reference to homicide, and that with reference to murder?" All the other jurymen seem to breathe freely—why, it is impossible to say. But nothing ruffled, and knowing evidently that human nature is human nature, and that brains cannot be made out of shavings, the Judge proceeds, as if instructing a school-boy, to state that homicide *is* murder, unless the perpetrator can show any mitigation or justification. Again asks the juryman "Supposing this were found not to be murder, but something short of it, is a man entitled to call another, and write about him in the papers, as a murderer?" More patient still, the judge replies 'He is, if a murder has been committed." And then, with even still greater simplicity and minuteness, he goes on to teach the juryman who, for the moment, is the judge in this all-absorbing case of Regina *vs* Don.

The audience waits to see the result. But no impression whatever has been produced upon this juryman. The whole matter must be debated over again in the Library, so they ask to retire, and the Court adjourns until a quarter past six o'clock in the evening.

As that hour approaches, the steps of the Eastern Districts' Court are crowded with a motley assemblage. The whole street is astir. Cabs, phaetons and carriages come rolling up to the great centre of attraction. The side-walks are full of pedestrians hastening to the scene. The evening is bright, clear, and warm, not a cloud is to be seen in the sky.

At last the door is opened, and in a few minutes the whole Court-house is packed, the galleries being besieged by ladies. All are there except Advocate Solomon. He has gone to prepare for a long journey, and leaves by evening train. He who ought to have been the prisoner is also not to be seen anywhere in the Court-house. Why, can only be conjectured. The address of the defending barrister, as also the summing up of the judge must have completely crushed out of him any spirit which may have carried him through the ordeal up to this point. There is a pushing and hustling from the door of the Library. It is the jury returning. Slowly, one after another they file into their box, and take their seats. As one looks at them they all appear to be honest Englishmen who cannot and will not bring dishonour upon Graham's Town, and yet as the last of them takes his seat, there is speculation still as to the result. The Judge President appears. The Court crier with stentorian lungs shouts aloud something which ought to be "Oyez!" but which sounds like "Silence." There is no need for the old time-worn custom to be repeated on this occasion, for instinctively all who were seated rise to pay customary honour to the personification of justice, and there is subdued silence in the Court-house. The Judge takes his seat. The names of the jury are called. They answer one after another. Every ear is strained, every eye looks towards those nine Englishmen who have sworn to do their duty to God and man. The expression on the Judge's countenance can never be described It speaks volumes It betrays a high-souled man trembling for the fate of the scales of justice which he has balanced so evenly Then comes the last, the crucial question, the one to which all this long case had pointed Gentlemen of the jury, is the prisoner guilty or not guilty ? *Two* words fall from the foreman, only *two* What are they ? *Not Guilty !* Such a burst of applause breaks out throughout the Court house as had never been heard before It is not suppressed It is the universal assent of true-born Britons to the fact that one man had dared to stand forth and vindicate, at a terrible cost, and at the peril of being cast into a felon's cell, the principles of truth and justice and the sacredness of the life of all who claim to be the subjects of our Gracious Sovereign Queen Victoria The Judge's features alter, the solemn sternness vanishes There are unexpressed thoughts in his soul The accused is called to stand, and he is told calmly the result, and a sentence or two is added indicating that the object for which he had been prepared to become a martyr is gained Thus the Pelser case is ended, and the prophecy which the manslayer himself had uttered is fulfilled, " I am in for a row "

The Rev Mr Don is seen emerging from the back of the Court-house in company with clerical friends It was characteristic of the man, of his humility, his modesty, and his calm dignity As the great crowd outside sees him walking quietly towards the telegraph office, a ringing cheer is raised which sounds loud and clear, as coming from English lips and hearts He lifts his hat in acknowledgement Justice has been vindicated, and a British jury have given a verdict which, as the sun set, was flashed over the whole Colony, significant of the fact that the liberties of British citizens cannot be invaded or tampered with Doubtless in many a home that night there was a feeling that Grahamstown's character was not tarnished, but that on the contrary in a critical moment of our colonial history she had taught lessons which never will be forgotten

VINDICATED

PUBLIC WELCOME TO THE REV JOHN DAVIDSON DON

> " The baleful dregs
> Of these late ages, this inglorious draught
> Of servitude and folly, have not yet,
> Blest be th' Eternal Ruler of the world !
> Defil'd to such a depth of sordid shame
> The native honours of the human soul,
> Nor so effac'd the image of its sire "

The Eastern Frontier of this Colony has had enough of " dark and bloody history ! " and the advance of civilisation enables pertinent exception to be taken to any efforts to make that history repeat itself   In the annals of our " Great Trials " one of its brightest records will be the victory achieved by " the native honours of the human soul " in the notorious Pelser Case, as it presented itself this month before the Eastern Districts' Court in the trial Regina *versus* J D Don, at Grahamstown   This community, consequent upon the action of two of its prominent members, was deeply interested in the result, at the eleventh hour legal acumen resolved upon the prosecution of only one person for the alleged libel , this individuality probably increased the interest of the townspeople in the case, and the verdict achieved on Monday evening last was sincerely welcomed by all   It was at once decided to do honour to one who had suffered much for expressing his convictions , the " hero of the hour " could not, however, arrive until Friday afternoon, and this delay was fortunate, as it enabled preparations to be completed   Yesterday evening, at six o'clock, was the hour appointed for the arrival of the Royal Mail cart from Grahamstown, and by it the Rev J D Don was a passenger The arrangements here took the form of presentation of addresses on the Market Square, immediately opposite to the Town Hall, the balcony of which was set apart for the accommodation of ladies   At half-past five this place was comfortably occupied, at six o'clock it was crowded   The commodious Square was dotted by groups of male adults whiling the time away in gossip, Maclean Street, opposite the Town Hall, held a large crowd of Native spectators   Shortly after five o'clock a number of well-filled vehicles, and many horsemen were to be seen passing westward of the Buffalo River in order to meet the Rev Mr Don at the Borough boundary, and form a cavalcade into town   At the outspan were a number of natives, principally school children, who made the welkin ring with their melodious voices in songs of joy   Soon the Royal Mail was sighted, but for a time the spectators were unable to comprehend what was the dark mass following behind   It proved to be a troop of native horsemen, who had ridden out as far as Crowe's (sixteen miles) to greet one who, in this trial, had championed their race!   On arriving at the boundary, greetings were exchanged with many friends, then the Rev J D Don took his seat in a private conveyance which had been provided for him, the cortege was formed up, and all proceeded towards the town at a spanking pace   Their approach was heralded by two native horsemen, one of whom carried his many-coloured handkerchief tied to a kerrie as a flag!   Remember that to them this demonstration was a Runnymede   The Royal Mail appeared, the head gear of the horses being decked with little bannerettes in red, white, and blue, a flag with the same colours flying at the back   People crowded forward to greet their townsman upon his return, but they were disappointed, the cart had only the mails and its driver   A rush back was made to the square again, and in a few minutes the "hero of the hour" arrived, being preceded by the Mayor's carriage, and two or three other vehicles   There was a waving of handkerchiefs from the balcony, and when Mr Don alighted he was accorded three lusty British cheers, which were followed by three others equally hearty for Attorney R W Rose-Innes, who the public anticipated had alighted with the Rev gentleman   It is a matter for regret, however, that Mr Innes was not present to acknowledge this mark of public appreciation of his skill towards winning the victory, unfortunately he was taken ill on the road, and had to be left at Crowe's hotel   When the excitement had subsided, the Mayor, Mr D T Hockly, proceeded to read the following address —

" To the Rev John Davidson Don, Presbyterian Minister, St
Andrew's Church, King William's Town, South Africa

Sir,—We, the undersigned inhabitants of King William's Town, have come to meet you on this occasion to give you a hearty welcome on your return among us, and to express the deep sympathy we have felt with you during the ordeal through which you have just passed   We, wish further, as far as it is in the power of your fellow-townsmen, to do honour to the courage with which you called attention to, and vindicated, the great principles of justice, so dear to right-thinking men of every nation

You have, both in your letter, and by your legal representative, protested that you have not in any way been influenced by political motives,   We, therefore, who are here to welcome you, come without any political feeling, and indeed have among us men of various shades of political opinion, but we wish most earnestly to express our hope that the great victory which you have gained will reap its legitimate fruits

At a time when the country seemed willing to rest in apathy, in connection with this matter, your voice was raised in unmistakable tones Some may have thought your language too strong, the event, however, has fully justified you, for it has proved your keen appreciation of what was necessary to bring matters to the right issue, and the careful manner in which you had studied the facts of the case before you spoke out

In conclusion, we would thank Almighty God, for having placed among us a man enjoying the responsible position to which you are called, who is endowed with a true perception of the high duties of citizenship, such a power of eloquence with which to enforce them, and such noble courage to stand or fall by what you believe to be right "

The address, worked upon vellum, is a high-class specimen of the printer's art The type used is known to the trade as two-line pica Pasen Script A pretty combination floral border, printed in gold, surrounds it, being supported by a thick red rule outside, with a thin red rule inside; the body of the address being printed in the dark blue ink The signatures which follow occupy eight sheets, and number about eight hundred names

Mr Don was about to reply, when the Mayor informed him that the Natives were desirous of also presenting him with an address, and had deputed a representative to do so At his Worship's request Mr J Tengo-Jabavu (editor of the *Imvo Zabantsundu (Native Opinion)*, then stepped forward, and read the following —

"To the Rev John Davidson Don, Presbyterian Minister St Andrew's Church, King William's Town, South Africa

Reverend and Dear Sir,— We cannot allow the occasion of your triumphant return to the sphere of your labour to pass without expressing to you the deep debt of gratitude which we all owe to you as a race We congratulate you on the issue of the matters laid to your charge, we heartily thank you for this herculean struggle in the sacred cause of Truth and Justice, and we cannot but admire and love you for the anguish of soul and sore trouble which you have had to endure to regain that precious fair-dealing (if but in words), which was, by a strong arm, being wrested from us of colour

It has now been made clear to all the world that the man who wantonly shot a Native, in a British Colony, and killed him, has been openly and boldly denounced as a murderer, and that, although the legal adviser of the Crown had declined to prosecute him, but prosecuted, or rather persecuted, him who protested, the Judges have acquitted the denouncer, and showed that he was justified in his criticism of public conduct It is not for us now, as is our custom, to ask the news as to how and what is to be done with the murderer Our duty here to-day is simply to rejoice that you are safely returned to our midst by the Providence of Him who rides over the storms and bids the surging elements to do His will We are grateful to think that in these days when prejudice seems to be getting the upper hand over Justice and good government, you have been the means of rousing that spirit of fair-play, which has won and achieved Empires that last, and we rejoice further that, as an Ambassador of Christ, and Minister of the mysteries of His Gospel, you have practically, and with all boldness, preached, under great persecutions, that which the holy and noble army of your predecessors have announced before you in this Land, viz "Thou shalt love thy neighbour as thyself" This, the triumph of your act, has allayed our suspicions as to the soundness of the system of Government, it has subdued our excitement and alarm, which had reached their utmost tension, and it has grounded and re-established the faith of the wavering, who had begun to fear that even religion itself was but a political dodge intended to weaken the minds of men into submission

Finally, we beg to assure you that our sympathy for you was deep and not feigned, that our anxiety as to the result you can imagine, for on it depended the fate of us all as a race, and that our joy is now unbounded And now that the strife is over, and you are returned to follow the life that now is, we humbly wish you God-speed, that as heretofore, you will not forget that we are the burden that is 'on thee laid and must bear, now with gladness, now with courage, till at a hereafter, when these thy labours shall with endless gifts be paid, and in everlasting glory, then with brightness be arrayed'

In conclusion, we beg to assure you that the sentiments herein expressed are not only on our behalf as Natives of King William's Town exclusively, but also on behalf of our countrymen throughout South Africa,—We are, Reverend and Dear Sir, yours most sincerely"

The speaker continuing, said The work was still in the hands of the printers, but he would hand to Mr Don this proof copy

The Rev J D Don said —Mr Mayor, Mr Jabavu, ladies and gentlemen, friends and fellow-citizens, - I thank you heartily for these gratifying addresses, and for this magnificent reception When I left town a fortnight ago, not knowing how long I should be away, I little thought that my return would be in this fashion Though I know and appreciate your kindly feelings towards myself, I should be foolish indeed if I took this as a tribute to myself personally, and not rather to the principles with which I have been identified, and which it has been my good fortune at this time to vindicate Indeed, I have felt, all through this business, that the *personal* aspect of it was altogether secondary I have done nothing remarkable I simply followed the dictates of conscience, without regard to consequences The outlook was sometimes dark, but I never hesitated or doubted the rightness of my action, or swerved from the cause on which I had entered, being sure that, because right, it would lead to a good issue I knew the risk, and was quite willing to go to prison, indeed, last Monday morning, I packed my portmanteau lest I should have to sleep elsewhere that night Even with this in view I considered that a great victory had been gained when the Judge President's summing-up of the evidence and charge to the jury was finished, no matter what the verdict might be I trust that noble charge will be read and studied throughout this land, for it contains an instructive statement of the law applicable to the case and a wholesome vindication of the right of free, honest speech and criticism, as well of the great principles at stake It was the proudest moment of my life when the Judge President addressed these words to me from the Bench "You have the satisfaction of knowing that the principles for which you have contended have been established" These were, the *sacredness of human life*, the *equality of all before the law*, and the *purity of the administration of justice* The vindication and maintenance of these principles is of vast moment, for the country not only now, but in the distant future It is only thus that the white and black races which exist here side by side can preserve a satisfactory relation to each other, working together, and each contributing its share to promote the prosperity of the country If these are jealously maintained and faithfully observed, there is no reason why there should not be that harmony which is necessary to the comfort and well-being of both That the country should recognise the great significance of the vindication of these principles, and rejoice in the result is a satisfactory and hopeful sign This is shown by the magnificent demonstration you have made, by the enthusiasm with which the verdict was received in Grahamstown, by the comments of the larger part of the press, and by the showers of telegrams I have received from all parts I thank the senders of these cheering tokens with all my heart They came in large numbers from Cape Town as well as King William's Town, from Somerset East, and none was more significant or more welcome than one from " Lovers of Justice at Burghersdorp " I have always said and it is now generally recognised, that my action had nothing to do with politics I was most thankful that the Judge President brought this out so clearly and fully in the exposition of my letter which he gave in his charge He apprehended my meaning at every point, and understood exactly my position I myself could not have explained my aim and meaning more truly and satisfactory to myself, had I been commenting on my own letter For this also I owe him a debt of gratitude The non-political character of my attitude being understood, there is one thing which I trust I may say without offence Let politicians of every colour, let statesmen and administrators of whatever party take note that *conscience* is a power, let them beware of coming into collision with conscience If one man's conscience is offended by public acts, that conscience may rouse thousands and tens of thousands of others, and the roused conscience of a community acquires irresistible force One may say of it that on "Whomsoever that stone shall fall, it will grind him to powder" To my Native friends and sympathisers, whose admirable address I highly appreciate, I would say that the profound interest they have shown in my case has deeply touched me The wide extent of their acquaintance with what was going on, and their appreciation of the significance of these proceedings for themselves and their children has surprised, but not astonished me Their intense sympathy with my position at Graham's Town as a prisoner on their behalf, and their joy in our common triumph, shown on the day of verdict, and to-day along the road, have gone to my heart Let them take note of this, that a large part of the white population of this country rejoice in the vindication of these principles as well they, are ready to do them justice, and desirous of living in harmony with them Let them take courage to face the future, to do the right, to abstain from what causes irritation and loss, and to work along with the white inhabitants for the common good There is one circumstance which damps our pleasure on this joyous occasion The absence of Mr Innes, to whom, under God, so much is due in connection with this result No man would have rejoiced more to be here, but he lies on sick bed, where I saw him three hours ago We sympathise with him deeply, and pray that he may be soon restored, and again take his place among us With heart full of gratitude to Almighty God, again I thank you all for your great kindness to me to-day

Three cheers were then given for the Rev J D Don, handkerchiefs were again waved from the balcony, the native children formed up on Market Square started singing, and the crowd dispersed Everyone seemed well pleased at so auspicious an ending to a grievous event What transpired on the 20th of November will long remain fresh and green in the community —
Cape Mercury

OPINIONS OF THE PRESS.

THE PELSER CASE

(The Cape Argus)

No case that has been tried in the Colonial Law Courts for some months has been watched with the interest that has followed the Pelser libel case through its curious history. It is apparent even from the brief telegraphic report of the concluding passages of the trial, that the verdict was no foregone conclusion, and that the case has been as fairly tried as either plaintiff or defendant could desire. A Grahamstown jury is as far removed from sympathy with Burghersdorp as from a leaning towards King William's Town; the learned Judge President at any rate allowed himself full time for impartiality, seeing that he occupied two hours in his summing-up, while the jury took so long to consider their verdict that the question evidently was keenly debated in the jury-room; and with all these evidences of fairness and an absence of popular passion, the jury found that the circumstances of the Pelser case justified the Reverend defendant in using the language of burning indignation published in the *Cape Mercury*. There has been some comment upon the conduct of Mr Maasdorp in conducting the prosecution. Such conduct was anything but seemly, seeing that it was pretty generally recognised that it was the Solicitor-General far more than Mr Pelser who was on his trial. We do not for a moment set ourselves to decide the awful question of whether Mr Pelser's life is justly forfeit for the act that he committed. It might be that, if he had been brought to trial a jury would have held that while he was not absolutely the murderer, which Mr Don's words implied, he was guilty of culpable homicide. The public scandal, which will now remain, is that the Solicitor-General's action in staying proceedings prevented the question being brought to the test. There never was a clearer case for trial; and as Mr Maasdorp chose to write to Mr Upington, assuming the entire responsibility for the course which he took, upon his head is the blame and disgrace of the failure of justice in the original case. It is to be hoped that the case will not be allowed to remain where it is. It would not be seemly to submit Mr Pelser to trial after the Crown has declined to proceed against him, for there should be no vacillation about the serious procedure of the administration of justice, but we trust that the next session of Parliament will not be allowed to go by without Mr Maasdorp being called to account, through the Ministers who, having gladly sanctioned his proceedings, are equally responsible with himself

There is another aspect of the case, scarcely less important How seriously all liberty of comment which is the very breath of a free community, has been imperilled by the mischievous use made of a statute certainly never destined to stifle free discussion, we need scarcely remind our readers Usually the question has been raised as one of the liberty to be allowed to the Press, but in this case, owing to the hap-hazard decision at the eleventh hour not to prosecute Mr Hay, the question is a little removed from the ordinary line We regard it as of none the less importance There are too few citizens such as Mr Don, ready manfully to speak out what they believe to be the solemn truth, and to take the consequences There are plenty of informers, glad enough to use the machinery of the Press for the exposure of abuses, but they always expect the newspaper proprietor to bear the whole burden of responsibility for the statements made They may be infinitely better able to bear the brunt of an action, better able to afford resistance to the detestable little acts of boycotting which, in "our small community," as we apolegetic-ally term it, are only too likely to follow from the simplest mention in print of that which is already in everyone's mouth, but the sole condition on which they will lend themselves to an attack on some monstrous commercial swindle or piece of administrative corruption, is, that on no account shall their name be divulged—that is to say, that the newspaper proprietor is to take the undivided danger Half the sympathy of the right-minded public is thus alienated The peril of disgraceful imprisonment, or a ruinous fine and costs, comes to be regarded as a business risk with the journalist, all in the way of his calling, whereas, if he had a leading lawyer, or merchant, or politician by his side in the dock, the public would soon find out that a vital question of social liberty was at stake Many a rotten concern has been propped up for years, to the ultimate ruin of the widow and orphan, many a fair-faced swindle in public life allowed to go on unchecked, because of the lamentable want of moral courage, which we are bound to say is the badge of too many men who profess to occupy a leading position amongst their fellow colonists Here is a minister, not very likely to be blessed with considerable worldly means, who has shamed us all, stood the test of his conduct and, after months of anxiety, come out triumphant We do not know how Mr Don stands with regard to costs—as far as the Government can avoid it, his prosecution should not have cost him a farthing—but if he is the sufferer in pocket, every colonist who does not want to live under an intolerable oligarchy owes it to him that his expenses should be made good to him, with something more if it be possible If any movement of the kind is made, we trust it will be heartily supported

---

THE TRIUMPH OF TRUTH

(The Cape Mercury)

The cheers which shook the dusty old coat of arms above the bench of the Eastern Districts' Court, and re-echoed from the recesses of that quaint old building on Monday evening, proved the correctness of the firmly held belief that in the last resort, the sense of honour and justice in the breast of every Briton may be depended on in the cause of law, order, and true liberty— that liberty which binds every man to do to others as he would be done by Once more, when the test has been applied, those living principles, which alone can make a nation great, have been upheld, and their champion in the person of the Rev J D Don completely vindicated During the past week the Pelser libel case has been the topic of discussion amongst thousands of colonists Everybody knows the story now—how a native was done to death by a shot in the back—how Mr Don stood manfully forward and characterised the deed as a foul crime— how Pelser obtained the fiat of the Attorney-General, putting in force the machinery of an unjust act, and arraigned a Christian Minister before a legal tribunal, which, after every point of the case was exhausted during four days, affirmed that in terming Pelser a wretched murderer under the circumstances, the truth had been spoken To the law Pelser appealed, and the law condemned him There can be no desire to torture the vanquished, and we refrain from saying a single word which could be construed into a howl of triumph over one whom we pity from the bottom of our heart Those who watched Pelser's face on the last day of the trial could have no other feeling, and whether he be tried for the crime or allowed to go free, the punishment of remorse must be greater to him than any mere physical degradation No one who saw that most wretched attempt to explain away the deed will ever forget it—the scene was unique There was one man, however, we believe, who felt it more keenly than Pelser, the one who, by his own confession, alone stands responsible for a gross miscarriage of justice, and whose instincts of honour must have reproached him as point after point was proved, and theory after theory was cut from his grasp, bringing out plainly the fact that he was—probably unwillingly and unwittingly—the advocate of lawlessness and disorder when the calling of his responsible position required his ability and energy to be on the side of justice and truth The Solicitor-General is not moulded in the Pelser form, and we cannot think otherwise than that the iron entered his soul when he remembered that the worry, anxiety, and expense forced upon Mr Don and ourselves, as well as the fact that Pelser had escaped his just trial, were the results of his mistake We are not going to treat him as he treated us in a place where we were powerless to reply, and taunt him with cheap sarcasm, because we hope never again will it be possible to lay the blame of miscarriage of justice at his door To finish with this aspect of the affair, let us say that we never did believe Mr Maasdorp to be blameworthy until he insisted that he, and he alone, was responsible for declining to prosecute

The case itself was so fully proved by the accused himself and the medical testimony, that had Pelser been in the place of Mr Don he could not have fearlessly awaited the slow flight of the hours that told of the jury being engaged in keen discussion The complete trial, with the full speeches of the Crown Prosecutor and Counsel, with the summing-up of the Judge President, will be published in pamphlet form, and we need only say here that the speech of Mr Solomon for the defence, was distinguished by a brilliancy which drew from Sir Jacob Barry the highest praise The charge of his Lordship to the jury was a masterly handling of the whole case, and when circulated is calculated to do a vast deal of good For nearly three hours his exhaustive analysis proceeded, and the treatment of the letter written by Mr Don was an eulogy of his motives, which, in itself, apart from the acquittal, was a complete victory

It must not be supposed that this case has merely justified Mr Don, condemned Pelser, and vindicated the liberty of the press, it marks a turning point in colonial history, indicating that the extreme swing of the pendulum towards lawlessness has been reached, and the return commenced to more peaceful ways The issue of this case is not seen by the supporters of unchecked shooting, but those who have the wisdom to "look into the future, far as human eye can see" know that the limit of safety has been reached and that the native is rapidly learning the value that is placed on the sacredness of life, and the lesson will find hideous expression on hidden pathways and lonely farms The writing is on the wall, but we trust that Mr Don's brave action will avert the evil threatened, and throughout this country all men will learn that every life has to be accounted for with an explanation that will satisfy justice

The cost at which the victory has been gained can never be fully understood by those who have not experienced the costliness and anxiety associated with the uncertainties of law, but the result has been worthy of it all, for what was said of Turkey is true of us—"The people are better than their rulers" Whatever the shortcomings of the Government or officers of the Crown charged with the administration of justice, when an appeal is made to the people themselves, all that we hold dear as principles of existence will be supported by the dictates of honesty and truth

---

THE PELSER LIBEL CASE

(The Journal)

The Pelser libel case terminated yesterday in a verdict of *Not Guilty*, so that the Jury held the Rev J D Don fully justified in the unsparing censure which he published, both against the wretched man who committed the crime, and against the system of justice that connived at his escape from punishment That verdict was confidently expected by all who had heard the evidence which was brought forward during the trial We think, indeed, that nothing further was needed than the inconsistent and self-contradictory evidence of Pelser himself at the outset of the case, to convince most people that a great crime had been committed But when it was further established by so many witnesses that the whole story of the assault, pretended to be made by the murdered man upon Pelser, was a mere fabrication that the deceased had no such weapon in his hand as Pelser pretended,—that he was seen at the moment of the fatal shot quietly walking in front of Pelser's horse,—and that according to concurrent medical evidence, the man must have been shot in the back, and not in front in the act of assaulting Pelser, as the latter pretends,—we have abundant proof that the death of the unfortunate Zachariah was nothing short of a deliberate murder This statement is not a whit too strong, since it was so clearly laid down by the Judge President that homicide is murder, unless any justifying or mitigating circumstances can be shown In this case we find none, since those which were sworn to by the perpetrator of the deed were manifestly untrue We deeply regret that Pelser cannot now be placed in the dock, and tried for the shocking, and to all appearances, unprovoked crime that he has committed The retribution of human justice, however, cannot reach him, but the future life of a man branded with the stain of innocent blood, and with the condemnation of all honest men, cannot be enviable, We must leave him to that penalty, and to

W

the contrition of which his bearing in court showed no sign, but which we may hope will come with reflection Meanwhile we are bound to thank the Court for its patient, able, and impartial handling of the case, and the defendant's Advocate for the skill and eloquence with which it was so successfully conducted on his part We thank the Jury too, that in a time when there is unfortunately much irritation between colonists and natives, they have refused to allow themselves to be biassed by any such feeling, and have returned a verdict which so far as it could go, tends to clear the Colony of the guilt of this great failure of justice Most of all we must thank the Rev Mr Don,—and we wish our thanks and those which the public sentiment of the country will so heartily render him, could be any small compensation for the pain, anxiety, trouble and expense that he has been put to in defending the right,—for his manly and Christian denunciation of the crime which our judicial system was so quietly hushing up He has rendered a great public service to his fellow-colonists, and averted great evils which were coming upon us It was time to speak out, when a spirit of seditious audacity was commencing to disregard the laws of the Colony, and take not merely the lands of the native people, but their lives also If punishment in this case cannot, unhappily, reach the criminal, yet Mr Don's action has done much to clear his fellow-citizens from the guilt of complicity or connivance, and it has done much also to check such crimes in future The more we plead for due restraint upon the law-breaking propensities of a portion of the natives themselves, the more we must insist on a just regard for their common rights as our fellow-subjects, who because they are the weaker and more backward race, may the more strongly appeal to us for fair dealing and protection Matters like this, we would remind our readers, excite deep attention in the minds of our countrymen at Home, and it is of the utmost importance that we should not disgrace ourselves in the eyes of those whose good opinion we value more than all the world's beside, by condoning the deliberate murder of innocent natives We have no doubt whatever that when the result of this trial is known in England, when it is seen how fully Mr Don has been justified by the lamentable facts, and by the jury's verdict, much indignation will be felt at the failure of justice Nor can any reasonable person doubt that it will be held there, as we have already urged, that a judicial system which leaves the decision of such cases practically in the hands of any single official, however eminent, is radically bad in this respect, and that at least in cases of actual or attempted homicide, the functions of a grand jury or some equivalent body of citizens should be called into action

A MOST WELCOME VERDICT.

(*Grocott's Penny Mail*)

The decision reached by the jury in the criminal libel case which came to an end on Monday evening, will have sent a thrill of feeling throughout South Africa Nor will the current be weakened by its transmission through the water or over the water to England. That the jury should have been ten minutes, after the Judge President finished his lengthy, particular, exhaustive, and luminous summing up both as to law and alleged fact, in coming to a decision, amazed everyone who had listened to the case with average intelligence and fairness That it was possible to come to any other conclusion than one of entire acquittal on each and all the charges in the indictment, and a complete substantiation of the plea of justification could scarcely have occurred to anyone The trial and the entire case out of which it grew with its collateral ramifications have been and still are a great deal more than a nine days' wonder Principles touching the most vital principles of law, good government, freedom of the Press, humanity, morality, and religion were involved in the trial It was not merely that a clergyman of blameless life, influential position, and intent on working for the common good, was placed in the dock at the instance of a man whose antecedents and especially whose dastardly and bloody deed on the 16th day of the present year, have been as unlike the antecedents of the Reverend Mr Don as cruel violence is unlike habitual humanity and forbearance The crowds who listened with intense interest as the trial proceeded, and the thousands who will read the details supplied by the local papers, or the vigorous comments which will be found in every newspaper of light and leading in the land—will see that very much more was affected by the trial and the verdict of the jury than the Reverend Mr Don or the man Pelser The sacredness of human life whatever the race or colour of its owner may be, the freedom of the Press to denounce the wrong, and especially that greatest of all civil and political wrongs—the wanton destruction of life without the destroyer being called to account and either convicted, justified, or excused by a jury of his countrymen, and other interests not less sacred, were at stake in the trial which has ended so satisfactorily Governments and all Crown officials are neither mentally nor morally infallible They are as subject to prejudice, ignorance, weakness of judgment, and unrighteous

motives and aims as those from among whom they are chosen
Errors of policy and administrative blunders will occur from
time to time, but their administration of justice might be and
ought to be without the shadow of suspicion of partiality, or
perversion by political and party considerations A worse case
against Crown officials than declining to prosecute Pelser we
never knew A large portion of the public neither can nor will
forget the state of feeling evoked in the early part of the year
in some quarters by the state of things in Bechuanaland while
the success of Sir Charles Warren's Expedition was not absolutely
assured, and while Niekerk and his coadjutors were detained in
custody Had we estimated the Solicitor-General's perspicacity
less highly than we do, or thought him capable of perverting
his high functions as Public Prosecutor, to political, party, or
racial ends, we might be ready to join in the hue and cry which
are pretty sure to be raised against him We cannot explain
satisfactorily to ourselves how he could come to regard Pelser's
deed as so unquestionably accidental, or necessary and justifiable
as to be above the need of judicial investigation On the other
hand, if he had been conscious of allowing party, political, or
racial considerations to influence his withdrawal of the order for
committal,—and such considerations could not have influenced
him, without his being fully conscious thereof,—how could he
be so blind as to allow the case to come before the entire country,
as it was sure to come in the prosecution of the Rev Mr Don !
Never was a young fellow allowed, advised, and encouraged to
put his head in the lion's mouth with greater certainty of ruin
to himself and triumph to the defendant, than was Pelser when
he was led to believe that he had a good case against the Rev
Mr Don What Mr Don had said in an eloquent letter of
public remonstrance and burning indignation, has now been
endorsed by Judge and jury, and will be endorsed by nearly the
whole Press of the Colony

The outspokenness of the letter containing the actionable
language was not greater than the boldness of the pleas hurled
against the indictment There could be no doubt about the
libellous character of the language Just as little was there any
attempt on the part of Mr Don to shuffle about the meaning of
of his words, or to escape the full consequences of what he had
done, by apology In similar circumstances he would act the
same bold part to-morrow He accepted the authorship of the
letter, and acknowledged the full meaning and his deliberate use
of the stinging words it contained He reaffirmed that the
defamatory words set forth in the indictment are true in
substance and in fact, and that it was right and for the public
good that they should be written and published He not only
offered the plea of justification, but in the opinion of jury, Judge
and crowded audience, he abundantly substantiated the plea.

We do not envy the feelings of the Government, nor of Pelser, nor of those who advised and abetted his suicidal attempts to scald and scrape, and render a little less offensive his own character by punishing the gentleman who had given the cruel deed its proper name, and depicted the heinous conduct of the Government in its true light. Sincerely do we congratulate Mr Don on his absolute and honourable acquittal. We thank him for having given what we consider the death blow to the Libel Act, so capable of being used to terrorize the Press into criminal silence or abject servility. We thank him for having demonstrated to the Natives that they may confide in the white man's love of justice. They will see that if Government fail in their duty of punishing or even of calling to account, the unscrupulous and reckless men who would shoot them down with as little compunction as they would shoot down a wild beast, there is refuge for them in the courts of law. The bench and the bar will not be intimidated by the Powers that be. Nor will they lack potent advocates in the Press or in high-minded gentlemen in various parts of the country. For morbid negro-philism we have the most absolute contempt. Not less un-mitigated is our hatred of wanton cruelty, habitual injustice, and murderous treatment of natives bad and exasperating as they often are. Cases of shooting thieves and natives intent on still more dangerous crimes, have occurred, where the killer of the native has been entitled to the sympathy and even the thanks of the authorities and the community. But Pelser's slaughter of his victim was at the very utmost remove from justifiable or excusable homicide, and it was a shocking mis-carriage of justice to treat it as such, and to decline to place him before a jury

IS PELSER A MURDERER?

(Het Volksblad)

We had at first intended to reserve any remarks we have to offer on the trial of the Rev Mr Don, charged with having libelled Mr Pelser, till the Grahamstown papers containing the full report of the case had reached us. But as this would involve too long a delay, and as we already have in our possession the report of the first portion of the proceedings, including the evidence of the two principal witnesses for the prosecution, Mr Pelser himself and the District Surgeon, we have quite sufficient to go upon

So far from anything new having been brought to light by the evidence of these two witnesses, we would, if it were necessary to go into detail, have to repeat exactly what we wrote in May last when the report of the preliminary examination in the case of Pelser was published. It will be remembered that after having shot the Kafir, Pelser reported to the Magistrate's clerk that he had shot the man in self-defence, and at the preliminary examination he swore that "his revolver went off and hit deceased." It is even now difficult to ascertain from the evidence given by Pelser at Grahamstown to which of these two statements Pelser elects to adhere. He repeats that the Kafir struck at his horse and at himself with an iron bar,—but on neither horse nor man were any marks ever seen—and repeats also that "the revolver went off before I anticipated it would, I was not prepared to fire,"—although he had armed himself with that revolver before he pursued the Kafir. We were wrong when we said that nothing new had come to light by Pelser's evidence. In cross-examination Advocate Solomon forced Pelser to admit that this was by no means the first case of assault in which he had been concerned. He admitted that he had been before now "before the court for assault, but his accuser did not appear,"—he had been bought off we hear. He went on to say that "he had never been before a Magistrate at any other time on any charge." But after a few more questions he confessed that ' he had been charged *several times for assault upon Natives*." "He might have been brought up in May 1884 for an assault upon Jan Jonas." "He remembered that charge." The charge was that Pelser had struck the native with the butt-end of a gun, and had discharged the weapon, the bullet grazing the native's head. Yet a while later, he says "Several charges have been made against me for assaults. I cannot remember any of them." This is the man who has met with such profound sympathy in certain quarters. When we find Pelser giving himself this certificate of character, it need no longer excite surprise to hear him swear that when the man shot by him "by accident" was seen by him to fall "he hurried off, he did stop to see whether he was much hurt, he went home," and only some hours later, in the afternoon, when the District Surgeon had arrived,—the spot where the man "accidently shot" lay dead, was again visited ! Of the doctor's evidence we need only quote two sentences to show how completely it upsets the theory set up by Pelser, that the shot was fired while the Kafir was in the act of attacking him with the iron bar. Doctor Paul says "My opinion as a medical man is that Pelser must have been behind the Kafir and slightly to his left hand." And again ' If I had seen the body and examined the wound *without reference to circumstances stated*, I should have said that the shot had been fired from behind sideways." So the doctor's unbiassed opinion agrees with that expressed by ourselves months ago   It is in fact self-evident, that if Pelser had fired at the Kafir while he was attacking him, the bullet must have struck him in the face or chest

But strange to say it was not Mr Pelser who was on his trial for murder or culpable homicide at the criminal sessions at Grahamstown, but it was the Rev Mr Don who was criminally prosecuted for libelling Mr Pelser, and we may safely add, the Government and the Solicitor-General   It is worth while quoting some passages occurring in Mr Don's letter upon which the charge of libel was based, which letter was published in the *Mercury* after it had become known that the public prosecutor had declined to prosecute Pelser   "I am reluctantly compelled to conclude," wrote Mr Don, "that our rulers have been influenced by political instead of such legal considerations as are alone applicable to the case   It may safely be assumed that if a white man had been the victim, the murderer would not have been untried and unpunished   It would seem that in the district of Burghersdorp, if a Dutchman shoots a Kafir, the crime must be overlooked, Government refuses to do its duty and the conscience of the whole community is offended   'What has thou done? The voice of thy brother's blood crieth unto me from the ground!' That poor man's blood crieth to heaven, not merely against the wretched murderer, but against the Government which refuses to prosecute, and the country which condones such conduct   I, for my part, will have no share in this responsibility   Therefore to clear my own conscience, I solemnly protest in the name of God, of law, justice and order, against the manner in which this foul crime has been dealt with"   And we say the country owes a debt of gratitude to the Rev Mr Don, for his ringing protest against that scandalous dereliction of duty of the Solicitor-General and the Attorney-General, who is responsible for the administration of justice without respect of persons   Mr Don no doubt has had to suffer intense anxiety and has had to incur considerable expense, in consequence of the manly stand he has taken, but he now has not merely the satisfaction afforded by the consciousness of having done his duty, but the satisfaction also of having successfully exposed iniquity, and of having reaped the reward which the champions of justice do not always meet with in this world

Whether by studied arrangement or not, circumstances were as favourable to Mr Don as they well could be   It is significant that in this case the usual course was departed from, and Mr Don instead of being put upon his trial in the place where he resides was brought before a Grahamstown jury   one less likely to entertain "philanthropic" notions than the men of King William's Town, and no man being entirely free from political bias, and there being very weighty political issues at stake in this trial, it is peculiar that Grahamstown was selected, which of all Eastern towns is the stronghold of the Ministry now in office, as was only recently proved by no one venturing to oppose the Ministerial candidate, Mr Wood. Judge Barry, who presided at the trial, is, of all colonial judges, perhaps the only one who is not regarded by "string the-nigger-up" party as imbued with "negrophilistic" proclivities. Advocate Maasdorp who prosecuted Mr Don and defended Pelser,—strange irony of fate that the Public Prosecutor appears in Court to defend a man who killed another—Mr Maasdorp was of all men most likely to do his utmost to secure a conviction, he being as much on his own trial as Pelser, and being as much put upon his own defence as Pelser himself. Over all these adverse circumstances, Mr Don has triumphed and the verdict so given is infinitely more significant than otherwise it would have been. Over every obstacle justice has in this instance proved victorious, and the political party now in power has once more proved singularly unfortunate in defending their conduct in Courts of Justice.

Will the *Star's* prediction, to which we called attention on Tuesday last, be now verified? Will the *Star* admit now—to use it own words—that "the Government has been upon its trial and the Solicitor-General upon his" That the charge, now proved, should "hurl the Ministry from office" and render Mr Maasdorp unfit to hold his position for a day longer?"—we candidly say that we do not expect any such display of sensitiveness on the part of the Ministry. They do not sacrifice fifteen hundred a year for honour. But of Mr Maasdorp we expect better things. We regret to say that, standing convicted as he does of so grave an error of judgment, there is but one honourable course open to him, and we hourly expect to hear of his having sent in his resignation. As to Pelser, time will show whether he is at last to be indicted for murder of which this jury has declared him guilty, they having found that Mr Don was completely justified in publicly stigmatizing Pelser "a wretched murderer"

RESULT OF THE PELSER TRIAL

(Eastern Province Herald.)

It was with much satisfaction that the intelligence of the Rev J D Don's acquittal was received here last Monday night. The public had closely watched this "Pelser Libel Case" from the very beginning, and as day after day passed, as witness after witness was examined, the conviction became stronger in the mind of every one that it was Pelser and not Don who should have been put on his trial What course the Solicitor-General will now pursue in regard to Pelser we cannot say, and it is not our province to suggest What we have to do with at present is the fact that, after a long and exhaustive trial, Mr Don has been acquitted of the charge laid against him This is another nail in the coffin of "Leonard's Criminal Libel Act," and we rejoice that it is so The whole of the evidence showed that further and fuller enquiry was necessary in this case, and the Solicitor-General never made a greater mistake in his life than he did by declining to prosecute Pelser We can make every allowance for the Solicitor The District of Albert was said to be disaffected, and caution was necessary Unfortunately, as often happens, a timid policy only increased the evil it was intended to check or avoid A firm front would have been best. The Solicitor-General should have "put his foot down," and have said, "It is my duty to enquire into this matter, and I shall do so" We have no hesitation in saying that if this unfortunate affair had occurred in the District of Albany or Fort Beaufort Pelser *would* have been indicted We do not say he would have been *convicted* either at Burghers-dorp or anywhere else, but it was the not trying him at all which has caused all the mischief The acquittal of Mr Don will cause people to breathe more freely It will show them that there is yet in this Colony liberty of thought, and liberty of speech—that when a great wrong is done, the people and the Press may yet speak out their minds without fear of pains and penalties We said some time ago that Mr Pelser had been badly advised, for it was plain from the outset that there was an under current of feeling that first of all prompted and then backed up these proceedings Mr Pelser will return to Burghersdorp a wiser, and it is to be hoped a less impetuous man He may thank his stars if matters are allowed to remain as they are He has had a lesson which will last him his life, and we hope he will profit by it We heartily congratulate Mr. Don and his friends on the result of this trial They acted from a strict sense of duty, and victory has been their reward They were willing to brave all for conscience sake, and they deserve the support of their fellow countrymen The trial was a criminal one, and therefore the expenses are borne by the Crown, but no doubt both Mr Don and Mr George Hay have been put to considerable inconvenience and some expense by these proceedings, and we hope their fellow countrymen will defray the costs by a public subscription The donations need not be large individually, but a trifle from those who are interested in matters of this kind —and who are not?—would preserve these gentlemen from loss, and would at the same time testify the sympathy of the public with them, and their thorough appreciation of such faithful conduct.

THE PELSER CASE.

(The Christian Express)

This famous case has now come to a close entirely satisfactory
to all lovers of justice in this country, whatever be their national-
ity, or their colour The great principles contended for, and
grave issues involved—these being the sacredness of human life,
whatever the colour of the skin, the purity of the administration
of justice, and the liberty of fair comment in the Press—will
make the case memorable outside of the law records, and beyond
the jurisdiction of the Eastern Districts' Court In the greater
court of English sense of justice —of English common sense and
fair play—the result has been hailed with the same unmistakable
delight and hearty satisfaction, as that which found vent in the
vociferous cheers within and without the court-buildings in
Grahamstown, on the evening of the day when the verdict was
pronounced Englishmen have many faults, but a liking for a
corrupt inefficient administration of justice is not one of them
That taste or preference is very un-English, and it is time it was
checked in this country Besides what has happened in the
region now British Bechuanaland, and some years ago in the
Western districts, the present instance would seem to show that
the taking of the life of a British subject is a less serious matter
than had been commonly believed, that such may be done, and
the doer escape even the form of a legal trial We hope this
case will prove a turning point in that unfortunate direction in
which opinion has been tending That an inoffensive man, proceeding on his master's business, could be shot a little before
midday, and left to welter in his blood unassisted for nearly two
hours before his death, that this could have been done in the
sight of other natives who were only some six hundred yards
distant, and dared not venture to go to his assistance, and that
a white man should have been made aware of this, and yet not
thought it worth his while to go to the spot, and stranger still
that the doer of such a deed should not have been put through
even the form of a trial,—all indicates either a low sense of justice,
or a state of terrorism in the district which is not creditable to
British rule We have no sympathy with those who are shot at
night, in their efforts to live by plunder and robbery rather than
by honest work They must take their chance, as they endanger
other men's lives not less than their own But this case does not
come at all within that class

We heartily congratulate Mr Don on the result of his stand for the vindication of justice In form, the prosecution stood Regina *versus* Don In reality, it turned out to be a triangular duel, which ended in a way very unlooked-for by two of the parties in this arrangement The prosecution, no doubt, hoped to convict Mr Don, or it would not have been undertaken The original affidavit of Pelser, and the prosecution following, were to find their mark in the one man innocent of the whole business , he might defend himself as best he could But before all was done, the attitude of the parties was quite changed This change was brought about by the evidence, slowly accumulating day by day, but also by the brilliant and acute address of Mr Advocate Solomon, and the summing-up of the Judge President, wonderful in its firm grasp of principles, and in its minuteness, which allowed not the slightest important detail on either side to pass unnoticed As it concerned those who raised this action, it amounted in substance to this — The evidence goes to shew that you have come out to shoot the wrong man Gentlemen, you must face the other way ' " And so it turned out Pelser's proof—his own evidence included—hopelessly shattered the prosecution , and the prosecution irretrievably shattered Pelser , while the intended victim, Mr Don, walked off the scene un- scathed, to receive general thanks and cheers from the interested public, and an ovation from his friends when he reached King William's Town

We have nothing but sincerest pity for the unhappy man whose rash and violent act—the most irretrievable in its con- sequences which one human being can commit against another— has produced such widespread mischief To him, earlier than to most of us, has come an awful impression of the irretrievableness of all wrong-doing, even of one wrong act The friends also, and even the casual acquaintances of the Solicitor-General are greatly puzzled How has it happened that one hitherto always esteemed as an able lawyer, and a man of high honour and English sympathies, could have allowed this case to have assumed its deplorable shape He has taken, as those who know him even but slightly, expected, the entire responsibility on his own shoulders, but there is an uncomfortable impression abroad, and a desire for a little more light on the first move- ments in this matter What germ or speck of suggestion led to the abandonment of the first prosecution, which should have been against Pelser ? What prompted the filing of Pelser's affidavit, which led to the second prosecution entirely in the wrong direction—as every one now sees ? It may have been on the Solicitor-General's part a serious error of judgment **Many** will take this possible view Others again will continue to believe in the active existence of certain influences from other quarters—general and administrative—influences subtile in

themselves, but destructive of English liberty and English
justice   A little light may be thrown on this difficulty, if our
readers will refer to the last of the opinions of the Press quoted
below, and which is part of an appeal for assistance to Pelser
By some it will be read with amusement, by others with indignation

On our Native friends, we hope, the recent judgment will have
the best effect, and will satisfy them that there is yet safety and
justice for them   What about the murdered man's widow, if
she still lives   Is there no redress for her?

THE PELSER TRIAL

(Port Alfred Budget)

The revelations which have now come before the public, in
what is known as the Pelser trial, will most undoubtedly shake
the confidence of the public in the administration of justice   A
man is shot down in broad daylight, without any reasonable
provocation being given, the deed is witnessed by others, is
investigated by a Magistrate, sent for further investigation to
the Solicitor-General of the Colony, but no prosecution follows
Yet an impartial jury, after hearing all the evidence in the
case, and the final summing up of the Judge President of the
Eastern Districts' Court, pronounce that the term murder, as
applied to such an atrocious deed, is a justifiable term   And we
feel sure that those who read the evidence for themselves will
come to the same conclusion as the Graham's Town jury   Well,
all this mal-administration of justice, this cloaking of a fearful
crime, would have been hushed up, had it not been for the courageous letter of the Rev Mr Don, of King William's Town
The rev gentleman had the courage of his convictions, and put
them forth in a public manner in the columns of a newspaper, and
for this he has been prosecuted, while the cowardly perpetrator
of the dastardly deed escapes scot free   This is justice with a
vengeance!!   The public have now had a fair view of the way in
which justice is being meted out in the Colony,—the veil has
been lifted for a moment and revealed a state of things almost
surpassing credence   We feel grateful to the Grahamstown
jury for the verdict given, which has absolved the public at
large from bloodguiltiness, we feel grateful to Mr Solomon for
his clear and masterly defence, which as it unrolled itself more
and more became more and more an indictment against the prosecution, we feel grateful to the learned Judge for his careful
and impartial summing up, but we feel most grateful to the

Rev Mr Don for his manly protest against shielding crime, and for his courage in choosing rather to stand his trial than withdraw his words of truth and justice. What the ultimate sequel of these proceedings is likely to be we do not care to prognosticate, but we should hope that those who have made such painful mistakes, and laid the whole Colony open to public scorn, will not be allowed to repeat such painful errors of judgment. That *scelerat*, the *Star*, tries to make the most of a bad case, but only succeeds in making it several degrees worse by suggesting that the native evidence was simply a conspiracy to ruin Pelser. With this single and miserable exception, we believe the whole Press of the Colony is unanimous in its opinion upon the late trial, and in its approval of the verdict given.

THE PELSER-DON CASE

(Graaff-Reinet Advertiser)

Pelser was badly advised or self-moved to bring this action. But he was probably under the same delusion as the editor of the *Burghersdorp Gazette*, who held that the refusal of a public prosecutor to prosecute was equivalent to an acquittal by a jury, and that shooting the Kafir could not be afterwards called murder, or a crime at all, and that if anyone did so call it, he who did so, came within the grasp of the Libel Act. Both the editor and Mr Pelser are now cured of their delusion. It is a very great pity the Solicitor-General took upon himself to decide that there was no case against Pelser. The case has now been clearly shown to be one to have gone before a jury. This case has caused much trouble in the country from the decision, and now, after the verdict, it will cause more. But it will be a lesson to the public prosecutors in future to send all such cases to a jury, and let the jury bear the responsibility of conviction or acquittal.

The Judge President concluded his remarks when, discharging the acquitted, with these words:—' You (addressing Mr Don) have the satisfaction of knowing that the principles for which you have contended have been established.' The principle for which Mr Don contended was free and open criticism of public men and their public acts. That principle has been established by this trial, and people who feel a little hurt by public criticism by the press, or through the press, must not think that they can with impunity take an honest journalist by the collar, cast him into the dock, and from there into prison, just to soothe the pain they feel. We should like this Pelser-Don case to end

where it is   We are afraid it will not   Mr Don and the Editor
of the *Cape Mercury* have been put to great expense by this trial,
and it remains to be seen whether they will let the matter rest
where it is

THE TRIUMPH OF TRUTH

(East London Dispatch)

The triumph of Truth, the victory of truth-speaking, is always
one of the most grateful things to human nature ; a fact which
shows of what sound elements poor human nature is compounded
after all   When to this is added the vindication of Justice, in
the teeth of her own professing agents, who have forgotten their
high calling and refused to adjust the scales, the appeal to the
better part of our average manhood is so much the stronger, and
quite irresistible   There is also this in the Pelser libel case and
its result , and there is much more   For our part we cannot
keep from one special wonderment, and that is, what on earth
led the prosecution in this case to face the ordeal of the trial?
It would have been an easy matter, under the circumstances, to
have treated Mr Don's famous letter with the kind of contempt
which would have been a fit accompaniment to the heroism
which brought Zachariah to his end   The actual facts being
what they were, it was on the face of it a beautiful simplicity
that courted the exposure   It appears to us that Pelser, whose
common instinct must surely have bidden him beware, was not
left to his own promptings, but was in all likelihood urged on
from behind , and the question remains, by whom ?   The man
has a large circle of relatives, but it is hardly likely that they
directly encouraged him in this risk   At any rate the relatives
of most men, with a discreet regard for their personal welfare,
would have advised under the circumstances to let well alone   But
he local branch of the Africander Bond is not to be forgotten ,
and to these gentry, or some of them, the prosecution of the
Scotch minister for his bold outspeaking, and the establishing
of a case against free criticism of free shooting, may have
seemed a very tempting piece of work   However this may be,
the present result is, save for the credit of two individuals,
distinctly the most beneficial result that has accrued in any cause
affecting society that has disturbed the atmosphere of our courts
for many years

THE ACQUITTAL OF THE REV J D DON

(P E Telegraph)

The acquittal of the Rev J D Don on the charge of criminal libel preferred against him will be a subject of congratulation among the just, humane, and law-abiding classes of the Colony It is at once a victory for justice and for the liberty of the press The Native population of this Colony, now rapidly growing in intelligence and influence, have been watching for the result of the trial with the intense interest In King William's Town and along the Border Mr Don was regarded as the champion of their rights as citizens, as the courageous man who had ventured to censure the conduct of the administration of justice in the Eastern Provence of this Colony in a case in which a black man had been, in his opinion, most cruelly murdered

PROSECUTION FOR CRIMINAL LIBEL

(The Cape Law Journal)

The acquittal of the Rev J D Don, who was tried for criminal libel at the November Sessions of the Eastern Districts' Court must commend itself to all as very satisfactory The case was one of the most peculiar character, having regard to the circumstances in which it originated In January of this year one Pelser, who lived with his father on a farm near Burghersdorp, shot a native at a distance of some few hundreds of yards from the homestead, and in the middle of the day Pelser never pretended that the native was on the farm for the purpose of stealing, nor was such a suggestion advanced by anyone But Pelser, who was proved to have given various statements of the occurrence at various times, finally rested his case upon a theory which, of itself, must be held to have proved conclusively that in error was committed when it was decided to let him go unindicted Pelser's case was that the man Zachariah was walking along in front of his (Pelser's) horse, Pelser riding behind to drive the man along, holding in his hand a loaded revolver, that Zachariah was carrying a small piece of iron, about two feet in length, with which he suddenly and fiercely made repeated attacks upon Pelser's horse and upon Pelser himself, that Pelser at last concluded his life was in danger and shot the man. Pelser having at first given an account irreconcilable with the wound, and the evidence of the native workmen on the line, was manifestly uncertain as to how he should explain the act of shooting Zachariah. He, however, adopted the somewhat venturesome theory that he did not mean to fire when he did, that the pistol went off, if not by accident, rather sooner than was intended, and that he intended to shoot the man to disable him. It is to be remembered that Pelser ventured to explain how, before the alleged attack was made upon him by Zachariah, he had complained that Zachariah was not walking sufficiently fast, and that he (Pelser) accordingly walked his horse close up against the man, who thereupon became irritated.

Seeing that the man Zachariah was proved to have been of a quiet and inoffensive character, this suggestion of Pelser's is in the last degree improbable, more particularly when considered with the evidence which was adduced against him. But the conclusion is forced upon us, and with irresistible force, that the man who would on his own admission, thus goad a respectable native by walking his horse up against him, as if to trample him under foot, only because the man walked slower than the horse, would not hesitate much about treating a European, who might be found trespassing, in the same way. No one can be surprised that the non-prosecution of Pelser, after a preliminary examination had been taken against him, and after the Solicitor-General had once decided to indict, occasioned a considerable amount of feeling in the minds of those who believe in maintaining the equality of the law. Most unfortunately, too, at the time of this occurrence there were in the Albert district, of which Burghersdorp may be called the capital, threats of lawlessness and of disorder, which ignorant and disloyal agitators imagined would prevent the principles of British justice being carried out in a British Dependency. No one who knows him would readily credit the Solicitor-General Mr A F S Maasdorp, with any other than the highest sense of duty, and we do not believe that these proceedings intimidated the Solicitor-General. But the fact remains that the real nature of Pelser's act was at least uncertain, it was either murder or culpable homicide—the self-defence theory was very shadowy. This appeared most strikingly throughout the trial of the Rev Mr Don, in which the Solicitor-General laboured painfully to make out some defence for Pelser. The fact of Pelser's conduct being such as to require such efforts for his exculpation was a convincing proof that this case was one which originally ought to have been put before a jury. But assuming that the non-indicting of Pelser was an error of judgment, the indicting of Mr Don for criminal libel, because he wrote a letter of vehement remonstrance to the *Cope Mercury* of King William's Town, in which the term "wretched murderer" was applied to Pelser, and in which the Solicitor-General's discretion was questioned, was one more, and even a greater error of judgment. Surely Pelser might have been left to his civil remedy. If he had been, and a Court of three Judges had confirmed the Solicitor-General's conclusion, that there was no crime, and that the comments were unfair, Pelser would have been compensated, as there can be no doubt that Mr Don could have satisfied any judgment against him, while if the Court had found that there was murder, it is possible that the ends of justice could have been secured or at least not defeated, as some think, by Pelser having been called as a witness for the Crown. Surely the community was not outraged by the severest comments upon a man whose conduct was such as the preliminary examination of Pelser made it appear to have been. Why, then, should the community have been taxed with the expenses of the hopeless struggle to prove Mr Don's comment unfair, and that Pelser was beyond doubt guilty of no more than excusable homicide? We are not disposed to discuss this case at length in these pages. At the close of the proceedings the Judge President told Mr Don that he had had the satisfaction of vindicating the principles for which he had contended. We cannot but agree with the opinion which has been expressed in other quarters, that the whole community is indebted to a man of the character and position of Mr Don, for lending himself at such cost to the cause of free discussion and impartial justice.

It has already been remarked in these pages (Vol I,, p 249) that "it seems to be unjust that a man, for simply doing his duty, should be put to so much trouble and expense, and therefore I think the law ought to provide that it shall be competent for the Court, on being satisfied that the defamatory libel complained of was true and that it was for the public benefit that such matters should be published in the manner in which and at the time when they were published, to condemn the party who set the criminal law in motion to pay all the costs incurred by the accused in defending himself" The prosecution, with its result, of the Rev Mr Don goes far to prove this suggestion to be fair and reasonable. A clergyman of the Scottish church, a gentleman and a scholar utterly without any interest in the matters upon which he wrote the letter, for writing which he was indicted, save as one who would not sit silent under what he conceived to be a gross injustice to the community, is tried for criminal libel and, notwithstanding that his defence succeeded, is mulcted in all the costs of that defence.

There are two or three further points which may be referred to in connection with this case. The compliment which Mr Richard Solomon's address to the jury elicited from the Judge President

x

was well deserved The speech was an admirable one in all respects and had it been adequately reported would have been worthy of being regarded as something very nearly approaching to oratory of the first order   The Judge President expressed pleasure "to find that such addresses could come from the Bar"   If his lordship was surprised, the reason for surprise may be explained in a measure by the fact that so few cases of this description, in which the principles of justice and liberty are at stake, occur Had this case resulted in a conviction, without doubt cases affecting the liberty of the subject would have multiplied Another reason why, perhaps, the Judge President appeared to discover oratory upon this occasion may be found in the fact that the arts of clap-trap oratory, the virtuous but inappropriate indignation of the "Old Bailey" school of practitioners, is never indulged in at the Eastern Districts' Bar

The Judge President's summing up was such as thoroughly to maintain the claim of the Judicial Bench to high character, fair judgment, and a jealousy for the best interests of justice There are times in the history of most countries when the people find the character and independence of their Judges to be the best safeguards of popular rights and privileges   We believe that the people of this Colony, with its interests tossed to and fro in the storms to which Responsible Government in a small community gives birth, have reason to congratulate themselves upon the fact that their Judges are removed from all political influence and can be trusted to administer justice without fear, favour, or prejudice

In the course of the trial the Judge President touched upon the subject of contempt of court   It transpired that one newspaper had at the beginning of the trial written an article full of sympathy for the accused, while another had erred by taking the other side   His lordship held this conduct to be a "gross contempt of court," but the offenders were not brought up to explain their conduct, which his lordship further observed was such as, if persisted in, must render Grahamstown an unfit place for the administration of justice   With great respect we would venture the opinion that the remedy lies with the Judges who, if they do not watch jealously over the dignity of their Court and office, by actually committing for contempt, may possibly induce the public to lose a little of that reverence even for Judges of the Supreme Court which ought always to be entertained   We will further note that in this trial, which may almost be called a political trial, the jury were suffered to be at large whenever the Court dispersed for refreshment or at the adjournment   In very largely populated towns this may be found to work no ill result, yet in the present case it is an open secret that the liberty accorded to the jury nearly resulted in an abortive trial. The exhortation of the Judge President, at the close of each day, that

the members of the jury should speak to no one connected with
the case was ill observed, and we cannot but feel that so long as
there is any likelihood of a juror fraternising or drinking with
one in the position which Pelser occupied in the late trial, so
long is there good reason why Rule of Court 50, as amended by
Rule of Court 12, 1880, should be observed

The cost of a trial of this description would of course be very
much greater if the jury were detained, but considerations of
justice should outweigh all considerations of expense, particularly
when political considerations and the action of Government
happen, as was the case here, to get mixed up, rightly or wrongly,
with the ostensible question at issue

THE POLITICAL TRIAL

(Imvo Zabantsundu)

The attention of the country has, during the last fortnight,
been rivetted by the great State Trial that ended at Grahamstown on Monday week in the acquittal of the so-called culprit.
The trial to which we allude is that instituted by the Solicitor-
General, Mr Maasdorp, countenanced by the Government in the
person of the Attorney-General and head of the law and the
Government, against the Rev J D Don, the much revered
minister of the Presbyterian Church of this town   We presume
that the circumstances of the case are well known to our Native
readers by this time, as we have taken care, from time to time,
to acquaint them of each step with respect to the proceedings
that arose out of the shooting and killing of one of our colour in
January last, by a Dutchman of the name of Pelser, near
Burghersdorp   To refresh the memories of our readers, however,
it will not be out of place briefly to relate the circumstances
But before doing so it may be stated for the information of our
people that the Solicitor-General is the officer who is, properly
speaking, the deputy of the Attorney-General in the Eastern
Districts and is charged with the very important and serious
duty of protecting the subjects of the Queen in the enjoyment
of their lives and property, and of bringing to justice all those
who in any way injure the lives or property of such Queen's
subjects

Having premised the above we may go on with the statement
of the facts   On the 16th January last, Zachariah a Christian
Native, was killed by Pelser, and it was taken for granted that
the perpetrator of the deed would, in the ordinary course, be
brought before a judge and jury   The Solicitor-General at first

resolved to bring Pelser to trial, but to the surprise of not a few the case was dropped like a hot potato, and Mr Maasdorp has been indiscreet enough to tell the public that "nothing further would have come of it had it not been for party politics" It was not, however, so dropped until after telegrams had appeared in the newspapers that the Dutchmen of Burghersdorp were purchasing arms and ammunition with a view to preventing the regular course of the law in this particular case An impression thus went abroad that this and other reasons had contributed to a failure of justice At any rate nothing more was heard of the matter, until the *Cape Mercury* by publishing portions of the preliminary examination, which showed that there was a sufficient case to submit before a judge and jury, called attention to a matter which might have been overlooked by the European public at least Our countrymen in Burghersdorp and Herschel were most indignant over the matter, as it was currently stated that it was not the first time Pelser had behaved harshly towards them, and the inglorious end of this case had put the seal upon the belief, which previous failures had already produced in the minds of the Natives, that the much-boasted justice of the English people was, so far as this Colony was concerned, nothing more than a mere name

Fortunately for our people, and, for the credit of the Colony we have still among us high-souled gentlemen who possess tender and refined consciences, and who still set store by the honour and credit of the British name and nation At the risk of incurring unpopularity, and drawing upon itself much odium in high circles, the *Cape Mercury* laid the facts of this scandalous business open for public inspection, and challenged the heads of the law either to explain or justify their masterly inactivity in a matter involving the shedding of the blood of a liege subject of the Queen in a British dependency There was no response The Colonial Press took the matter up in the same strain All in vain The Crown officers were as deaf to the voice of the Press, as Baal was to the voice of his despairing worshippers But a solemn and serious protest from the incisive pen of Mr Don was alone destined to break open the grave of official indifference He, with true Scottish tenacity of purpose, vigorously demanded for the unhappy Zachariah that precious justice for which the ancestors of the Scottish and English people had freely shed their blood but two or three generations ago, and demonstrated to grasping and imperious kings that they feared God more than they feared earthly tyrants and potentates, and were zealous for public liberty In his vigorous denunciation of corruption in high quarters, Mr Don had but to call Pelser a "wretched murderer" and the whole machinery of the law was set in motion to disgrace, if not to crush him That public money should, in these straitened times, have been spent in effecting the degradation of a minister of Christ's Gospel in a Christian country, to say nothing of the fact of the country being a British Colony, for venturing to unburden his conscience on a public scandal, is a circumstance unparalleled in the annals of the great English nation It could be easily understood, indeed, none would begrudge the expense, if the expenditure had been devoted to probing the unsatisfactory features of the case, which a cultured and a Christian mind and a humane disposition could not contemplate with equanimity   And it is amazing that this overtaxed community has, so far as our observation goes, not been struck by this aspect of the question   We do not intend to analyse the evidence adduced in this deplorable affair   Mr Maasdorp's lame and pitiful address, Mr Solomon's brilliant oration, and the eloquent, exhaustive, and luminous summing-up of Sir Jacob Barry are before the public, and they disclose facts of a most damning character to Pelser, and if there were in the community any sceptics of the time-honoured proverb that ' Murder will out," they must have received a rude awakening when Pelser asked for and the Attorney-General agreed to issue his fiat, and Mr Maasdorp put on the copestone by consenting to prosecute the Rev John D Don with the result that,

> " God helped the right, God spared the sin
> He brings the proud to shame,
> He guards the weak against the strong—
> Praise to His holy name' '

We must confess that we have rarely witnessed anything in our life with more pain than the attitude of Mr Maasdorp in this miserable trial   It must have been an unedifying spectacle to behold his abortive attempts to demolish evidence that he should have availed himself of in exacting justice for the deceased and his relatives, and we would have admired and loved the Solicitor-General the more, and considered his failure to prosecute Pelser as a pardonable error of judgment, if, on discovering the material evidence so utterly went against the complainant in this case, he had dared to uphold the dignity of his office by declining to carry on the prosecution to so inglorious an issue As, however, he has not chosen to do so, it is so much the worse for him

Albeit the fact stands prominently forward that Mr Don has struck a blow for the rights and liberties of the Native people of this land, the results of which will last for all time   The monster of brutality and lawlessness must have received a blow under which it merely reeled when our friends Mr Saul Solomon and Mr Dormer grappled with it in 1879 in the Koegas Tragedy We venture to say Mr Don's herculean struggle with it at Burghersdorp, its very den, has laid it low, and nothing but the united and persistent efforts of the order-loving and law-abiding inhabitants of this country whether Dutch or English, assisted by well-disposed Natives, will avail to keep it where it is The hearty rejoicing throughout the country at Mr Don's victory, as evidenced by the Press, clearly shows that the Briton's love of fair-play is still there True there have been one or two papers that have laboured to cheapen that victory, but it is a notorious fact that Mr Don has been highly commended by all whose approbation is of real value

We are now curiously awaiting to see what is the next step our Government will take towards Pelser, for unless he is brought to justice it will be hard to induce our people to admire and believe in the anxiety to mete out even-handed justice to all irrespective of colour, caste, or creed

IMPORTANT PAPERS BEARING ON THE CASE.

PELSER'S LETTERS TO 'BURGHERSDORP GAZETTE"

No 1

OUR TIMES

TO THE EDITOR OF THE "BURGHERSDORP GAZETTE"

SIR,—It is at times becoming unbearable What with the severe drought on the one hand and the unceasing thefts on the other, our patience and forbearance is coming to an end We have already had to seek refuge for our cattle, because the Kafirs along the line of railway take the liberty of slaughtering whenever they please, and as many as they please

Were it not for the thefts which are so constantly committed along the line, there would have been no necessity to flee, because we have thousands of morgen of ground along the said line which can still support a large number of stock But we dare not venture to allow anything to graze there, as by doing so we would be placing it within reach of the thieves

Since we have placed our cattle beyond their reach, they more frequently attack our sheep Within two weeks we have lost twenty-three sheep To whom shall we now look for protection? To the Government? certainly not! because it locates the thieves and murderers on our farms without affording us assistance.

Since the Railway has been commenced here we have lost about two hundred sheep and twelve head of cattle

Before long there will be a second Hans Botha here   But God preserve me from it—and may our Government come to the assistance of us farmers before we feel ourselves necessitated to assemble a body of farmers to drive the Kafirs on the line of railway into Kafirland by force

(To be continued next week)

W J PELSER

No 2

OUR TIMES

TO THE EDITOR OF THE " BURGHERSDORP GAZETTE "

SIR,—Where is our Government꞉ Are Firbank & Co and their Kafirs our rulers ? If so then we shall certainly rebel, as there has been enough crying in the wilderness

Before three more months have passed, a deed will be done which will put an end to our sufferings

A statement of all stock that has been stolen will be sent to the Government, so that it may see how we farmers along the line are being robbed   It is absurd to state that the Government is unable to give us relief, because there is no money to maintain an adequate police force money has been borrowed to construct the Railway

The contract has been given to those who have no stake whatever in our Colony   Money was borrowed to construct the Railway , workmen have been brought from England to do the work   Robbers from Kaffirland to rob us   And why—and why then can money not be got for police for our protection ? But no, we are not thought of except only when we have to pay It is at present hard to be a farmer, but believe me it is harder still to be a farmer here along the line of Railway   When a railway is brought into the country, it is a curse to us farmers Piet, Hendrik, and Klaas alone are Masters, and if you speak much, then your life is in danger   If you fire a shot at your kraal, then it is said you have shot a Kafir, and it costs you but two guineas to release yourself from custody and the loss of a whole day from home

Everything tends to one point—our notice has been published Dawn has appeared, and we can already see in the distance our deliverance coming

Farmers—to a man—let the motto " Unity is strength " still show its power. Our meeting is to be held at Burghersdorp on

the 3rd January, and we expect all farmers who have been
robbed to be there with a list of their stolen stock

(To be continued next week)

W J PELSER

CASES AGAINST PELSER

Copies of the Record in the two cases of assault against W J
Pelser, referred to by Mr Advocate Solomon in his cross
examination of Pelser —

At Burghersdorp on this 15th day of May, 1884, before me,
C W Andrews, R M, and in presence and hearing of the
prisoner William Jacobus Pelser, charged with the crime of
assault with intent to do grievous bodily harm

Appeared, Jantje Jonas, a native employed on the Railway
Works, and residing at the camp on Wonderboom Spruit, in the
District of Albert who being duly sworn states   I know
prisoner   On or about the 3rd instant I left Burghersdorp
after sunset in company with Snowball and Dick to return
to the camp   On the way we were passing the back of Mr
Pelser's house   It was then after dark   Prisoner came up to
us from the house with a gun in his hand, and asked us what
we were doing   I replied that we were going home   Prisoner
then said to me ' Go on," and at the same time struck me a
blow on my back with the butt-end of the gun   This blow he
followed up with several other blows with the butt-end of the
gun   My hat fell off   Prisoner pushed me with the gun, and
told me to go on   He then fired the gun, I can't say whether
he fired at me, as he was behind me   The bullet grazed my
head, causing the scar I now show   I fell down on the ground,
and whilst on the ground, prisoner again struck me a blow with
the front part of the gun on my back   My head was bleeding
from the wound caused by the bullet   I got up and followed
my companions who, had already gone ahead of me during the
assault   Upon overtaking them I persuaded them to return
with me to pick up my hat   We went back to where I had
dropped my hat, and I was about to pick it up when prisoner
again came up and struck me a blow on the back with the gun
I picked my hat up and went on   When about three yards
from prisoner, he again fired the gun   I did not see him fire
I heard the report, and heard the bullet pass me on my right
I then went on to the camp   I did nothing whatever to provoke
this assault, and am unable to assign any reason for it   I was
walking along the road at the time   The wound on my head
was examined by the District Surgeon

Cross examined by **Mr** Harrison, who appears for prisoner We had each had a glass of brandy in the town We did not take any liquor away with us We were not drunk Prisoner did not tell us not to shout, and to go quietly past I did not seize his gun When I reached the camp, I reported to the clerk there that I had been shot

(Signed) JANTJE JONAS

his X mark

Witnesses { (Signed) W CLIFTON PRICE
{ (Signed) J SPRANGER HARRISON

Before me (Signed) C W ANDREWS, R M

Snowball, a native residing at the Railway Camp at Wonderbroom Spruit, sworn, deposes I know prisoner and last witness I remember being in his company one evening about the beginning of this month when we were going home to camp from town, and passing the homestead of the prisoner Dick was also with us We were walking together, Jantje being nearest to the house When prisoner came up and asked what we were doing We told him we were going to the camp He had a gun in his hand, with which he struck Jantje several blows, on his back Dick and I walked on in front, leaving prisoner and Jantje together It was after dark, and I did not see what further took place I heard two shots fired in quick succession Afterwards Jantje overtook us without a hat, and asked us to return with him to fetch it He told us he had been shot in the head, and showed us the wound, and I saw blood We went back with him to fetch his hat Jantje picked it up, and we all walked together to the camp Prisoner did not come up when Jantje got his hat Prisoner did not then again strike Jantje Prisoner was not there then

Prisoner has no questions

(Signed) SNOWBALL

his X mark

Witnesses { (Signed) W CLIFTON PRICE
{ (Signed) J SPRANGER HARRISON

Before me (Signed) C W ANDREWS, R M

Dick, a native residing at Wonderbroom Spruit Camp, sworn, deposes I know prisoner, I remember passing his house one evening early in the present month in company with the two last witnesses Prisoner came from the house with a gun, and asked us what we wanted there, Jantje was walking on the side nearest the house He replied that we were going home Prisoner said " *Go on,*" and struck Jantje several blows with the gun I did not see where the blows took effect Snowball and I went on When a short distance away I heard two shots fired After the first shot, I saw Jantje on the ground We were then about five yards ahead of Jantje Prisoner left

z

Jantje, and came up to us and told us to go on   After the first shot was fired, I saw prisoner strike Jantje with the gun   After that I heard the second shot fired   I saw a wound on Jantje's head   None of us were drunk   We had each a glass in town   We took no brandy with us to camp

Cross examined   It was moonlight   We went back to get Jantje's hat   Prisoner was then going towards the house. Prisoner did not beat Jantje again when he took his hat

(Signed) DICK, his X mark

Witnesses { (Signed) W CLIFTON PRICE
{ (Signed) J SPRANGER HARRISON

Before me   (Signed) C W ANDREWS, R M

Ferdinand Paul, District Surgeon, residing at Burghersdorp, sworn   I know Jantje Jonas. I examined him on the 5th instant, and found an abrasion of the skin about the size of a shilling on the crown of his head, and two abrasions above the left eye   I also found considerable abrasions between the shoulders, and under the left shoulder blade   The abrasion on the head did not appear to have been caused by a graze from a bullet, it appeared rather to have been caused by a fall or a blow

Prisoner has no questions

(Signed) F PAUL

Before me (Signed) C W ANDREWS, R M

Prisoner released on his personal Bail in £25, to appear at any time within six months to answer the charge preferred against him

(Signed) C W ANDREWS, R M

[A true copy, W F BERGH, A R M, 4/9/85]

CORRESPONDENCE

BETWEEN THE

MAGISTRATE OF BURGHERSDORP, THE SOLICITOR-GENERAL, AND THE ATTORNEY-GENERAL

Office of the Solicitor-General,
Grahamstown, 4th May, 1885

QUEEN *versus* PELSER

THE HONOURABLE THE ATTORNEY-GENERAL, CAPE TOWN

SIR,—As a great deal of discussion has found its way into the public press on the subject of the above case, and as my decision has, in certain quarters, been ascribed to unworthy motives on the part of the Government or myself   I beg to forward to you herewith all the papers (marked A) upon which my decision

was based, leaving it to you to deal with them as you may think
fit It is unnecessary for me, I would hope, to assure you that
my decision not to prosecute Pelser was based solely on the
evidence I had before me, but as doubts have been cast on my
judicial independence in the matter, I have thought it right,
though unsolicited, to lay before you a short statement of the
reasons which guided me in my decision

It will appear from the recorded evidence that in the month
of January last the accused was suffering severe losses from
stock thefts, which were committed by day as well as by night,
and therefore had strong objections to allowing natives to roam
about his farm at will

On the 16th of that month the deceased, a Kafir, came into
the farm of the accused with the object as here alleged of looking
for a horse belonging to his master, but without producing a
pass for that purpose   He was told to go back for his pass but
refused, and in defiance of the accused went off across the farm,
being at the time armed with an iron rod two feet in length
Thereupon the accused mounted his horse, being armed, as afterwards appeared, with a revolver, and after sending off one of his
men in quest of some police who had been about the farm that
morning went in pursuit of deceased   He overtook the latter at
some distance from the homestead and turned him back towards
it, with the object of handing him over to the police, but before
they had gone very far the deceased suddenly turned round and
attacked the accused with the iron rod to which I have already
referred whereupon the accused shot him in self-defence, the discharging of the revolver being apparently precipitated by the fact
of the horse upon which the accused was riding becoming unmanageable, and he therefore more at the mercy of the deceased
This was the account of the occurrence given by the accused
himself

In opposition to this view was the evidence of some natives,
employed in digging holes for the erection of the telegraph, who
attempted to prove that the accused was guilty of deliberate
murder, by shooting the deceased in the back, in cold blood, at
a distance of two yards   Of these witnesses only one viz Mtlaziza swears distinctly that he actually saw the shot fired, while
two others, viz Alfred Peters and Veldschoen Gewakweka would
appear (in so far as their evidence is consistent with itself) only
to have looked up after the shot was actually fired   In addition
to this, these witnesses pretend not to have noticed that the
deceased was armed in the manner described, though he was
conversing with them for some time, and they consequently had
every opportunity of becoming aware of the fact, though it was
distinctly sworn to by four other witnesses for the prosecution,
and though as a matter of fact the iron rod was found lying near
to the corpse when first visited by the officials

The evidence of these witnesses was further discredited by that of Mr David Man, Sub-Inspector of Telegraphs, under whom they were working at the time   Alfred Peters swore at the preliminary examination that after the occurrence he went and immediately reported it to Mr Mair and gave him all the particulars   Mr Man on being examined denied this, and stated that hearing Alfred Peters telling the other natives something about a Kafir having been shot, he questioned him and received for answer that a Kafir had been shot by a farmer, but that Alfred Peters told him this as a mere matter of rumour without any details, and not as having seen it himself, and from what he said, he (Mair) concluded it was a mere idle rumour, and took no further interest in the matter   This conclusion of Mr Mair's, is further strengthened by the fact that though the body of the deceased was lying at a distance of only 560 yards from where these witnesses were working, and though the deceased seems to have been alive for sometime after he was shot, they acted as if they were wholly ignorant of the occurrence, seeing that none of them visited the body, nor showed any further interest in the matter

Lastly, the evidence of these witnesses was entirely upset by that of Doctor Paul, the District Surgeon, who stated that it was impossible for the wound on the corpse to have been occasioned in the manner described by these witnesses, whereas the explanation of the occurrence given by the accused was quite borne out by the *post-mortem* examination

On all these grounds, and influenced no doubt by the demeanour of Alfred Peters, Veldschoen Gewakweka and Mtlaziza in the witness-box, the Resident Magistrate came to the conclusion (see his letter of January 28th, 1885) that these witnesses were swearing falsely in order to secure a conviction on the charge of wilful murder, and accordingly did not commit the accused for trial, but forwarded the papers to me for instructions   The documents arrived in my office on January 31st, 1885, and were perused by me on the same day with the result (as you will observe from the documents themselves), that not having the prisoner's declaration before me, I gave instructions to have the prisoner committed for trial, and recorded my intention to indict

The prisoner's declaration was accordingly taken on February 11th, and he was thereupon committed for trial   The completed preliminary examination arrived in my office on February 14th, and the evidence was thereupon again carefully reperused by me on February 16th, with the light thrown upon it by the prisoner's declaration, and the letter of the Resident Magistrate of January 28th, and after mature consideration of all the circumstances, I came to the conclusion that the Magistrate was right in his view of the case, that it would be impossible to find a jury to convict the accused, and that it was foreign to my duty, as Public Prosecutor, to press a prosecution which was based upon evidence which I was myself convinced was false

I may add that in arriving at this conclusion, I was materially assisted by the conduct of the accused after the event, by the fact of his reporting the unfortunate occurrance to the authorities, and to his showing every readiness to assist the prosecution in the inquiry

Unfortunately some excitement seems to have prevailed at the time of the preliminary Examination among the farmers in the neighbourhood of Burghersdorp in consequence of the prosecution, and some ill-advised persons were no doubt guilty of some indiscreet vapourings I need not say that, in deciding to drop the prosecution, I was in no way influenced by that circumstance To have allowed, on the other hand, the indiscretions of others to tell against the accused, would, I venture to submit, have been criminal

In accordance with the rule of the Civil Service, which prohibits Government Officials from taking part in newspaper controversies, I have hitherto refrained from joining in a discussion which has been consequently carried on in a somewhat onesided manner, but as my silence appears to be misconstrued, and as an attempt is being made in certain quarters to shift my responsibility (a responsibility I shall be at all times ready to meet) on to the shoulders of the present Government, I would respectfully suggest that in the interests of justice the present is an occasion on which the rule of the Service may properly be departed from I would therefore suggest that to meet the partial reports of the evidence which have found their way into the newspapers, a full report of all the enclosed papers be published, together with this explanation

I may state further, that never at any time has any former Government interfered with the exercise of the judicial discretion conferred upon me by Section 36 of Act 21 of 1864, and it is of course unnecessary to tell you, Sir, that the present Government has not made the slightest attempt to influence me in the present case In fact the only communication I have ever received from your Office on the subject was the Telegram (marked B) herein enclosed, which I received on February 9, and to which I replied by telegram on the same day, and again on February 16, copies of which telegrams (marked C and D) are also herein enclosed In conclusion, I beg to state that ever since my appointment to the office of Solicitor-General, I have kept myself aloof from party politics, as was my bounden duty, and I hope to be enabled to do so

> I have the honour to be, Sir,
> Your most obedient Servant
> (Signed) A F S MAASDORP
> Solicitor-General

Copy of the letters and telegrams which passed between the Magistrate of Burghersdorp and the Solicitor-General, and between the Attorney-General and Solicitor-General, during the progress of the proceedings against Pelser

Office of the Resident Magistrate of Albert,
28th January, 1885

47 B]

CASE OF WILLEM JACOBUS PELSER, CHARGED WITH CULPABLE HOMICIDE

The Solicitor-General, Grahamstown

SIR,—I have the honour to forward herewith for your consideration, a copy of the Preliminary Examination in the above case

The accused man has been charged in the first instance, on his own statement, with the crime of Culpable Homicide, and, as yet, he has been allowed to remain out of prison under heavy bail   I have taken his own recognizance to appear on the 1st proximo, for £1,000, and two sureties each in the sum of £500

I have had some hesitation in charging the accused man with murder, on the testimony of the telegraph labourers, who state that they saw him shoot the deceased *full in the back* as he was driving the man in front of him, because I doubt the veracity of these witnesses in respect of the most material points of the case, for the following reasons —

They swear that the Kafir man, when he came to them, had nothing in either of his hands, whereas all the witnesses who saw him at the thrashing-floor, saw a piece of iron, or a switch as they thought, resembling the bar or bolt of iron produced at the examination, which iron was found by the Chief Constable close to his body, as if it had dropped from his hand when he fell after having been shot   The deceased must have passed these witnesses after leaving the thrashing-floor, and he must have had the piece of iron in his possession when he accosted them   In this respect they appear to have sworn falsely, for the purpose of representing the deceased as having been defenceless, and of convicting Pelser of murder   The statement of Mair, their employer, also shows that they did not report the alleged murder to him as they swore they had done

Then again they swear most positively that the accused was driving the Kafir in front of him, in which case the two men would have seemed to have been coming towards the witnesses—the Kafir in front and Pelser behind—and that then Pelser shot the Kafir *full in the back*   If that were the case the bullet would have penetrated through the back into the chest in a straight direction, unless deflected in its course by a bone   That does not accord with the evidence of the District Surgeon, who found that the bullet had entered the *flesh* of the back in *an oblique direction*, the wound being oval and the bullet having been stopped by the vertebra, otherwise it would have passed out by the right shoulder You will observe that Dr Paul believes it possible that the wound might have been caused by a revolver having been fired at the deceased under the circumstances described by Pelser himself, who seemed to have supposed that he had hit the deceased man in the head It is, however, in my opinion, not competent for me as examining Magistrate to decide upon the credibility of witnesses, and I have deemed it better under the circumstances of the case, to take your directions, under Section 44 of Ordinance No 40 of 1828, as to whether Pelser ought to be committed for trial on a charge of murder, or the lesser crime of Culpable Homicide

I have therefore remanded him until the 4th proximo, by which time I hope to receive your instructions in the matter

I have the honour to be,

Sir,

Your obedient Servant,

(Signed) Alex Stewart, R M

Endorsement on this letter as follows —

Let the prisoner be committed for trial on the charge of Culpable Homicide Indict

(Signed) A F S M
31/1/85

Sent 31/1 '85
(Signed) M H W

Office of the Resident Magistrate of Albert,
11th February, 1885

Registered]

CASE OF WILLEM JACOBUS PELSER, CULPABLE HOMICIDE

The Solicitor-General, Grahamstown

Sir,—Adverting to my letter of this date, referring to the above case, I have the honour to state for your information, that very considerable excitement has prevailed in this town and district in connection with the examination which has just been closed, and that I anticipate very serious excitement when the case is tried Under these circumstances I would suggest that it might be desirable, in the interests of justice, that the case be removed to trial to another district—say Queenstown

I have, &c,

(Signed) Alex Stewart, R.M

Office of the R M of Albert,
11th February, 1885,

No 63/83]

CASE OF WILLEM JACOBUS PELSER, CHARGED
WITH CULPABLE HOMICIDE

The Solicitor-General, Grahamstown

SIR,—Adverting to my letter, No 47 B, of the 28th instant, I have now the honour to forward herewith copy of the statement of the prisoner in the above case and the Schedule to the Preliminary Examination

I have, &c ,
(Signed) ALEX STEWART, R M

Office of the Resident Magistrate of Albert,
16th February, 1885

No 69 B]

CASE OF WILLEM JACOBUS PELSER, CULPABLE
HOMICIDE

The Solicitor-General, Grahamstown,

SIR,—Adverting to my letter of the 11th instant, I have the honour to forward herewith copy of the Bail-bond entered into by W J Pelser with his sureties This was inadvertently omitted to be forwarded with the other documents

I have, &c ,
(Signed) ALEX STEWART, R M

[B]

Annexure " B " referred to in my letter

(Signed)   A S F M

4, 5, 83

Telegram 9th February

From   To
Secretary, Law Department,   Solicitor-General,
Cape Town   Grahamstown

Urgent   The Attorney-General is anxious to know at what stage the proceedings in the case against Pelser at Burghersdorp for shooting a native have arrived   Please wire at once,

[C]

Annexure "C" referred to in my letter

(Signed) A F S M

4/5/85

From
  Solicitor-General

To
  Secretary, Law Department,
                    Cape Town

Re Pelser   The Magistrate has been instructed to commit for trial on charge of Culpable Homicide, upon which charge I have decided to indict

(Signed) MACLEOD B ROBINSON,
                    Clerk to Solicitor-General

9/2/85

———

[D]

Annexure "D" to in my letter

(Signed) A F S M

4/5/85

From
  Solicitor-General

To
  Attorney-General,
                    Cape Town

Re Pelser   Upon seeing the preliminary examination as completed, I have declined to prosecute

(Signed) MACLEOD B ROBINSON,
                    Clerk to Solicitor-General.

16/2/85,

2 A

THE COSTS OF THE DEFENCE

The costs of the defence amounting to £800, are being defrayed by public subscription, and contributions are coming in from widely separated parts of the Colony. It is believed that many persons in England and elsewhere will be glad to have opportunity for showing their practical sympathy with the Rev Mr Don, and all such are respectfully requested to send their donations without delay to Dr Smith, Secretary, Free Church Missions Committee, Edinburgh

CPSIA information can be obtained
at www.ICGtesting.com
Printed in the USA
BVHW011032260421
605870BV00013B/366